# AGENTS *of the* APOCALYPSE

*A Riveting Look at the Key Players of the End Times*

# DR. DAVID JEREMIAH

Tyndale House Publishers, Inc.
Carol Stream, Illinois

Visit Tyndale online at www.tyndale.com.

*TYNDALE* and Tyndale's quill logo are registered trademarks of Tyndale House Publishers, Inc.

*Agents of the Apocalypse: A Riveting Look at the Key Players of the End Times*

Designed by Jennifer Phelps

Published in association with Yates & Yates (www.yates2.com).

**Library of Congress Cataloging-in-Publication Data**

Jeremiah, David, date.
   Agents of the Apocalypse : a riveting look at the key players of the end times / Dr. David Jeremiah.
      pages cm
   Includes bibliographical references.
   ISBN 978-1-4143-8049-0 (hc)
1. Bible. Revelation—Criticism, interpretation, etc.  I. Title.
   BS2825.52.J46 2014
   228'.06—dc23                                                                2014024615

ISBN 978-1-4143-8050-6   Softcover
ISBN 978-1-4964-0105-2   ITPE edition

Printed in the United States of America

21   20   19   18   17   16   15
 7    6    5    4    3    2    1

## Special Thanks

*I would like to extend my deepest gratitude to Thomas Williams for his assistance in crafting the dramatization component of this book. I had the idea of bringing the characters of the Apocalypse to life to open up the Scriptures for you, the reader, but I could not have done that without his remarkable skills.*

# CONTENTS

# INTRODUCTION

*AGENTS OF THE APOCALYPSE* came about because so many people urged me to write another book on Revelation. I can well understand the current interest in the end times. We live in an increasingly chaotic and godless world, and many Christians believe the dark shadows of the Apocalypse are looming on the horizon. In the last century we saw brutal persecution of Jews and faithful Christians in nations such as Germany, Russia, and China. Today God's people continue to face torture and death in countries throughout the Middle East, Africa, and Asia. Even in Western nations, which have long upheld Christian principles, the repression of Christian expression and practice has begun. And if history is any guide, this discrimination against believers is bound to increase.

I encounter Christians every day who are anxious about the future, not only because of this increase in anti-Christian sentiment but also because of the decline of economic and social stability. In times like these, people tend to look even more closely at the book of Revelation, because perhaps above all others, it encourages Christians to keep hope alive. It recognizes the hard facts of worldwide disintegration and persecution, yet it assures God's people of certain victory.

Because of the critical importance of Revelation and its relevance for our current reality, I recognize the need for fresh books to help keep its message alive. But that need also presents a big challenge. Revelation is hardly a fresh subject for authors to write about. No doubt thousands of books have been written on the topic, and I have already contributed several to that number myself. So when I was urged to write again on the subject, the burning question in my mind was, *How can I write a book that will present this important message in a new and captivating way?*

The answer that found its way into my mind was to use dramatized accounts to make the prophecies in Scripture come to life. But at first I could hardly accept the idea. I wanted to present the biblical truths of Revelation, not speculative fantasy that might lead readers to wonder about its accuracy. Yet the value of story as a vehicle for truth had been impressed on me by a man who is widely recognized as the most influential writer on Christianity in our time: C. S. Lewis.

Lewis was a young atheist when he first read *Phantastes*, a novel by the nineteenth-century Scottish Christian author George Macdonald. Lewis reported that a new quality, a "bright shadow," leaped off its pages and that his "imagination was, in a certain sense, baptized."[1] Though the book did not prompt Lewis to convert on the spot, it was the starting point in his journey to faith. Years later, Lewis's close friend J. R. R. Tolkien, the author of *The Lord of the Rings*, described the ancient myths of gods who died and were reborn as stories that prefigured Jesus' crucifixion and resurrection. Lewis eventually became convinced that the story of Christ as presented in the Gospels "is simply a true myth."[2]

In response to those who were suspicious about the power of story to present truth, Lewis said, "Reason is the natural organ of truth; but imagination is the organ of meaning."[3] He was saying that stories can align reason with imagination and mind with emotion. When truth is put in imaginative form, it can be driven not only into the mind but also into the heart.

So I asked myself, *Could stories be used to drive the message of Revelation into the human heart?* The more I thought about it, the more convinced I became that they could. While the book of Revelation presents an overview of the future, it provides little detail. That is not its purpose. Yet the cataclysmic and triumphant events it portrays will affect real people in real situations. The players identified by Revelation in this end-times drama will also be real people—either people who go bad and wreak destruction, such as the Antichrist and the false prophet, or faithful people such as the martyrs and the two witnesses, who stand against these demonic individuals.

Capturing these players through the lens of story allows Revelation to come to life in a new way. It enables us not only to see the overarching truths of Scripture but also to experience them vicariously. It gives us the chance to see the actions of these individuals up close and personal as they play out this cosmic drama.

In this book I've devoted one chapter to each of the most prominent players in Revelation—those who are the primary agents of the Apocalypse. After I did the research on the key players or groups of players, I asked my friend Tom Williams if he would write the dramatizations that illustrated the biblical truths. He agreed to do so, and we have ended up with this unique book.

I want to emphasize that in the writing of these fictional accounts, nothing presented in the Bible has been altered. The dramatized elements are constructed firmly on the facts of Revelation. The stories merely fill in the gaps that Revelation does not address. They present possibilities about how the biblical events could play out. I recognize fully that these scenes cannot fill in the gaps with perfect accuracy, but they offer one possibility among many with one goal in mind: to drive the truths of the end times not only into the mind but also into the heart. My hope is that these stories will serve as a reminder that the book of Revelation isn't just theoretical; it's intended to depict real-life individuals and situations.

Each chapter in this book is divided into two sections. The first is the dramatized account, which is followed by a section called "The Scripture behind the Story." My hope is that the dramatization will whet your appetite to explore the biblical truths behind the story. This second section digs deeper into Scripture, with discussions about what Revelation says and how it can be interpreted and applied. This setup enables you to separate the facts from the fiction and understand the biblical foundation that undergirds the story. Thus you get everything from this book that C. S. Lewis would want. The story drives the truth into your heart, and the Scripture behind the story drives it into your mind.

It is my heartfelt prayer that this book will impress the truth of Revelation into both your mind and your heart, and that it will strengthen your resolve to stand firm for Christ in the face of the worst of circumstances. I also pray that this book will help you to realize the overarching truth of Revelation: that the Christian's victory in Christ is an absolute certainty.

*Dr. David Jeremiah*
FALL 2014

*chapter one*

# THE EXILE

It was a Sunday morning in the first century AD, and the members of the Ephesian church were gathering to worship in the spacious atrium in the villa of Marcellus, a wealthy Roman convert who freely offered his home as a meeting place.

As the members arrived, their faces were taut with uncertainty. Tension filled the air, like a mooring line ready to snap. The meeting began as usual, with a hymn, but today the church sang with little feeling. Their minds were distracted by the ominous rumors coming out of Rome. After a prayer and a reading from the prophet Isaiah, Tychicus, one of the deacons, stood to address the congregation.

"Dear brothers and sisters, the church leaders have asked me to inform you of evil tidings. A decree has just been posted in the forum telling us that the Roman emperor Domitian has assumed the title 'master and god.' He has demanded that everyone in the empire swear an oath to worship him. He has already launched an aggressive

1

campaign to enforce the edict in every city under Rome's jurisdiction. What is worse, he has especially singled out Jews and Christians because he suspects our disloyalty to Rome."

A voice from the crowd called out, "Are the rumors true that the edict has already been enforced in some of the other churches?"

The deacon nodded soberly. "A fortnight ago Roman soldiers invaded all the Christian homes they could find in Pergamos and demanded that every member immediately take the oath of worship to Domitian."

"Did they do it?" another tremulous voice asked.

A pained look crossed Tychicus's face. "It grieves me to report that two-thirds of them gave in and took the oath."

A gasp rippled through the crowd. "What happened to those who would not bow?" someone asked.

"I am sorry to tell you that they were brutally flogged and executed. And we can be sure the same thing will soon happen here in Ephesus."

The room fell silent. Finally someone asked, "What can we do?"

At that moment, an aged man who had been sitting to the side stood slowly, aided by the staff in his hand. Unlike the other faces in the room, his showed no distress. In fact, he positively radiated joy. "It was almost as if his face glowed," one member later observed.

The apostle John faced the group. "My dear brothers and sisters," he began, "you ask what we can do. There is but one answer." At the age of ninety, his voice still rang out clear and strong. But there was a warmth in his delivery that dissolved much of the tension in the room.

"We can stand ready to give back to our Lord Jesus Christ what He has given to us. He gave us life by giving up His life, and we must do no less for Him."

"Perhaps we should stop meeting for a while," Marcellus said. "That would keep us from being so visible and identifiable."

"No, that is exactly what we must not do," John replied. "We must look at this trouble coming our way as a test of our faith. Will we love our Lord enough to stand firm and suffer with Him? Or will we turn our backs on the One who gave us the greatest gift of love in history? With such trouble coming, we need more than ever to meet together in order to support and encourage one another to stand strong. If we stop assembling, we will isolate ourselves and lose the strength we draw from each other. We must never stop meeting, no matter how severe the persecution."

"As long as this threat remains, we have decided that we should meet all over the city in separate homes," Tychicus said. "The Romans will never be able to find us all. Some of us may fall, but the church in Ephesus will survive."

"And, I hope, grow even stronger in the face of the persecution," John added. "Sometimes I fear that we are becoming complacent and that the love we originally had for our Lord and for each other is beginning to cool. Persecution could rekindle that love by drawing us together as we face a common danger."

"Why is God letting this happen?" a voice cried out from the back. "We have been loyal and dedicated. We have done many good things in Christ's name. Yet the more good we try to do, the more the world seems to hate us."

"Do not marvel, my brothers and sisters, if the world hates you," John replied. "Our Lord and Savior was perfect in every way, and yet the world hated Him. People hate what they do not understand. We should look on this coming trial as a great honor. We are being chosen to share His cross and His sacrifice for us. Many who have already died for Christ have received their suffering with joy. In the years since His death and resurrection, all my fellow apostles, including that late-coming firebrand Paul, have been called to suffer death for Him. I am the only apostle remaining who has been denied that honor. And now that I see it on the horizon, I welcome it with all my heart. I urge all of you, my dear brothers and sisters, to remain steadfast and true to Christ, no matter the cost. You will receive a reward in heaven that will make your sacrifice seem as a mere trifle."

John resumed his seat, leaning heavily on his staff. After another hymn and several prayers, the assembly dismissed.

As usual, the members clustered around John with questions or prayer needs, or simply to bask in the man's magnetic presence. But today a tense undercurrent ran through the conversations. It wasn't long before Marcellus pushed his way through the group and stood facing the apostle. His face was as red as wine, and his eyes blazed with anger.

"How can you ask us to do this?" he demanded. "I have a wife and five young children. Do you expect me to just stand by while they are tortured and slaughtered? I will not do it! The rest of you can meet next Sunday like cattle waiting for these Roman butchers. But not I! You must find another place to meet. There will be no worship here until this crisis has passed. I am perfectly willing to live for Christ, but it's too much to ask me to die for Him!"

Without another word, Marcellus turned on his heel and walked away. Soon the remaining members dispersed to their homes. How would they react when the Romans came? They weren't entirely sure. Would they face the crisis with the courage of their apostle John or with the fear of Marcellus?

* * *

The following Sunday, a small group of families assembled in John's home to worship. Five of the expected twenty-three members were not in attendance. Nothing was said about those who were missing, but the morning prayer included a petition that all would regain their courage and stand fast. After a few hymns, a Scripture reading, and more prayers, John stood to speak.

Suddenly the door burst open, and eight Roman soldiers barged in. They were dressed in armor and carried swords. The startled Christians stared wide eyed, and mothers drew their children close to them.

The commanding officer opened a small scroll and read the emperor's demand. "You must cease to worship your God," he proclaimed. "It is lawful to worship only Domitian."

After the reading, one of the soldiers held up a bronze statue. It was over a foot tall and bore the precise image of the emperor's face.

The commander rolled up the scroll and said, "The emperor Domitian requires that you show your compliance with his order this day by bowing down before his image. If you refuse, you will be put to death."

Not one of the Christians moved. This was a fragile moment, and they all knew it. If any of them broke and bowed to the image, others might lose courage too and do the same. After a tense moment of silence, the commander nodded to his men. They drew their swords.

A woman near the front shrieked and fell to the floor. She knelt before the image and swore the oath. Her husband quickly followed, as did four other members. But the rest of the assembly held firm, some of them mouthing silent prayers.

"The six of you who yielded have saved your lives, for whatever they are worth." The commander made no effort to hide his contempt.

As the six scrambled out the door, the officer strode toward John. "I believe you must be the one your people call John the Apostle."

"I am he," John replied.

The commander turned to his soldiers. "We have finally found him, men—the ringleader of all the churches in Asia Minor. This is the chief rebel who has led thousands of citizens to deny the authority of Rome and worship a man who was executed as a criminal."

The commander turned back to John. "Word of your disloyalty has reached the ears of the emperor himself, and he has a special punishment reserved for you. Instead of slaying you outright, he wants to make you suffer until you wish you were dead. Your fate will show your followers the futility of resisting Rome."

The commander seized John and shoved him out the door. The other soldiers followed and bolted the door from the outside, trapping the Christians who remained within. One soldier produced a torch, lit it with his flint, and set fire to the house. As the soldiers led John toward the Roman garrison, John could see the house begin to blaze.

They were fifty paces away when the commander stopped and turned toward the now-flaming cottage. "What is that noise?"

"It is singing," John replied. "My faithful brothers and sisters are singing a song of praise to their true Lord, Jesus the Christ, whom they will meet face-to-face within this very hour."

John leaned heavily on his staff, struggling for breath, but they forced him to march on. Upon arrival at the garrison, he was handed off to a prison guard, who clamped chains on John's ankles and dragged him out to the yard. The soldiers stripped him to the waist, chained his wrists to a post, and flogged him with a metal-studded whip. Then they locked the apostle inside a damp, reeking cell. For several days he lay there suspended between life and death.

Yet in spite of his shredded back, the filthy conditions, and the meager food portions, John never cursed his guard. The soldier, impressed by John's perseverance, began to slip additional food to him. Over the next few weeks, John's wounds healed, and eventually he was able to stand and limp about his cell. One day the guard called for him to come close.

"I have learned what is to become of you," he whispered. "You are to be taken to the Isle of Patmos, where you will be exiled for the rest of your life."

"Patmos!" John repeated. He knew of the island—an infamous dumping ground for Rome's convicted prisoners. "When will I be sent to exile?"

"In two days. You will not be fed well on the voyage—and not at all on the island. I will bring you a small sack with bread and grapes that you can slip under your robe and smuggle aboard the ship."

"Thank you, but if it's all the same to you, I would much prefer a roll of parchment and a vial of ink."

"I will do what I can."

*　*　*

Two days later John boarded a ship leaving the Port of Ephesus for the three-day voyage to Patmos. Beneath his robe he carried a flat leather bag containing his parchment and ink.

The ship—a converted Roman merchant vessel—was propelled by a single square sail and forty oars below deck. The departing exiles were forced to man the oars—with the exception of John, who was still wearing ankle chains, and three others, who were exempted because of age or disability. They were kept on deck near the prow of the ship.

As the ship sailed into the port on Patmos, John looked out on a landscape of barren hills, arid fields of sand and salt, and rocky crags dotted with brambles and stunted trees. As the prisoners disembarked, each was given a three-day ration of dried meat and fish. "That's all you get," the quartermaster told them. "When it's gone, you're on your own."

John soon learned that the exiles were on their own in other ways as well. They would not only have to gather their own food but also would have to find shelter. While there were two or three crude settlements that had been built on the ruins of ancient towns, these struggling villages provided no protection from the island's population of exiled criminals. The only law was self-preservation and survival.

Incoming exiles either found their own shelters among the island's caves or built huts from rocks and deadwood. When John was aboard the ship, he had heard rumors that the far side of Patmos was the least populated. He reasoned that food and shelter would be more readily available there, so he headed out on a trek across the island.

The aged apostle was nearing exhaustion when he stumbled upon an abandoned cave. It overlooked the sea, and a trickling stream flowed nearby.

Born and raised a fisherman, John gathered some tough vines and wove together a serviceable net. He hobbled down to the shore and climbed onto a promontory that was strewn with boulders. When he reached a ledge overhanging the deeper water, he dropped the net, retaining his hold on its long leaders, and waited. Two hours later he returned to the cave, his makeshift net filled with three large crabs and two silver fish.

\* \* \*

As the days wore on, each like the one before it, John began to feel that his life had become meaningless—that he was doomed to live out his remaining time on earth without purpose. He often wondered why he hadn't been martyred like his fellow apostles.

One bright Sunday, after his morning worship and midday meal of fish and berries, John hobbled off toward his favorite spot overlooking the sea. He sat down on his usual rock, shaded by a towering boulder, and gazed out on the gray-green water. Placing his parchment on his lap, he took out a quill to write a letter.

That's when it happened.

A great voice boomed from just behind him. "I am the Alpha and the Omega, the First and the Last." The mighty words reverberated through the heavens like rolling thunder.

John dropped his quill and began to tremble. Nearly paralyzed with terror, he could hardly bring himself to look toward the source of the voice. But there was something so compelling about that voice that he finally had no choice but to turn around.

Before him stood the most magnificent and majestic Man he'd ever seen. His face shone with the brilliance of the sun. He was clothed in a shimmering robe of pure white that was bound about His chest with a golden band. His hair was white—not the lank, faded white of advanced age, but the vibrant, glistening white of pure snow.

The Man's eyes burned into John's soul like piercing flames. In His right hand He held seven brilliant stars. When He spoke, the words rolled off His tongue like tidal waves. Everything about the Man exuded such perfect beauty and glory that John's senses were overwhelmed. He fell to the ground in a dead faint.

He was awakened by a gentle touch on his shoulder.

"Do not be afraid," the Man said, His voice so infused with love and warmth that John's fear dissolved like wax in the sunlight.

"I am the First and the Last," the Man said again. "I am He who lives and was dead, and behold, I am alive forevermore. And I have the keys of Hades and of Death."

John realized that he was once more in the presence of the Lord he adored. He basked in waves of unforeseen joy.

The golden voice told John to take up his quill and record the wonders about to be revealed to him—wonders concerning things existing and things yet to come. John, now filled with expectation, sat again with the quill in his hand and the scroll on his lap.

The voice spoke: "What you see, write in a book. . . ."

Immediately the Lord began to dictate warnings, rebukes, and commendations to the seven churches that had looked to John as their patriarch. As John completed the final letter, the vision of Christ vanished, and His voice called from somewhere above: "Come up here, and I will show you things that must take place after this."

In that moment, the familiar landscape of Patmos faded, and John gazed awestruck at what no earthly human being had ever seen— the very throne room of heaven. Vision after vision followed—some horrifying to behold and others majestic beyond imagination. As the last vision faded, the apostle heard these final words: "I am coming quickly!"

Suddenly John found himself sitting back on his rock in the shade of the boulder. He had been given a vision of things to come—a message that would assure the Lord's churches across the world that although terrible persecution loomed in their future, their ultimate triumph in Christ was certain.

"Yes, Lord, please come quickly," he said as he rolled up the scroll.

* * *

# THE SCRIPTURE BEHIND THE STORY

The apostle John, in writing his great book from the Isle of Patmos, joined an exclusive band of chosen servants who had received similar instructions from the Lord and had done their work under adverse circumstances. Moses wrote the Pentateuch in the wilderness. David wrote many of the psalms while fleeing from the murderous King Saul. Isaiah wrote while watching his nation degenerate, and according to tradition, he died a martyr's death. Ezekiel wrote while he was in captivity in Babylon. Jeremiah's life was one of trial and persecution. Peter wrote his two letters just before he was martyred. Paul wrote his letters amid being beaten, shipwrecked, stoned, and robbed, and while facing hunger, thirst, cold, nakedness, slander, and just about every other kind of tribulation known to humankind (2 Corinthians 11:24-28).

And John received the most extensive revelation of future events shown to any writer of the New Testament while he was banished to Patmos—a small, rocky island in the Aegean Sea. He was shut out from the world but shut in to God, and from that lonely island he gave us the book we know as the Revelation of Jesus Christ.

God very well may have allowed John's banishment so he could be alone with Him and receive this monumental vision of the future. Sometimes the work He has for us requires removal from our normal environment. Abraham's call, Joseph's slavery, Moses' flight from Egypt, and Daniel's captivity come to mind. Many writers I know get away to a mountain retreat or even a hotel room so they can concentrate fully on their task. My schedule calls for frequent flying, and I tend to do my best writing, planning, and thinking in the isolation of an airplane at thirty thousand feet.

As we open the book of Revelation, it quickly becomes apparent that we are about to encounter a message with a high purpose. Though it bears certain similarities to prophetic passages in Daniel, Ezekiel, and Matthew, Revelation is unique. It tells us what kind of book it is in the first few paragraphs.

### A Prophetic Book

> The Revelation of Jesus Christ, which God gave Him to show His servants—things which must shortly take place. And He sent and signified it by His angel to His servant John.
>
> REVELATION 1:1

This verse displays the prophetic nature of what John wrote through the use of one key word and one key phrase. The key word is *revelation*, which is the translation of the Greek word *apokalypsis*, or "apocalypse." In the Greek New Testament, this is the first word of the entire book.

When we hear the word *apocalypse*, we think of horrible disasters associated with the end of the world. But in Greek, the word simply means "an uncovering; an unveiling; a manifestation of." The primary purpose of the book of Revelation is not to paint a picture of the end times, although it does do that. It was written primarily to unveil, or uncover, the majesty and power of Jesus Christ. The book is neither a puzzle nor an enigma but a disclosure of who Jesus is.

The key prophetic phrase used in verse 1 is translated "must shortly take place." This expression describes something that suddenly comes to pass. It indicates rapid progression after something commences. The idea is not that the event may occur soon but that when it does, it will occur suddenly. It's like a California earthquake: we don't know when the next will come, but we know that it will. And it will come suddenly and without warning.

### A Personal Book

> John . . . bore witness to the word of God, and to the
> testimony of Jesus Christ, to all things that he saw.
> REVELATION 1:1-2

The book of Revelation is cosmic and far reaching in its scope, yet it is also very personal. This is a message that John received personally from the Lord. John writes to those with whom he is intimately acquainted, referring to himself as a "brother and companion" in tribulation (1:9).

Christ said to John, "What you see, write in a book and send it to the seven churches which are in Asia: to Ephesus, to Smyrna, to Pergamos, to Thyatira, to Sardis, to Philadelphia, and to Laodicea" (Revelation 1:11). The seven letters we find in chapters 2 and 3 were personal letters written to actual congregations in Asia Minor (modern-day Turkey) at the end of the first century AD.

According to theologian John Stott, "The seven cities mentioned form an irregular circle, and are listed in the order in which a messenger might visit them if commissioned to deliver the letters. Sailing from the island of Patmos . . . he would arrive at Ephesus. He would then travel north to Smyrna and Pergamum, south-east to Thyatira, Sardis and Philadelphia, and finish his journey at Laodicea."[1]

Each of the letters begins with the phrase "I know your works," and each contains a promise to the one "who overcomes." But each message between these bookend phrases was personally tailored to the needs of the church to which it was addressed. As such, the letters must be read in their own context.

Even so, there are applications for us today. Although John wrote these letters with first-century churches in mind, they accurately identify the kinds of Christians who show up in church in every age—including today. Anyone who reads the letters will likely think of individuals or churches that fit some of the descriptions. I believe the Lord's recommendations to these seven churches could solve all the problems modern churches face. This principle seems confirmed by the fact that all seven letters were contained in a single parchment, meaning that each of the churches was required to read the letters written to the others.

### A Pictorial Book

> He sent and signified it by His angel to His servant John,
> who bore witness to the word of God, and to the testimony
> of Jesus Christ, to all things that he saw.
>
> REVELATION 1:1-2

On thirty-nine occasions, John indicated that he was recording things he saw. His words paint vivid pictures to reveal the future through memorable symbols and images.

Symbols occur throughout Scripture as vehicles for divine revelation, but this book contains more symbols than any other. Sometimes the symbols represent people. For example, in the first chapter, Jesus is seen as a judge with a two-edged sword coming out of His mouth. In chapter 13, the Antichrist is presented as a beast coming out of the sea, and the false prophet as a beast originating from the earth.

Why is there so much symbolism in the book of Revelation? First of all, symbolism is not weakened by time. Well-chosen symbols span the centuries and allow us to apply them not only to ancient or future times but also to our own. They create a compelling drama that encourages persecuted and suffering saints throughout the ages.

Second, symbols impart values and arouse emotions. To call a tyrant a beast evokes a primal fear that the word *dictator* misses. It is more colorful to refer to the corrupted world system as Babylon the Great than to dull it with a mundane list of descriptions.

Take a look at what Eugene Peterson says about how the imagery in Revelation affects him: "The truth of the gospel is already complete, revealed in Jesus Christ. There is nothing new to say on the subject. But there is a new way to say it. I read the Revelation not to get more information but to revive my imagination. . . . [John] takes truth that has been eroded to platitude by careless usage and sets it in motion before us in an 'animated and impassioned dance of ideas.'"[2]

Last but not least, these symbols functioned as a kind of spiritual code that was generally understood by believers but not by outsiders. John's book was circulated to the churches during the reign of Domitian (AD 81–96). If it had been written in more direct, prosaic language and happened to fall into Roman hands, those associated with the book would have been executed. Historian Ethelbert Stauffer writes, "Domitian was . . . the first emperor to wage a proper campaign against Christ; and the Church answered the attack under the leadership of Christ's last Apostle, John of the Apocalypse. . . . Domitian was the first emperor to understand that behind the Christian 'movement' there stood an enigmatic figure who threatened the glory of the emperors. He was the first to declare war on this figure, and the first also to lose the war—a foretaste of things to come."[3]

*A Profitable Book*

Revelation is the only book in the Bible that motivates its readers by promising a blessing for those who will read and obey it. The promise is made at the beginning and the end:

> Blessed is he who reads and those who hear the words of this prophecy, and keep those things which are written in it; for the time is near.
>
> REVELATION 1:3

> Behold, I am coming quickly! Blessed is he who keeps the words of the prophecy of this book.
>
> REVELATION 22:7

The word *blessed* means "happy; blissful; joyous." It may seem strange to associate joy with the sometimes chilling drama of the book of Revelation, but Dr. Martyn Lloyd-Jones helps us understand why this is a logical reaction for those who read the book: "Revelation was written in order that God's people who were passing through terrible persecutions and terrible adversity might still be able to go on rejoicing. It is a book that showed them the ultimate victory of the Lord over Satan and all the other forces of evil. . . . It was written for men and women who had been in trouble, and it was meant to help *them*, not only people who would live 2,000 years later. . . . If your understanding of the book of Revelation does not help you rejoice, you are misunderstanding it."[4]

PROFITABLE FOR PERSONAL APPLICATION

John was not interested in merely stimulating the imaginations of his readers. His goal was to influence their lives and change the way they lived. Scripture is a guide for conduct as well as the source of doctrine. Seven times in the book of Revelation we read this phrase:

"He who has an ear, let him hear" (2:7, 11, 17, 29; 3:6, 13, 22). What we read in this book should govern our conduct.

Our conduct today is affected by what we know of tomorrow. The book of Revelation tells us of God's plan for the future and assures us that we are on the winning side. It often appears that the enemy is winning, but Revelation puts everything into perspective. Satan may win some present battles, but the outcome of the war has already been determined—and Satan knows it. When we know that truth as well, it gives us courage to persevere through the downturns. Like castaways who keep on rowing because the map shows an island ahead, we'll have the courage to press on.

Perhaps this is the reason the devil tries to discourage people from reading this amazing book. "The devil has turned thousands of people away from this portion of God's Word. He does not want anyone to read a book that tells of his being cast out of heaven, bound in a bottomless pit for a thousand years and eventually cast into the lake of fire to be 'tormented day and night for ever and ever.' Nor is he anxious for us to read of the ultimate triumph of his number one enemy, Jesus Christ. The more you study the Book of Revelation, the more you understand why Satan fights so hard to keep God's people away from it."[5]

### PROFITABLE FOR PUBLIC ASSEMBLY

The dramatization at the beginning of this chapter portrays an assembly of the first-century church, inspired by the writings of the early church leader Justin Martyr (AD 100–165). He describes the nature of their worship in his *First Apology*: "On the day called Sunday there is a meeting in one place of those who live in cities or the country, and the memoirs of the apostles or the writings of the prophets are read as long as time permits. When the reader has finished, the president in a discourse urges and invites [us] to the imitation of these noble things."[6]

| The Beatitudes of Revelation |
| --- |
| 1.   Blessed is he who reads and those who hear the words of this prophecy, and keep those things which are written in it. (Revelation 1:3) |
| 2.   Blessed are the dead who die in the Lord from now on. (Revelation 14:13) |
| 3.   Blessed is he who watches, and keeps his garments, lest he walk naked and they see his shame. (Revelation 16:15) |
| 4.   Blessed are those who are called to the marriage supper of the Lamb! (Revelation 19:9) |
| 5.   Blessed and holy is he who has part in the first resurrection. Over such the second death has no power, but they shall be priests of God and of Christ, and shall reign with Him a thousand years. (Revelation 20:6) |
| 6.   Blessed is he who keeps the words of the prophecy of this book. (Revelation 22:7) |
| 7.   Blessed are those who do His commandments that they may have the right to the tree of life, and may enter through the gates into the city. (Revelation 22:14) |

Public reading and exhortation were an integral part of gatherings in the early church. Paul told young Timothy, for example, to "give attention to reading, to exhortation, to doctrine" (1 Timothy 4:13).

Revelation 1:3 indicates that the public reading of the Revelation will meet with a special blessing from God.

### PROFITABLE FOR PROPHETIC ANTICIPATION

The third verse of Revelation 1 ends with the phrase *the time is near*, and Revelation 22:10 declares that "the time is at hand." Many people have interpreted these phrases to mean that fulfillment of the prophecy must be just around the corner. This has resulted in rash predictions about when the Rapture, the Tribulation, the Millennium, and the second coming of Christ will occur.

However, the expression "the time is near" does not necessarily mean the event will occur immediately. It indicates nearness from the standpoint of prophetic revelation, which operates according to its own timetable. To say that an event is near means it is the next major occurrence on the prophetic calendar. These events were near in that sense when John recorded them; they were the next major event on the calendar. And they are even closer today. Prophecy is God's way of giving us fair warning so we can prepare our hearts and minds to be ready for what is ahead.

### A Practical Book

More than a century ago, William E. Blackstone wrote a little book called *Jesus Is Coming: God's Hope for a Restless World.* It had a significant impact on the Christian world and spurred much of today's interest in the study of prophecy. In his book, Blackstone devotes an entire chapter to the practical benefits of studying prophecy, which he calls the true incentive to a holy life. He writes, "No other doctrine in the Word of God presents a deeper motive for crucifying the flesh, for separation to God, to work for souls, and as our hope and joy and crown of rejoicing than this does."[7]

Blackstone goes on to give forty benefits listed in the Bible for those who study prophecy. I don't have space to mention forty, but I would like to share three practical paybacks that come to us from studying prophecy—and especially the book of Revelation.

#### STUDYING PROPHECY MOTIVATES US TO LIVE PRODUCTIVE LIVES

Some people think a keen awareness of the second coming of Christ will turn us into lazy souls who stand around gazing upward in some kind of useless trance. But in reality, the opposite is true. In the greatest sermon ever preached on the Second Coming (the Olivet discourse in Matthew 24–25), Jesus listed the "signs of the times" and described the events surrounding His return. Then He told a series of stories illustrating the importance of being productive and prepared. "Blessed is that servant whom his master, when he comes, will find so doing," He said (Matthew 24:46).

Denis Lyle, a Baptist pastor in Belfast, Northern Ireland, tells of a tourist who visited a beautiful mansion on a lovely lakeshore in Switzerland. The house was surrounded by well-kept gardens connected by tidy pathways. There wasn't a weed in sight.

"How long have you been caretaker here?" the tourist asked the gardener.

"I've been here twenty years."

"And during that time how often has the owner of the property been in residence?"

The gardener smiled. "He has been here only four times."

"And to think," the visitor exclaimed, "all these years you've kept this house and garden in such superb condition. You tend them as if you expected him to come tomorrow."

"Oh no," replied the gardener, "I look after them as if I expected him to come today."[8]

Jesus is coming back—coming any minute, coming soon, maybe coming today. These are some of His last words recorded in the Bible: "Surely I am coming quickly" (Revelation 22:20). The more aware we are of His impending return, the more motivated we'll be in our work for Him in these last days.

### STUDYING PROPHECY MOTIVATES US TO LIVE POSITIVE LIVES

The book of Revelation also promotes a positive mind-set. As we study it, we begin to realize that everything that is happening in our world today is heading somewhere. In the book of Revelation, as in no other book, we see God's sovereign hand upon the affairs of the world. We see Him in control even though so much here on earth seems out of control.

John says that Jesus Christ is "the ruler over the kings of the earth" (Revelation 1:5). This is not a statement about the future reign of Christ. It is a statement about His present reign. Jesus not only *will be* King, He is *already* King over the kings of the earth.

Vernard Eller drives home this point quite forcefully:

> We are here at the heart of John's message. . . . It is this: things aren't what they seem! From everything . . . most of us can see, it appears clear that "the kings of the earth" are where the action is: theirs is the clout that makes things happen; theirs are the actions determining the course of history. . . .
>
> No, things are not what they seem! Contrary to their own inflated opinion, that crew does not hold the reins of history. John's very first notice of the kings of the earth is to proclaim that they have a ruler, they are being ruled. That ruler . . . already has won the decisive victory and established his control. . . . God's is real power clothed in apparent powerlessness; Evil's is apparent power which is really powerlessness. Things are not what they seem! Jesus is Lord— and that not only of us . . . who accept his lordship but of everyone else, up to and including the kings of the earth.[9]

As the conditions of our world worsen, Jesus said we shouldn't hang our heads in depression or shake our heads in confusion. We should lift up our heads in expectation, for our redemption draws near (Luke 21:28). After Paul told the Thessalonians about the sudden return of Christ for His people, he said, "Comfort one another with these words" (1 Thessalonians 4:18).

Our world is in a state of depression, and anti-depression pharmaceuticals are being swallowed at a faster rate than ever before. According to a recent study, the use of antidepressants has skyrocketed in the past several decades. In fact, one in ten Americans now takes an antidepressant medication. Among women in their forties and fifties, the figure is one in four.[10]

When I read those statistics, I thought of Proverbs 12:25: "Anxiety in the heart of man causes depression, but a good word makes it glad." I believe there are times when medication is absolutely called for, but *meditation* is often better. When we read the book of Revelation, some of the very first words we encounter are these: "Behold, He is coming with clouds, and every eye will see Him" (1:7). As we visualize our Lord's return, we're treating our souls to a "good word."

### STUDYING PROPHECY MOTIVATES US TO LIVE PURE LIVES

Here's a final benefit from the study of Revelation: it fosters purity in our lives. Several years ago, a prominent minister named Dr. J. C. Massee went to a show he felt he shouldn't have attended. After a few minutes, he abruptly rose and left. His friends followed him out, asking what was wrong. Dr. Massee explained that Jesus could come at any moment. "I don't want Him to [find] me here!" he said.[11]

The Bible says, "When He is revealed, we shall be like Him, for we shall see Him as He is. And everyone who has this hope in Him purifies himself, just as He is pure" (1 John 3:2-3).

The study of Revelation isn't just for "prophecy freaks" or "Second Coming scholars." It's for every Christian who loves Jesus Christ and is anticipating His appearing. It's comprehensible and it's compelling, and it will change our lives. It is a practical book with tangible benefits, and those who study it are happier, holier, healthier people.

### A Purposeful Book

Revelation 1:7-8 presents the twofold purpose of the entire book, which is to affirm Christ's return and His ultimate reign over the earth.

> Behold, He is coming with clouds, and every eye will see
> Him, even they who pierced Him. And all the tribes of the
> earth will mourn because of Him.
>
> REVELATION 1:7

The Bible most often expresses the second coming of Christ by using the Greek word *parousia*. This is the Greek term for "coming" or "advent," but it came to be applied in a technical sense to the arrival of Christ. The Greek word carries specific connotations that are helpful: a *parousia* is an entrance that immediately changes the existing situation it enters.

Picture a teacher who momentarily steps out of the classroom. At his departure, the students become loud and boisterous and begin to throw wads of paper. But when the teacher steps back into the room, everything changes. At his *parousia*, the students quiet down, and order is restored. This is a snapshot of what will happen when the King returns. Everything will change—evil will be shut down, order will be restored, and justice will reign.

Revelation 1:7 stands in a long line of biblical truth. Daniel predicted that the Messiah would come through the clouds: "I was watching in the night visions, and behold, One like the Son of Man, coming with the clouds of heaven!" (Daniel 7:13). In His Olivet discourse, Jesus spoke of His coming in similar terms: "The sign of the Son of Man will appear in heaven, and then all the tribes of the earth will mourn, and they will see the Son of Man coming on the clouds of heaven with power and great glory" (Matthew 24:30).

John expanded upon Jesus' words to describe what every person will experience at His second coming. When the King returns, "every eye will see Him" (Revelation 1:7). In that moment, the great question for all of us will be whether our eyes are filled with tears of joy and thankfulness for what the King has done for us or tears of sadness and terror for the judgment that awaits us.

## THE REIGN OF THE KING

> "I am the Alpha and the Omega, the Beginning and the End," says the Lord, "who is and who was and who is to come, the Almighty."
>
> REVELATION 1:8

*Alpha* and *omega*—the first and last letters of the Greek alphabet—point not only to the eternity of Christ but also to His all-inclusive power. In Genesis we read of how Satan subverted the first humans and usurped the title "the ruler of this world" (John 12:31). Since then, we humans have lived in what C. S. Lewis called "enemy-occupied territory." The earth still belonged to God, but He did not move immediately to drive Satan out.

This was not due to a lack of power; it was a matter of timing (Ephesians 1:10). As the Alpha and Omega, He is greater than the bounds of time. He precedes the beginning of Creation and survives the end of humanity's day. He is the eternal, omnipotent God. And when the time was right, Jesus began His campaign to regain His rightful sovereignty over the earth.

The book of Revelation is the account of that campaign. It tells of His appointment by the Father to the throne, His battle against the forces of evil, His final victory, and His relationship with the redeemed.

Because of Christ's triumph, His people are presented as overcomers. In the first three chapters of Revelation, Christ makes seven promises to "him who overcomes," and a similar phrase occurs five more times in the book. The simple meaning of the word *overcome* is "to conquer" or "to win the victory." The promise of victory is certain, but its final reality awaits the return of the King.

The prophet Daniel foresaw this victory long before John did, and he wrote about it with the same clarity: "I was watching in the night visions, and behold, One like the Son of Man, coming with the clouds of heaven! He came to the Ancient of Days, and they brought Him near before Him. Then to Him was given dominion and glory and a kingdom, that all peoples, nations, and languages should serve Him. His dominion is an everlasting dominion, which shall not pass away, and His kingdom the one which shall not be destroyed" (Daniel 7:13-14).

Likewise, the New Testament leaves no doubt about Christ's ultimate victory: "He who testifies to these things says, 'Surely I am coming quickly.' Amen" (Revelation 22:20). It is in the heart of every believer to join with the saints of old in longing for that day as did John when he completed his scroll: "Even so, come, Lord Jesus!" (Revelation 22:20). Yet while we wait, let us remember this:

> [W]e still live in the time of John's crisis and . . . the Revelation he received from Jesus is still the definitive answer to today's big questions. . . . It's time for us to rediscover the book of Revelation and its message of hope.
>
> In a world where [more than 100,000] Christians are martyred for their faith each year, we still need the Revelation which Jesus gave to John.
>
> In a world where the Church remains terribly flawed and where every week sees another church close down and its building turned into a nightclub, a restaurant or a mosque, we need the Revelation which Jesus gave to John.
>
> It's a Revelation which changes everything. It's a Revelation that God is on the Throne. And he is working out his strategies from the control room of Heaven.[12]

*chapter two*

# THE MARTYRS

IT WAS AFTER TEN O'CLOCK on Sunday morning when Daniel Goldman, an up-and-coming attorney in a Turin, Italy, law firm, finally rolled out of bed. He poured his cup of wake-up coffee, eased into his recliner, and flipped on the TV. He had nothing to do before Rachel got out of church; they would eat lunch at their favorite restaurant afterward.

*Rachel Elon.* Daniel warmed at the thought of her name. He had met the raven-haired beauty at a bar mitzvah five months earlier. Their attraction had been immediate and mutual, and as love blossomed, they had begun to talk of marriage.

A woman in the marketing firm where Rachel worked had invited her to a Christian gathering, and within a few weeks she had become a Christian. This morning was her second time to attend the little church.

Her conversion did not bother Daniel. As far as he was concerned, she could follow whichever religion made her feel good—or none at all. He had quit attending a synagogue the day he left for college, and his only connection with his parents' Jewish faith was an occasional wedding or bar mitzvah.

A newsflash snapped Daniel out of his reverie. According to chaotic reports from around the world, thousands of people had suddenly vanished. People had disappeared from workstations, cars, airplanes, ships, and military stations, causing widespread devastation. Cars had crashed. Planes had plunged to the ground. Gas plants had exploded. Cities were darkened by massive power outages. Daniel watched, incredulous, as casualty estimates rose into the millions.

Before long the panicked news anchor announced something strange: "From the reports we have so far, it appears that all who have vanished were professing Christians. Here in our studio we have retired pastor Marco Conti to make some sense out of this."

The former clergyman explained the Christian belief called the Rapture, which maintained that all Christians would be taken into heaven so they would be spared the political and natural upheavals that would precede the second coming of Christ.

"Do you think this is what has happened?" the anchor asked.

"Of course not." Marco chuckled and shook his head. "Enlightened Christians today see all biblical miracles—including virgin births, resurrections, and prophecies—as myths intended to convey larger truths, such as humanity's ability to find spiritual life within."

"Yet it seems that all who have disappeared were practicing Christians."

"Well, not all," the pastor said with a smile. "I'm still here."

Daniel looked at his watch. It was time for Rachel to be out of church.

He called her cell phone. No response. He kept calling for the next half hour. Finally, he drove to the little church building.

Cars—including Rachel's—were still in the parking lot. He stepped inside the open door. The pews were empty, but a half dozen men and women stood around, looking dazed.

"What's happening?" Daniel asked.

"Look at the pews," a woman replied, her voice breaking.

The benches were strewn with Bibles, bulletins, and purses. Daniel searched until he found a lavender-colored Bible he recognized as Rachel's. He slumped to the floor, barely realizing that the sobs he was hearing were his own.

\* \* \*

Daniel remained in a stupor for days. He plodded about his life mechanically, performing his duties at the law firm without his usual enthusiasm and creativity. The firm itself was in turmoil, having lost fourteen of its fifty-plus employees in the cataclysmic disappearance. The increased workload significantly stretched the remaining attorneys and their staffs. Daniel, however, was grateful for the distraction of overtime.

The first nation to recover its balance was Great Britain. The architect of the recovery was their brilliant prime minister, Judas Christopher, who identified the most urgent problems and formed teams to conscript workers for cleanup and reconstruction and to fill critical vacated positions. Within weeks, although people were still reeling, Britain was back on its feet as a functioning society.

Other European nations did not fare so well, and many countries were sinking deeper into chaos with each passing week. Most of Europe's leaders pleaded with the British hero to bring order to their own devastated nations. Prime Minister Christopher graciously offered his help, and slowly but steadily Europe regained its footing.

In the evenings Daniel watched the aftermath unfold on TV while he worked. The British prime minister appeared often, always displaying confidence and an air of concern. But something about him made Daniel's skin crawl. He sensed that the man's charm was a facade and that his eyes were on something far beyond helping people who were struggling. Daniel knew from various blogs he'd read that Christopher had demanded a fair amount of internal control from those desperate nations in exchange for his leadership.

One day, when Daniel was at work, his phone rang.

"I need to see you in my office." It was the firm's senior partner.

As Daniel entered, his boss couldn't look him in the eye, and his fingers fiddled compulsively with a pencil.

"Daniel," he said, his eyes still averted, "I have to let you go."

Daniel tried to absorb the blow. "Why? What have I done wrong?"

"You've done nothing wrong. You have been loyal, your work has been impeccable, and you have consistently taken on additional responsibilities."

"But . . . but we all know the firm is shorthanded after the big disappearance. You've been desperately trying to recruit new lawyers. So why are you firing me?"

"I'm not at liberty to say. Please don't ask questions. It will do no good. But I am giving you a generous severance package. It has already been deposited to your account."

Still reeling, Daniel returned to his desk and boxed up his belongings. Stunned though he was, the young lawyer had no doubt he would find another job quickly. All the law firms in Turin had been desperate for attorneys since the mass disappearance. In the next few weeks, Daniel submitted his résumé to every firm in the city. They all turned him down.

One evening, after a month of hitting dead ends, he sank deep into his recliner, wondering what he would do next. He had plenty of money; he had quite a bit saved even before the severance package. But it wouldn't last forever.

The phone rang. "Daniel Goldman?" The voice was familiar, but Daniel couldn't place it right away. "Matthew Pearlman here."

"Matthew, my old friend! I haven't seen you in ages. How in the world are you?"

"Not bad. I just heard that you've been fired. Join the club."

"Not you, too! But you were a partner in your firm."

"Yeah, it didn't matter. We're all being fired, Daniel."

Daniel didn't know where Matthew was going with this, and there was a moment of awkward silence.

"Care to have coffee?" Matthew asked. "We need to talk. In person."

*　*　*

Once they were tucked away at a remote table in the local café, Matthew wasted no time. "This is Judas Christopher's doing. We've learned that he is anti-Semitic down to the marrow. He has forced our own gutless premier to get rid of all the Jews in Italy."

"But why—?"

"Firing us is just his first step. Jews in other Italian cities are quietly being rounded up and shipped away on trains. We don't know where they are being taken, but no one has returned. We've just learned that Turin is next, and the purge could begin at any moment."

"Who is this *we* you keep referring to?"

"An underground network organized to help Jews in this crisis." Matthew leaned toward Daniel. "We have set up a secret head-quarters in the basement of an abandoned factory building. We call it the Exchange. We're linked to Exchanges in other cities through a communication network that gathers information to help Jews escape into France. You need to come see us."

Matthew gave Daniel a pointed look. "Come tonight. There may not be much time."

That night, following Matthew's instructions, Daniel went to the Exchange. He parked his car three blocks away and walked to the old warehouse. Like a burglar about to break into a house, he looked in all directions before entering the alley between the last standing wall of the building and the equally damaged factory adjacent to it. Once inside, he descended the stairwell to the basement and knocked softly on the metal door.

He was admitted immediately into a space that had formerly been the warehouse locker room and recreation area. Matthew greeted him with a broad smile. Eighteen or twenty others, both men and women, sat at mismatched desks around the room. Matthew sat Daniel in a chair that looked like a Salvation Army reject, and after introducing him to his associates, he got straight to the point.

"As I told you, we collectively run an underground operation to help Jews anywhere flee from Judas Christopher's purge. We also have another purpose: we are all Messianic Jews, which is another name for Christians who—"

"You? A Christian?" Daniel was incredulous. "But you were always such a staunch Jew!"

"The big disappearance forced me to do some serious soul-searching," he said. "And since my conversion, I have joined these brothers and sisters in devoting ourselves not only to saving our fellow Jews' lives but also to saving their souls."

"Why would you want to become a Christian *now*?"

"Well, I didn't know much about Christianity before. But the fact that only Christians were taken in the Rapture got my attention. I knew that had to mean something. So I got a Christian Bible with a commentary and learned that all this had been predicted. The more I studied, the more I realized that Christianity is actually the fulfillment of Judaism. So I became a believer in the crucified and resurrected Messiah."

"And what about these other people working with you?" Daniel asked. "How were they converted?"

"The Rapture opened their minds to Christianity, just as it did for me. Our paths crossed through various circumstances, and we've been getting together to share what we're learning."

Matthew's face glowed as if lit by some inner fire.

"You are really into this," Daniel said.

"Yes. It has been revealed to me that I am one of 144,000 Jewish evangelists throughout the world who have been called to bring people to belief in our Messiah."

Daniel rolled his eyes. "Come on, Matthew. How can you possibly know all this?"

Matthew was ready for the question. He took his Bible—only weeks old, but already showing signs of wear—and pointed to passage after passage explaining how Jesus' coming made sense of hundreds of prophecies from the Hebrew Scriptures. He went on to show passages from the New Testament that explained the current disturbing events, and horrors looming on the horizon, and his mission.

Matthew closed his Bible and looked gravely at his friend. "Daniel, you can see that the death and resurrection of our Messiah as well as everything we're experiencing now were prophesied in this book. Now I urge you to do two things."

"I'm listening."

"First, I beg you to turn to our Messiah before it's too late. Second, you need to get out of Italy immediately."

Daniel was ready on both counts. Matthew took him to an adjacent room, where he opened the book of Romans and explained the gospel to him in greater detail. Daniel committed his life to following Christ, knowing full well that the cost could be steep. But now that he understood the sacrifice Jesus had made on his behalf, he was willing to lay down everything—even his life, if necessary.

Matthew explained that first thing in the morning, Daniel was to go to the bank and withdraw all his savings. Soon after he returned home, a FedEx truck would pick him up. He was to take only one suitcase, and he would be driven directly to the sister Exchange in Grenoble, France, along with other Jewish refugees.

Yet another shock awaited Daniel at his bank the next day: the government had already confiscated every euro he had. The gravity of the situation was really starting to sink in now. He rushed home, locked the doors, and shuttered all the windows.

As he stuffed his suitcase, he heard a furious pounding at the door. Peering through a slit in the blinds, he saw five armed men in Italian military uniforms. The knock came again, loud enough to rattle the windows this time. Daniel grabbed his suitcase and headed for the back door. He heard the front window shatter, followed by the stomping of heavy boots. At that moment, shouts and pounding erupted at the back door. He turned and bounded down the basement stairway. Just as his pursuers clambered into the basement, he managed to shatter one of the narrow windows just above ground level and wriggle out, leaving his suitcase behind.

Daniel ran down the alley behind the houses in his neighborhood. He could hear the soldiers shouting behind him, but they were too far back to see him. Soon he was gasping for breath, and his knees were buckling. He knew he wouldn't be able to run much longer. He rounded a corner and almost collided with a garbage can. He crawled inside and pulled the lid over him. Moments later the soldiers rushed by, cursing and bellowing.

Trembling with terror, Daniel remained there for more than an hour before he dared to take out his cell phone. He called Matthew and explained what had happened.

"Whatever you do, don't come here." Matthew's voice was tense. "They're onto us, and we've scattered. Jews all over the country are being caught and shipped to gas chambers modeled after those in Auschwitz and Dachau. We're all in grave danger. You must get to France immediately, but not by the highway. You'll have to walk across the countryside at night."

As soon as dusk fell, Daniel Goldman began his westward trek toward France, creeping through fields and woods under cover of darkness. Obstacle after obstacle slowed him down—barking dogs, fences, creeks, and farms to be skirted. At one point he fell into an unseen ravine, and a farmer nearby must have heard him, because several shots were fired in his direction. He managed to escape unscathed, but hunger continued to stalk him. He snatched corn from the fields and fruit from wooded areas whenever he could, but it was barely enough to keep him going.

Finally, after four long nights, he had covered the thirty-plus miles to the border. He made his way over the Alps through a gap near the highway and reached France just as the sun rose behind him. It was now safe for him to hitchhike, and following his friend's instructions, Daniel found the sister Exchange the Jews had set up there.

\* \* \*

The Grenoble Exchange fed and housed Daniel until he secured a position with a local law firm. He worked in relative safety for three years, donating much of his salary to the Exchange and volunteering for them in the evenings. He continued to grow in his faith, meeting with fellow members of the Exchange in the evenings to study Scripture and discuss how to apply it to their lives.

One by one, the prophesied disasters Matthew had pointed out to Daniel in his Bible began to materialize. Countries around the world endured a marked increase in droughts, water contamination, and infectious epidemics. A massive earthquake devastated several nations, killing millions of people.

Ominous signs also appeared on the political front. All the countries in Europe united their government and military forces, which meant that France was no longer safe for Jews. Daniel was fired again, but this time he was better prepared, having stashed his savings in his apartment rather than at a bank.

Daniel knew that a job search would be futile, so he joined the Jewish underground at the Grenoble Exchange. Smuggling Jews across borders was now pointless, because no country was free from persecution. Yet the Exchange continued its mission to help Jews.

They concentrated their efforts on conversion and built a network of underground churches.

In the ensuing months, the entire world became a cauldron of misery and death. Crops failed. Diseases ran rampant. Food became scarce and exorbitantly expensive, and violence erupted over food rations. People in every nation were dying of starvation on a daily basis. Yet these horrors produced one positive effect: they brought startling success to Daniel and the Messianic Jews of the Exchange. Some people were beginning to see the futility of depending on their own efforts and were turning their eyes upward for help and hope.

Judas Christopher's iron fist now gripped virtually all of the civilized world. Not long after he became the leader of the united European nations, he demanded that every person on earth acknowledge him as their god. To enforce compliance, he decreed that no one would be allowed to buy or sell any commodity, including food, clothing, and shelter, without a government-issued number. And no number would be issued to anyone who refused to worship him.

On the night following the decree, the Jews who ran the Grenoble Exchange met to address this new crisis.

"This Antichrist, Judas Christopher, has just pronounced a death sentence on all worshipers of the one true God," one member said.

"The question is, what can we do about it?" someone else asked.

"Whatever we do," Daniel responded, "we cannot bow before this monstrous beast. That would be our eternal death sentence."

"You're right, but I don't see a solution. Death seems inevitable for us all."

"Not necessarily," another member replied. "We can hide in the wilderness or in buildings that were abandoned after the Rapture. We can feed ourselves by hunting and foraging."

"There's also a growing number of Gentiles who detest Christopher's tyranny," Daniel added. "No doubt many of them would be willing to offer us shelter."

"Is it really necessary that we refuse the assigned number?" someone asked. "Under ordinary circumstances, of course, we should not compromise. But what we are facing now is far from ordinary. It's literally a matter of life and death. Would it really be wrong to accept the number just to survive, while in our hearts we retain our allegiance to the true God?"

"You make a good point," another member said. "Even the apostle Paul told the Corinthians that they could freely eat food that had been offered to idols. 'Don't ask questions,' he said. 'Just do it. Those idols are not real gods, and you know that all food comes from the true God.'"

"But he also said not to eat such food when others knew it had been offered to idols," Daniel said. "The light we shine to others is critical. That's one reason so many martyrs were willing to die—they would not deny their Lord just to save their own necks."

"Amen!" The chorus of voices echoed through the room.

"We must model for others the courage these ancient martyrs modeled for us."

The meeting ended with the adoption of a strongly worded resolution to reject the government-issued numbers and to encourage all Messianic Jews to do the same. The group formed several task forces. Some located dwelling places where Jews could hide. Others sought out Gentiles known to be sympathetic to the persecuted Jews. Still others devised methods for distributing donated food and clothing.

\* \* \*

It was not an exaggeration to say that this new decree amounted to a death sentence for those who would not declare their allegiance to Judas Christopher. Although some families managed to survive, eking out a living from forest game, edible plants, and occasional bundles of goods smuggled to their hiding places, the threat was imminent. Jewish Christians were hunted down, tortured, and killed. They were impaled, stretched on racks, flogged to death, fed to wild animals, burned at the stake, beheaded, hurled from cliffs, dismembered, or flayed alive. But in the midst of the bloodbath, the Exchange continued its ministry, the members pouring their energy into converting, feeding, housing, and hiding the beleaguered Jews whenever possible.

Late one night Daniel sat at a large table with twenty other Exchange leaders. They were meeting to arrange shelter for a recently uprooted Jewish man who now sat among them. He had just lost his home and his wife to the persecution. His seven-year-old daughter sat on his lap, her eyes wide with terror.

Suddenly the door burst open, and the man who had been standing guard rushed in, slamming and bolting the door behind him.

"They're here! They have found us!"

Immediately everyone headed for the escape tunnel. Within moments, the door splintered and Christopher's troops rushed in. The Jews emerged from the escape door and scattered as they dashed toward the nearby woods.

Five members of their group were caught immediately, but Daniel and the others made it into the forest. Gunshots crackled behind them, followed by the scream of the little girl. Daniel stopped short and then turned back, leaving the protective covering of the trees. The girl's father lay motionless on the ground. The girl fell to her knees beside him, shrieking in terror.

A soldier reached down and grabbed her long hair. Daniel didn't take time to think—he plowed headlong into the soldier, bowling him to the ground, and then scooped up the girl and ran back into the woods. Three soldiers came barreling behind him.

With the girl in his arms, Daniel knew he couldn't outdistance his pursuers. He stopped and set her down.

"Run for it!" he whispered urgently. "Go as far into the woods as you can. There's a family that will take you in, hiding in a hut."

The girl stood frozen until Daniel turned her around and shoved her forward.

"Run!" he barked.

The girl obeyed, and Daniel turned to keep the soldiers from following. The scuffle lasted only seconds before a rifle butt smashed into his head and he fell to the dirt, unconscious.

*  *  *

Daniel awakened in a filthy prison, his head throbbing. A score of other prisoners were packed into the cell. Next to him sat three fellow workers from the Exchange.

"Did any of the others escape?" he mumbled.

"Two did. Ben, Leah, and Simon were killed outright, and the rest of us are here."

"True martyrs, those three—steadfast to the end." Daniel felt the tears welling up in his eyes.

It wasn't long before several uniformed guards unlocked the cell and took five prisoners away. An hour later they returned and took five more. Daniel, his three companions, and one other prisoner were taken next. The guards led them to a gloomy chamber furnished with ominous looking devices.

Daniel recognized some of them—a rack, a whipping post, and a bloodstained table where he knew prisoners were slowly eviscerated.

A guard grabbed him and forced him to the post. They stripped off his clothes, chained his wrists high above his head, and flogged him with metal-studded whips until his back was shredded nearly to the bone. They laid another prisoner across a rack with his hands and feet bound and the ropes stretched taut until his joints popped. The man cried out in agony. The other three were held in chains, forced to watch as they awaited their turn.

Unable to stand, Daniel and his companion were dragged out of the chamber to an enclosed yard, where an executioner stood waiting with an ax in hand. The man's foot rested on a wooden block with reddish-brown streaks staining its sides.

Two soldiers stepped forward to deliver Daniel to the block, but he insisted that he would stand and walk himself. As he approached the block, he began to sing—softly at first, but with growing volume and feeling. It was an old song he'd learned from his companions at the Exchange:

> *O victory in Jesus,*
> *My Savior, forever.*

Then he knelt, placed his head on the block, and uttered a prayer as the executioner raised his ax.

A moment later, Daniel arose from his kneeling position feeling no pain. He looked around him and saw, to his amazement, that he stood beside a huge altar shaped like the one he'd seen pictured in Solomon's Temple—only this one was made of pure, shimmering gold. Standing with him were many of his Jewish Christian friends and other believers who had been martyred before him, including the three who had been killed in the attempted escape from the Exchange. As he gazed around him in awe, his three cell mates arrived and stood beside him, looking healthy and whole.

Even as he basked in the glory of this place, Daniel couldn't help but feel a stab of pain as he remembered the suffering the Christians were still facing on earth.

As if with one voice, he and his fellow martyrs cried, "How long, O Lord, holy and true, until You judge and avenge our blood on those who dwell on the earth?"

A voice answered, beautiful and resonant as rolling thunder, urging them to take a well-earned rest as they waited a little while longer. The suffering of their fellow servants would soon cease.

At that moment, Daniel felt something being draped over his

shoulders. It was a magnificent robe, dazzling white and fringed with gold. All his questions melted away as he rested, confident that all was well in the mighty hands of his Lord and Savior.

\* \* \*

# THE SCRIPTURE BEHIND THE STORY

The history of redemption has been written in the blood of martyrs, much like Daniel in our story.

Early in the Old Testament, we read of Pharaoh scheming to destroy all male children born to Hebrew women. When Jews were under the rule of the Persian Empire, Satan inspired Haman, the wicked favorite of King Ahasuerus, to devise a scheme to kill every Jew in the country. In the second century before Christ, Antiochus Epiphanes became one of Israel's unrelenting enemies, attacking Jerusalem and executing Jews who refused to bow to Zeus. Herod tried to destroy Jesus by slaughtering all the infant boys in Bethlehem.

The first pages of church history tell of Stephen, who was stoned to death for insisting that the Jewish religious leaders had murdered Jesus (Acts 7). Herod had the apostle James executed (12:1-2). Polycarp, bishop of Smyrna, was burned at the stake for his refusal to worship Caesar. Revelation 2:13 mentions Antipas, a member of the church at Pergamos who was executed for his faith. Still others died under the cruel reign of Emperor Domitian because of their Christian testimony.

Many Roman Christians suffered in the arenas. Medieval believers endured the Inquisition. The Huguenots and other Protestants were massacred or exiled during the Reformation. Hundreds of Chinese believers lost their lives during the Boxer Rebellion, and Russian Christians were sent to slave labor camps or to Siberia.

The people of God's chosen nation have suffered martyrdom

throughout history. So intense was Hitler's persecution of the Jews in Europe that some believe the Jewish population in Europe was reduced to less than the number of Jews who left Egypt under Moses.[1] In Germany in 1938, hundreds of synagogues were destroyed within a few days, and the shopwindows of thousands of Jewish-owned establishments were shattered. The Auschwitz concentration camp was equipped to execute thousands of Jews per day; Hitler's torture camp Treblinka destroyed more than one million people in just a few years.

The infamous Adolf Eichmann, expressing Nazi hatred for the Jews, said, "I shall leap laughing into my grave, for the thought that I have five million human lives on my conscience is to me a source of inordinate satisfaction."[2]

Moses' prediction of Jewish persecution has been fulfilled in literal ways throughout history:

> The LORD will scatter you among all peoples, from one end
> of the earth to the other, and there you shall serve other gods,
> which neither you nor your fathers have known—wood and
> stone. And among those nations you shall find no rest . . . ; but
> there the LORD will give you a trembling heart, failing eyes,
> and anguish of soul. Your life shall hang in doubt before you;
> you shall fear day and night. . . . In the morning you shall say,
> "Oh, that it were evening!" And at evening you shall say, "Oh,
> that it were morning!" because of the fear which terrifies your
> heart, and because of the sight which your eyes see.
>
> DEUTERONOMY 28:64-67

John says that the end of it all has not yet arrived. There will be more martyrs in the future. "When He opened the fifth seal, I saw under the altar the souls of those who had been slain for the word of God and for the testimony which they held. And they cried with a loud voice, saying, 'How long, O Lord, holy and true, until You judge and avenge our blood on those who dwell on the earth?'" (Revelation 6:9-10). These souls under the altar testify to the untold suffering and persecution that will occur during the Tribulation period.

### The Context of Their Martyrdom

> When He opened the fifth seal, I saw under the altar the
> souls of those who had been slain for the word of God and
> for the testimony which they held.
>
> REVELATION 6:9

Who are these martyrs? To help us answer this important question, we must first remember that John places them in the future, when the church of Jesus Christ has already been raptured and the dead in Christ have been resurrected. So then, these martyrs are not from the church age we are living in now.

Also, since the martyrs ask for judgment on their oppressors on the earth, their murderers are obviously still living. This strongly suggests that these martyrs are faithful saints who are killed during the Tribulation period.

After the church is taken away, God will turn His attention to Israel once more. During the seven-year Tribulation period, many Jews will return to God, as Daniel Goldman did in our story. In his letter to the Romans, Paul wrote, "I do not desire, brethren, that you should be ignorant of this mystery . . . that blindness in part has happened to Israel until the fullness of the Gentiles has come in. And so all Israel will be saved, as it is written: 'The Deliverer will come out of Zion, and He will turn away ungodliness from Jacob'" (Romans 11:25-26).

This is another way of saying that Israel as a nation will be saved. The partial blindness of the people will be taken away, and many Jews will turn to God and reject the Antichrist during the Tribulation.

Because of this, the Antichrist will martyr so many of them that their blood will run like a river.

But if not one believer will be left on the earth at the beginning of those seven years of Tribulation, how will people be saved? For one thing, God will send forth His two witnesses into the world to prophesy and perform mighty miracles. There will also be 144,000 Israelites who are "sealed" for God's service during this period (Revelation 7:4).

It is possible that another means will also be used. Dr. Henry Morris has suggested a "silent" witness:

> Millions upon millions of copies of the Bible and Bible
> portions have been published in all major languages, and
> distributed throughout the world. . . . Removal of believers
> from the world at the rapture will not remove the Scriptures,
> and multitudes will no doubt be constrained to read the
> Bible. . . . Thus, multitudes will turn to their Creator
> and Savior in those days, and will be willing to give their
> testimony for the Word of God and even . . . their lives
> as they seek to persuade the world that the calamities it is
> suffering are judgments from the Lord.[3]

In the Tribulation period, martyrdom will be as common as it is uncommon in the West today. Those who trust in God at that time will be called upon to demonstrate their faith—often with their very lives. "They overcame him by the blood of the Lamb and by the word of their testimony, and they did not love their lives to the death" (Revelation 12:11).

Although believers during this period will experience intensified persecution, this is not a new thing for God's people. The psalmist describes martyrdom this way: "For Your sake we are killed all day long; we are accounted as sheep for the slaughter" (Psalm 44:22). During Israel's captivity in Babylon, three young Jewish men portrayed the mind-set of martyrs when they were willing to die rather than worship the Babylonian king's golden image. When they were threatened with death by fire, they responded, "If that is the case, our God whom we serve is able to deliver us from the burning fiery furnace, and He will deliver us from your hand, O king. But if not, let it be known to you, O king, that we do not serve your gods, nor will we worship the gold image which you have set up" (Daniel 3:17-18).

Zechariah the prophet spoke of the future day of tribulation as a time when two-thirds of the entire Jewish population would be killed. But, God promised, "I will bring the one-third through the fire, will refine them as silver is refined, and test them as gold is tested" (Zechariah 13:8-9).

The book of Revelation identifies the enemies of God as those who have shed the blood of His people (Revelation 16:6; 17:6; 18:24; 19:2). Jesus spoke of this coming period of intense suffering in His sermon at the Mount of Olives: "All these are the beginning of sorrows. Then they will deliver you up to tribulation and kill you, and you will be hated by all nations for My name's sake. And then many will be offended, will betray one another, and will hate one another" (Matthew 24:8-10).

Biblical scholar Richard Bauckham summarizes martyrdom during the Tribulation period with these words: "Revelation portrays the future as though all faithful Christians will be martyred. . . . It is not a literal prediction that every faithful Christian will in fact be put to death. But it does require that every faithful Christian must be prepared to die."[4]

### The Cause of Their Martyrdom

I saw under the altar the souls of those who had been slain for the word of God and for the testimony which they held.

REVELATION 6:9

The martyrs of Revelation 6 were slain for the same reason John was exiled: "I, John, both your brother and companion in the tribulation and kingdom and patience of Jesus Christ, was on the island that is called Patmos *for the word of God and for the testimony of Jesus Christ*" (Revelation 1:9, emphasis added). These saints, too, have been sacrificed on the altar of devotion to their God for their witness and for their adherence to the Word of God. We must remember that when the church is raptured, the restraint of the Holy Spirit will be removed from the earth. The rulers of that day will target followers of Christ as they vent their anger and rebellion against God.

The "testimony which they held" is likely a reference to the judgment these believers will preach. As the events of the Tribulation intensify, they will warn of even more severe judgment to come. They will preach repentance and reckoning, and they will be killed for their message.

These Tribulation preachers will join a long line of courageous prophets who spoke out against wickedness in their generation:

- Samuel prophesied to Eli that because of his evil sons, Hophni and Phinehas, the judgment of God would be upon his house (1 Samuel 3).
- Elijah denounced Israel's prophets of Baal, and as a result, his life was threatened (1 Kings 18).
- Isaiah prophesied that because of their unfaithfulness, the people of Judah would be carried into captivity and the Temple and Jerusalem would be destroyed (Isaiah 64).
- Jeremiah's prophecy was so offensive to his listeners that he was put in stocks and chains (Jeremiah 40).
- Jonah passed on God's message to the people of Nineveh that if they did not repent, the city would be destroyed in forty days (Jonah 3).

- Jesus Himself prophesied judgment in His message in the Olivet discourse (Matthew 24).

Dr. W. A. Criswell offers this reminder that it is part of a prophet's very nature to proclaim judgment:

Whenever there is a true prophet of God, he will preach judgment. These modern so-called ministers of God speak all things nice. . . . There is not any hell and there is not any devil and there is not any judgment of God. . . . In our enlightened and sophisticated day . . . we stand up and we speak of the love of Jesus, and we speak of peace, and we speak of all things pretty and beautiful. But remember . . . the same Book that tells us about the good, tells us about the bad. The same Revelation that speaks to us about heaven, speaks about hell. The Bible that presents the Lord Jesus as the Savior, is the same Bible that presents to us the devil as our enemy and adversary of damnation and destruction. The two go together. If there is not anything to be saved from, we do not need a savior.[5]

### The Consequence of Their Martyrdom

When He opened the fifth seal, I saw under the altar the souls of those who had been slain for the word of God and for the testimony which they held.

REVELATION 6:9

At this point in John's account, the scene shifts from earth back to heaven. Here John sees a vision of those who will be martyred for their faith in Christ. They are "under the altar," which is also where the blood of the sacrifices during the Old Testament was poured out (Exodus 29:12).

The word used to describe the death of these Tribulation martyrs is unique to the apostle John. It is translated as "slain" but could also be translated as "slaughtered." *Slaughtered* is a sacrificial word that speaks to the special nature of these Jewish witnesses. "To the world they were destroyed, but to God they were offered as a sacrifice unto Him. They gave their lives for the Lord and the Lord looked upon them as His. They are *His* martyrs."[6]

### The Cry of Their Martyrdom

> They cried with a loud voice, saying, "How long, O Lord, holy and true, until You judge and avenge our blood on those who dwell on the earth?"
> REVELATION 6:10

The martyrs' cry for vengeance is another evidence that they are not church age sufferers. The cry of the church age martyr is the cry of Stephen, the first martyr of the church: "Lord, do not charge them with this sin" (Acts 7:60). But those who are persecuted during the Tribulation will be able to call for God's judgment in perfect propriety because the age of grace has ended. This is the day of the judgment of God.

Louis T. Talbot observes, "A man prays according to the attitude God is taking toward the world in the dispensation in which he lives. This present age is the age of grace. God is showing . . . mercy to the worst of men, and we are told to pray for them that despitefully use us. But in the Tribulation period God will be meting out judgment upon the earth."[7]

### The Comfort of Their Martyrdom

> A white robe was given to each of them; and it was said to them that they should rest a little while longer, until both

the number of their fellow servants and their brethren,
who would be killed as they were, was completed.

REVELATION 6:11

The Lord provides five comforts for these martyred souls:

## 1. A REFUGE

The vision of these faithful servants under the altar is meant to
convey their redemption and protection. Donald Grey Barnhouse
explains, "We are not to think that John had a vision of an altar with
souls peeping out from underneath. The whole teaching of the Old
Testament is that the altar was the place of the sacrifice of blood. To
be 'under the altar' is to be covered in the sight of God by that merit
which Jesus Christ provided in dying on the cross. It is a figure that
speaks of justification. . . . These martyred witnesses are covered by
the work of the Lord Jesus Christ."[8]

## 2. A ROBE

God, in His gracious love and mercy, rewards each martyr with a
white robe. This gift raises an interesting question: What kind of
bodies do these martyrs have? If these are saints who died during the
Tribulation, Scripture clearly states that they will not receive their resurrection bodies until the end of the Tribulation (Revelation 20:4-6).

Scholars are divided as to whether saints who die receive temporary bodies in heaven prior to their resurrection bodies or whether
only their spiritual beings are in heaven at that point. Dr. John
Walvoord offers one possible answer based on this passage in
Revelation:

> The martyred dead here pictured have not been raised from
> the dead and have not received their resurrection bodies. Yet
> . . . they are given robes. The fact that they are given robes

would almost demand that they have a body of some kind.
A robe could not hang upon an immaterial soul or spirit. It
is not the kind of body that Christians now have, that is, the
body of the earth; nor is it the resurrection body of flesh and
bones of which Christ spoke after His own resurrection. It
is a temporary body suited for their presence in heaven but
replaced in turn by their everlasting resurrection body given
at the time of Christ's return.[9]

### 3. A REST

When the martyrs ask how long it will be until their deaths are
avenged, they are told to "rest a little while longer" (Revelation 6:11).
This particular time under the fifth seal is the first of two periods in
the Tribulation when believers will be martyred. The Lord does not
answer their prayer for vengeance because the cup of human iniquity is not yet full—some "fellow servants" and "brethren" still must
suffer death. Only when the second contingent of martyrs has been
slaughtered will God act in judgment.

In the interim, as the martyrs wait to be avenged, they are to rest:

> I heard a voice from heaven saying to me, "Write: 'Blessed
> are the dead who die in the Lord from now on.'"
> "Yes," says the Spirit, "that they may rest from their
> labors, and their works follow them."
>
> REVELATION 14:13

### 4. RETRIBUTION

From the same altar in heaven where the martyrs cry out will come
an angel with a sharp sickle (Revelation 14:18). This is the angel of
judgment, sent to avenge them. He will "thrust his sickle into the
earth and [gather] the vine of the earth" (verse 19), which represents
the wicked deeds of humanity. Then he will throw the clusters of

grapes "into the great winepress of the wrath of God" (verse 19). The prophecy concludes: "The winepress was trampled outside the city, and blood came out of the winepress, up to the horses' bridles, for one thousand six hundred furlongs" (verse 20).

This picture of judgment is one of the most graphic depictions of God's wrath against the evil deeds of humanity in the Bible. In this passage, the prayers of the martyrs are answered as God tramples the wicked, causing their blood to flow like the juice from a grape that is crushed by a winepress.

### 5. A REWARD

The martyred saints will be honored in heaven forever, but even before that, they will be honored on earth during the Millennium: "I saw thrones, and they sat on them, and judgment was committed to them. Then I saw the souls of those who had been beheaded for their witness to Jesus and for the word of God, who had not worshiped the beast or his image, and had not received his mark on their foreheads or on their hands. And they lived and reigned with Christ for a thousand years" (Revelation 20:4). During the Millennium, these saints will experience the justice and peace that eluded them during their lifetimes. Having experienced resurrection on the other side of their martyrdom, they will be invited to rule alongside Christ in His righteous, holy, and joyful Kingdom.

### The Courage of Martyrdom

Vibia Perpetua was a beautiful, twenty-two-year-old woman of noble birth who lived in Carthage in the year 203. She was married and had an infant son, whom she was nursing. She had been studying Christianity when Emperor Septimius Severus issued a decree forbidding conversions to Judaism and Christianity. Ignoring the decree, Perpetua was baptized. Two days later, her conversion was discovered, and she was imprisoned and condemned to death.

Pepetua's pagan father came to the prison with her son in his arms to plead with her to renounce Christ and save her life. "Daughter," he said, "have pity on my gray hairs; have pity on thy father. Do not give me over to disgrace. Behold thy brothers, thy mother, and thy aunt: behold thy child who cannot live without thee. Do not destroy us all."

Perpetua wept at her father's grief and tried to comfort him. "My father, you see this pitcher. Can we call it by any other name than what it is?"

"No," he said.

"Nor can I call myself by any other name than that of Christian," she replied. "In this trial, what God determines will take place. We are not in our own keeping, but in God's."

Her father left her, weeping bitterly.

On March 7, Perpetua and another Christian woman were led into the arena. First they were scourged, and then a wild bull was loosed on them. Perpetua was gored and mangled, yet she remained alive until gladiators entered the arena and stabbed her to death.[10]

When we think of Christian martyrdom, we tend to think of the many stories of ancient witnesses like Perpetua who sacrificed their lives for their beliefs. But it isn't just in ancient history that people have died for their faith. Today, Christians around the world are suffering martyrdom as well.

For example, in the summer of 2005, two young Bangladeshi men, twenty-one-year-old Lipial Marandi and twenty-seven-year-old Tapan Kumar Roy, showed the *JESUS* film to guests in their home. They were threatened with death if they did not cease the showings. They did not comply, and two weeks later, in the dead of night, their accusers entered their home and hacked them to death with machetes.[11]

Stories like this are not rare. Studies from several organizations show that in our world today, a Christian is martyred every four to five minutes. To get a picture of Christian persecution today, consider the following facts:

- More Christians were martyred in the twentieth century than in all previous centuries combined.
- It is illegal to be a Christian in North Korea, and some fifty thousand Christians have been sent to labor camps there.
- Christians are persecuted in more than 65 of the world's 193 countries.
- In Nigeria, nearly 300 churches were destroyed, and 612 Christians were killed in 2013.
- Since 2010, the treatment of Christians has rapidly worsened in Iran. The regime monitors church services, bans Farsi-language services, and arrests converts.
- In India, anticonversion laws have been adopted in five states, and these laws are frequently used as a pretext to disrupt church services and harass Christians. Pastors are frequently beaten or killed, church buildings are destroyed, and converts are forced to flee their homes.
- More than one million of the 1.5 million Christians in Iraq have fled the country since the fall of Saddam Hussein, due to increasing persecution.
- In August 2013, thirty-eight churches were burned down and twenty-three others were damaged in an upsurge in violence against Coptic Christians in Egypt.[12]

As we can see from history and from current events, persecution and martyrdom are the norm for Christians. And as Revelation 6 shows us, it is also the norm for the future. The dark lord of this fallen world cannot tolerate opposition to his program to annihilate everything good and godly.

These martyrs—past, present, and future—provide ample examples of courage that should inspire us to a deeper commitment to Christ and a determination to stand strong for Him, no matter the cost.

*chapter three*

# THE 144,000

Eli Jacobs plodded home from the synagogue, head bowed and shoulders sagging. The Orthodox Jewish scholar looked older than his fifty-six years. Especially on this day.

Eli was discouraged. His once burgeoning congregation in Hadera, Israel, had dwindled like water in a drought until only twelve members remained. No longer able to support a rabbi, the congregation had pleaded with Eli, a former professor of religion at Jerusalem's Hebrew University, to become their lay leader.

Eli couldn't argue—after all, he didn't have the responsibilities that came with being a husband and a father. He'd always been so deeply immersed in his studies that he'd never married. "What kind of son are you?" his mother had chided relentlessly. "You're married to your books. How are you ever going to give me grandchildren?"

Although Eli had devoted his life to Judaism, he often felt that somewhere along the way, his religion had taken the wrong road.

Most Jews in Israel were now Zionists, more secular than religious. Few had any expectation of an actual Messiah. And although Eli was deeply devoted, even his own beliefs no longer touched his heart. He performed his synagogue duties with a growing sense of detachment.

One evening Eli sat in his study at home, feeling weary even though he'd done little work that day. As usual, his radio was tuned to Kol Ha Musica, Tel Aviv's classical station. He stared without seeing at the open Torah on his desk until a stirring choral work began to penetrate his malaise. He had heard the piece many times; it was Sir Arthur Sullivan's "The Lost Chord." But tonight its music spoke to his heart as never before.

The lyrics portray a weary composer sitting at his organ, letting his hands wander idly over the keys. They unwittingly strike a magnificent chord of music "like the sound of a great Amen." The chord leaps from the organ into the composer's soul, and though he tries desperately to find it again, he cannot. Finally he gives up, realizing that only in heaven will he ever hear that chord again.

"It is my own story," Eli muttered. "I have often sensed something undefined that I long to know fully, but like that chord, it eludes me." He closed his Torah, switched off the radio, and went to bed.

The next morning Eli sat in his usual booth at the restaurant down the street, ordering his typical breakfast. Moments later, he heard his name spoken in a Scottish brogue thick as molasses. He looked up to see a gray-haired, ruddy-faced man of about sixty standing beside his table.

"Professor Jacobs?" the man said again.

Eli nodded.

"I am Wallace Duncan, a Christian pastor just sent to Hadera from a missionary society in Edinburgh. May I sit down?"

Eli nodded.

"I've been wanting to meet you," Duncan said, "because it seems that you and I may be the only non-Muslim religious leaders in the city. Though our beliefs differ widely, I thought you might be willing to help me get my bearings as I begin my work here."

The Scot explained his mission: at present, some seventy-five Christians lived in Hadera, and they had begged the missionary society for a pastor. He had been sent to organize the separate house churches into a unified whole.

"Hadera has more Christians than devout Jews," Eli said, shaking his head.

As the conversation continued, the two men found they had much in common: they loved the same books and music and were both avid fans of American baseball. An hour later they parted, agreeing to meet again the following Friday.

The pair met for breakfast every Friday for the next three weeks, and their friendship grew. With the current turmoil in Europe, it was inevitable that the Jewish professor and the Scottish pastor would discuss politics and the growing influence of British prime minister Judas Christopher. "I've even heard rumbles that the European Union wants to unite into a single empire and make Christopher its head," Eli said.

"I'm convinced these are the first tremors of an imminent upheaval that will bring about the worldwide disasters predicted by your Tanakh—what we Christians call the Old Testament—and by several New Testament books as well," Duncan replied.

Eli fell silent, and his eyebrows furrowed.

"What is it?" Duncan asked.

There was something about Duncan that made him easy to talk to, and Eli found himself pouring out his doubts about the faith he'd given his life to. When he finished, he smiled ruefully. "I guess I'm an Orthodox Jew who wonders whether he still believes in Judaism."

Duncan remained silent for a moment, his chin resting on his clasped hands. "Eli, do you know much about Christianity?"

"Only by hearsay. I've never studied it."

"I hope you will not find my question offensive, but I must ask. Would you be willing to hear how Christianity fulfills the majority of the Tanakh prophecies?"

"Yes, I'm ready to listen," Eli responded, surprising himself.

"Very good. We'll begin at breakfast next Friday."

* * *

The following Friday morning, Eli was full of questions as he entered the restaurant to meet with Pastor Duncan. His friend was not there, and Eli noticed that patrons and café employees were clustered around the TV.

"What's going on?" he asked.

One of the waitresses answered without taking her eyes off the screen. "Thousands of people have disappeared out of Israel—just vanished off the face of the earth. They're saying that seventy-five people are missing from Hadera."

"And millions upon millions have vanished around the world," a patron added. "There have been disasters everywhere. Two air crashes in Tel Aviv alone."

After waiting in the restaurant for a while, Eli decided his friend must not be coming. *Was he one of the people who went missing?* Eli wondered.

Eli no longer had an appetite, and he returned home to watch the news. Every channel—at least those that were still airing—reported a world in turmoil. Apparently people had disappeared in the same instant—wherever they were, whatever they were doing. It soon became clear that all those missing were Christians, though almost a quarter of American and British pastors remained.

"So only Christians have disappeared," Eli muttered, shaking his head in wonder. "I have no idea what all this means, but it must say something about the validity of Christianity."

In the next few weeks he began studying the Tanakh prophecies with his synagogue members. But like the Ethiopian eunuch in the book of Acts, the people floundered without anyone to explain what they were reading. Eli sank into discouragement.

"Self-Styled Prophets Create Turmoil in Jerusalem," the front page of Tel Aviv's newspaper screamed. Eli's pulse quickened as he read the story. Two unknown street preachers, calling themselves the two witnesses, were roaming the streets and parks of Jerusalem, calling Jews to repent of their sins, recognize the rabbi Jesus as the true Messiah, and return to their ancient calling to be a holy nation.

Eli dropped his newspaper. "Maybe these men can answer my questions." Within the hour, he was on a bus to Jerusalem.

Once he arrived, he learned that the two men—the "two witlesses" as the locals called them—often spoke in Jerusalem's Sacher Park. He hailed a cab so he could see for himself.

The park teemed with strolling couples, joggers, picnicking families, and the hollow pop of tennis balls. Yet an odd sound reached him from the distance—a jumble of dissonant shouts and invective. Curious, he followed the noise, and he soon saw the cause. An angry mob was hurling rotting fruit and raw eggs at two men standing on a bench. As he watched, police officers appeared and dispersed the unruly crowd.

The two men, dressed in threadbare black suits, strode to a drinking fountain, where they tried to wipe off their splattered clothing. Eli followed them.

As he approached, the taller man said, "Greetings, Professor Eli Jacobs."

Eli's mouth fell open. "How—how do you know who I am?"

"God revealed it to us. We have known you were coming since you left Hadera."

Eli gaped in disbelief. "Who on God's earth are you?"

"We are two of God's prophets. Come. Let's find a comfortable place to talk."

They led him to a nearby park bench under the shade of a spreading cedar. At their urging, Eli told his story, from his growing doubts about Judaism to his futile attempts to find the current meaning of ancient Tanakh prophecies.

"Have you ever read the Christian book of Revelation?" the shorter witness asked. When Eli admitted he had not, the man said, "Then we will read it with you. Tomorrow bring your Tanakh, and we will bring our Bibles. We will open your eyes to truths you have never suspected."

Over the next few evenings, the two witnesses showed Eli how Jewish prophetic books such as Daniel and Ezekiel match up with the apostle John's Revelation. They went on to compare these prophecies with world events, emphasizing Judas Christopher's expanded influence across Europe in the chaotic wake of the Rapture. "These events foreshadow the worldwide disasters prophesied in the books we've been studying."

Eli shook his head, trying to take it all in. "I wish I knew what we could do about it."

"That we can tell you," the taller witness said. "God has taken Christians out of the world to focus on His promise to bring His chosen people, the Jews, back to Him. In fact, God sent you to us because you have a role to play in that plan. You are to be His evangelist to all who will listen."

"But I am just one person. How can I—"

"No, you are not just one person any more than Elijah was in the wicked days of King Ahab. Just as God reserved seven thousand Israelites who did not bow to Baal, so He has chosen thousands of Jewish leaders like you to become evangelists throughout the world. All of them are new converts who came to Christ after the Rapture. Many of them are already at work."

"You see, you are not the first God has sent to us," the second witness said. "There will soon be 144,000 of you—12,000 from each of the ancient tribes of Israel—who will lead a worldwide movement to evangelize the world for Christ before the end comes."

"But I am not even a Christian."

"Aren't you ready to become one?"

"I am." Eli's voice was sober, but it also held an undercurrent of exultation. "I believe that Jesus Christ is truly the Son of God."

He let that truth sink in for a moment. "What now?"

"Come again tomorrow, and we will tell you."

\* \* \*

That night in his hotel room, Eli Jacobs dreamed of vague, distant chords from a breathtaking song. When the song ended, his heart ached for some beckoning mystery just beyond the horizon. Though he could not remember the melody after he awoke, he knew he had just heard a lost chord like the one that had so tantalized the composer Sullivan. Its elusive echoes filled him with unspeakable joy.

When Eli arrived at the park that afternoon, an even more clamorous mob surrounded the two witnesses. As he approached, the rioters began to pelt the speakers as before, but this time the missiles were not refuse and eggs; they were stones.

In a burst of outrage, Eli raced toward the barbarians, bellowing at them to stop. But as he drew closer, he stopped short. Though the air swarmed with rocks being hurled at short range, the witnesses stood unscathed. Finally the frustrated crowd gave up and turned away.

"What just happened?" Eli cried. "How is it possible that none of those stones hit you?"

"God has promised to protect us from harm until our task is complete," one of them said.

"Which brings us to the reason we asked you to return," the other added.

The three men sat on a bench as the two witnesses began their explanation. "As you and the other evangelists go out into the world, many will reject your message. You will endure the same kind of vitriol you just saw spewed at us. When people hear that the droughts, plagues, earthquakes, and contamination now beginning to cover the earth are God's warnings, they will, as they say, shoot the messenger and take out their anger on you."

"Well, that's not pleasant to hear," Eli said. "But it will be worth it if our apostate nation returns to its original calling."

"That's absolutely right!" the taller witness said. "The good news is that God has sealed and secured you for this purpose."

\* \* \*

Eli returned to Hadera buoyant and encouraged. On the following Sabbath, he gave his testimony to his congregation of twelve. He told them how the Tanakh prophecies meshed with the New Testament, how they explained the disappearance of the Christians and predicted coming world events. Three of the young men, college students, accepted his explanation eagerly and immediately became believers.

The remaining members stalked out of the synagogue. "How could you betray our heritage like this?" they demanded.

Eli and the three new believers met in his home that afternoon, recognizing that they were possibly the only Christians in a city of nearly one hundred thousand.

Eli explained what they were up against. "According to the prophecies, horrible persecutions will soon afflict Israel and Jews all over the world. We must persuade our people to acknowledge the resurrected Jesus as the prophesied Messiah, turn away from their sin, and resume their role as God's holy people."

To Eli's surprise, all three students felt the urgency of the call and were ready to join the evangelistic campaign. One went to England, one to New York, and the other to Germany.

Eli remained in Israel and, modeling his ministry after the apostle Paul, began traveling from town to town preaching in local synagogues. More often than not, the presiding rabbis ejected him before he had a chance to complete his sermon. But many people were responding. Typically a quarter to a third of those in attendance heard his message and believed. Of these, three or four usually felt the call to join the evangelistic effort. Eli was heartened.

An evangelist in Austria, fearing that phone and e-mail connections were no longer secure, organized an amateur ham-radio network to connect as many of the Jewish evangelists as possible. Eli bought a radio and learned through the network that the young man he'd sent to England had sent out new missionaries, who had also sent out missionaries, who had in turn sent out still others until Messianic Jews now preached Christ in all English-speaking nations. Other evangelists reported similar successes in every country in the world.

Soon there were 144,000 evangelists preaching across the globe, and in their wake came intense persecution. When the disasters foretold by the two witnesses began to descend upon the unrepentant world, people blamed the Messianic Jews for the calamities. It wasn't long before these evangelists began to encounter the same fury that had been hurled at the witnesses.

People hated them—not only for their message but also because their holy and pure lives exposed the immorality of the hearers. The audiences struck back, spitting at the evangelists and barraging them with curses and violence. Still, because the Lord had sealed these preachers for this very purpose, they were able to persevere unscathed.

\* \* \*

It was in the city of Be'er Sheva in southern Israel that Eli experienced his most spectacular success—and his first taste of persecution.

Of all the places Eli had been, the local synagogues in Be'er Sheva had been particularly receptive to his message. Led by God's Spirit, these new converts combined their resources to rent the local Andre

Minkoff Auditorium and invite the public to a major address by the controversial Professor Jacobs.

Nabal Cohan was owner of one of Be'er Sheva's many strip clubs. When he heard of the upcoming event, he called together the proprietors of related establishments—gentlemen's lounges, escort services, bars, casinos, and brothels—for an emergency meeting. More than seventy people attended.

"Gentlemen, we all know that an epidemic of Messianic Jewish preachers has infested our nation," Cohan began. "One of the most notorious of these will be speaking at the Minkoff Auditorium tomorrow night. I'm sure you know what their preaching has done to businesses like ours in other cities."

"Yes," the manager of a casino responded. "After this professor spoke in Ashkelon, business in our trades dropped 30 percent."

Several owners cited additional examples of financial losses and closures in other cities.

"I see that you understand the problem," Cohan said. "So the question is, how do we stop this guy?"

People tossed out ideas into the fog of tobacco smoke. Hire a hit man to put Jacobs down. Kidnap him and smuggle him out of town. Plant a car bomb. Send thugs to beat him to a pulp. Plant hecklers in the auditorium to drown out his speech.

No one could agree until the manager of an escort service said, "Why get rid of Jacobs when we can use him to our advantage?"

"How so?" Cohan asked.

"We could discredit him publicly. Think what that would mean: his speech would be canceled, and even better, the people he has already converted would discount his message and revert to their former habits. They will be ours again."

"It won't work," someone else replied. "We won't catch him doing anything wrong. These Messianic Jews are as upright as a saloon piano."

"Did I say he had to do something wrong? We simply make it *appear* that he is doing something wrong."

"I suppose you have an idea," Cohan said.

"All we have to do is pick him up, force him into one of our establishments, and then set him free once he's inside," the man continued. "He'll make a beeline for the door, and we'll have a news crew waiting with their TV cameras as he comes out. Think what it will do to his cause when that footage is broadcast all over the world."

"And think what it will do for *our* cause," Cohan added gleefully.

The plan was adopted unanimously.

*  *  *

That evening after dinner, Eli returned to his hotel room. As he slid his key card into the door, two burly men appeared behind him. One clapped a hand over his mouth while the other clutched his arm.

"Don't say anything," his captors ordered. "You've said way too much already." They dragged him down the back stairway and forced him into a waiting sedan.

As the car sped away, Eli quipped, "If you're taking me to dinner, don't bother. I just ate." Getting no answer, he continued, "Well, then, while we're on our way to wherever, let me tell you about the Messiah our ancestors rejected."

As Eli continued to talk about Jesus, the car pulled into an alley and stopped at a dimly lit delivery entrance. The sign above read "The Salome Club" in both Hebrew and English. Eli did not resist as the two men shoved him through the door and into the club's seating area. One held him captive while the other approached Nabal Cohan, who was standing several feet away.

"We got him, Boss."

"Did he give you any trouble?"

"Didn't resist at all. Not even when we brought him in here. But

I'll tell you, I'm glad to be rid of him. He preached to us the whole way. Almost turned me into a Messianic Jew."

"Okay, everything is ready," Cohan said. "Release him and tell him he's free to go."

But when Eli was set free, he didn't scurry toward the door as his captors had expected. Instead, he stepped in front of the stage where girls were performing and faced the audience. "Ladies and gentlemen, let me tell you about the Messiah our ancestors rejected."

Eli had uttered little more than three sentences before a drunken patron stood and shouted, "Get that freak out of here!" A chorus of voices took up the cry, and a bouncer rushed forward to force the professor out the front door.

But before he reached Eli, another cry rang out: "Let him speak! The guy's got guts!"

"Yeah, let's at least hear what he has to say," someone in the crowd echoed.

At that moment a chair flew through the air and knocked the bouncer to the floor. More chairs followed, sailing across the room from all directions. Several drunken patrons began throwing punches, and others quickly joined the fray. In moments, the chaos escalated into an outright brawl. Drinking glasses were shattered, tables were flipped over, and beverages were splattered everywhere. It was a good ten minutes before sirens screamed and police burst through the door.

An hour later, Eli Jacobs sat on a cot, staring through the bars of a municipal jail cell. He had been charged with inciting a riot. "When will my hearing come up?" he asked a prison guard.

"Maybe never," the guard sneered. "The law in this city sides with the businesses you're trying to ruin. Can't risk losing the taxes. You may rot in this cell with your trial conveniently forgotten."

"Well," Eli replied, "the apostle Paul endured much worse."

That night he dreamed once more of a choir singing the same magnificent song. When he awakened, his soul ached with an unquenchable longing to hear the tune again, to immerse himself in its ecstatic chords.

The morning guard greeted Eli with a pleasant surprise. One of the leading city magistrates had become a Messianic Jew after hearing Eli preach in nearby Ashkelon. After reviewing the evidence, he ordered the prisoner released. That evening, as scheduled, Eli Jacobs delivered his message at the Andre Minkoff Auditorium.

\* \* \*

Three and a half years after the Rapture, the world was rocked by new traumas—from Judas Christopher's desecration of the Temple and unprecedented reign of terror against the Jews to cataclysmic plagues and natural disasters.

When it seemed that the horror could not get worse, it did. Christopher was elected president of the European nations, and from that position of power, he ground the rest of the world under his heel—largely by economic coercion and military conquest. Natural disasters increased exponentially all over the world, causing widespread death and unprecedented misery.

Eli and the rest of the worldwide network of 144,000 evangelists, now sure they were in a race against time, spent every waking hour calling people to repentance. Heartening successes were interspersed with violent rejections. But the people they had led to the faith became shining beacons of love and holiness, and many became diligent champions of the Good News—some through the example of their changed lives and others through their deaths for the sake of Christ.

The worldwide spiral into chaos seemed inevitable until Christopher's tyranny began to foment rebellion. Several North African and Asian nations reached the tipping point. They formed an alliance and marched their armies against Christopher, whose forces were amassed in Israel, preparing to vent his deep-seated hatred of the Jews by destroying Jerusalem.

Eli Jacobs sat in his cottage in Hadera, his eardrums assaulted by the cacophony of bombs, missiles, gunfire, artillery salvos, and screaming warplanes. Christopher's battle against the allied rebels had spread over all Israel. Eli learned through the ham-radio network that a massive Chinese army had just crossed the Euphrates River and was now marching toward the battlefront. Sensing the end of the Tribulation was near, he remained at peace, confident that he was in his Lord's hands.

That night he had a dream so vivid he couldn't distinguish it from reality. He found himself in a place of splendor beyond imagination. A great throne towered before him, surrounded by a dazzling rainbow of gem-like colors. Before the throne lay a sea as smooth and as clear as glass. Magnificent creatures hovered above it.

He was so absorbed in the majesty before him that it was some time before he realized he was not alone. On one side stood the student he had sent to England. On the other side stood the other two men from Hadera. Then, looking about him in awe, Eli realized that he was standing among a great throng—the rest of the 144,000 whose efforts had brought so many people to their Messiah.

At once, as if on cue, Eli Jacobs and the others began to sing.

"I know this song!" he exclaimed. It was the beautiful tune that had so often eluded him on earth.

He lifted his voice with unparalleled joy. As he and his fellow evangelists sang their praise to God, he realized this was not a dream. He now stood in the throne room of heaven itself.

* * *

# THE SCRIPTURE BEHIND THE STORY

During the Tribulation, the Antichrist will work to consolidate his power and exalt himself in the Holy of Holies in Jerusalem. While he is crushing those who refuse to bow before his statue, the greatest spiritual awakening of all time will take place. And this awakening will come through the ministry of the 144,000 sealed Jewish evangelists.

Their story is another dramatic demonstration of the way God takes care of His people during an era of trial and tribulation, reminding us that "God has not cast away His people whom He foreknew" (Romans 11:2).

The 144,000 who faithfully serve the Lord during the Tribulation period are introduced in Revelation 7:1-8 and discussed again in Revelation 14:1-5. Here is what the Bible tells us about them.

### They Are Selected from the Twelve Tribes of Israel

I heard the number of those who were sealed. One hundred and forty-four thousand of all the tribes of the children of Israel were sealed.

REVELATION 7:4

In spite of the absolute clarity of this passage of Scripture, some scholars still identify the 144,000 witnesses as representatives of the church of Jesus Christ. Let me be very clear: the 144,000 witnesses do not represent the church. Just as the redeemed elders are already in heaven, so is the church—raptured between chapters 3 and 4 of Revelation. Furthermore, in Revelation 14, the 144,000 and the elders are present in heaven as two distinct groups. According to J. A. Seiss, no error "so beclouds the Scriptures, and so unsettles the faith of men, as this constant attempt to read *Church* for *Israel*, and Christian peoples for Jewish tribes."[1]

The matter of the sealed witnesses' identity is so significant that the names of the tribes of Israel from which they come are listed in Revelation 7:4-8. In this passage, we are told that twelve thousand witnesses are selected from each of the twelve tribes.

Throughout Scripture, the number twelve is consistently associated with Israel. The Jewish high priest wore a breastplate bearing twelve precious stones, the table of showbread displayed twelve holy loaves, and there are twelve gates in the city of God—all representing Israel's tribes. Matthew 19:28 tells of a future day when Jesus is sitting on His throne and the twelve apostles will "sit on twelve thrones, judging the twelve tribes of Israel."

These depictions of Israel around the number twelve all lead up to this culmination in Revelation: the sealed individuals from the twelve tribes of Israel.

### They Are Sealed on Their Foreheads

> I saw another angel ascending from the east, having the seal of the living God. And he cried with a loud voice to the four angels to whom it was granted to harm the earth and the sea, saying, "Do not harm the earth, the sea, or the trees till we have sealed the servants of our God on their foreheads."
>
> REVELATION 7:2-3

This text gives us no specific information about what this "seal of the living God" is like except that it served to protect the servants of God from His judgments on the earth. Revelation 14, however, identifies the seal as "His Father's name written on their foreheads" (verse 1).

This is not the first time that God sealed off some of His people from tribulation and divine wrath:

- When God sent the great Flood upon the earth, He sealed Noah and his family from the rest of the human race so the waters would not hurt them (Genesis 6–8).

- God told Lot and his family to get out of Sodom before the fire descended, thus sealing them from terrible judgment (Genesis 19).
- God sealed the firstborn of all the Jewish families who applied sacrificial blood to the doorposts of their homes in Egypt (Exodus 12).
- God sealed Rahab and her household by means of the scarlet cord when He destroyed Jericho (Joshua 2, 6).
- Even though Elijah didn't realize it, God had sealed seven thousand Israelites in his day who had not bowed their knee to Baal (1 Kings 19).

### *They Are Servants of the Living God*

> Do not harm the earth, the sea, or the trees till we have sealed the servants of our God on their foreheads.
>
> REVELATION 7:3

The seal of the living God will not be merely an external mark; it will also be a moral badge. These witnesses are described as "servants of our God." They are people who have not bowed to the Antichrist but have devoted themselves sincerely to God.

When Jesus talked about being sealed (John 6:27), He was referring to the Holy Spirit's descending on Him and enabling Him to do the mighty work of God that He was sent to do.

Perhaps the seal in Revelation 7 is the same as the seal of which Paul spoke:

> He who establishes us with you in Christ and has anointed us is God, who also has sealed us and given us the Spirit in our hearts as a guarantee.
>
> 2 CORINTHIANS 1:21-22

In Him you also trusted, after you heard the word of truth, the gospel of your salvation; in whom also, having believed, you were sealed with the Holy Spirit of promise.

EPHESIANS 1:13

Do not grieve the Holy Spirit of God, by whom you were sealed for the day of redemption.

EPHESIANS 4:30

The prophet Joel connected the ministry of the Holy Spirit with the powerful ministries that will take place in the end times:

It shall come to pass afterward
That I will pour out My Spirit on all flesh;
Your sons and your daughters shall prophesy,
Your old men shall dream dreams,
Your young men shall see visions.
And also on My menservants and on My maidservants
I will pour out My Spirit in those days.

And I will show wonders in the heavens and
        in the earth:
Blood and fire and pillars of smoke.
The sun shall be turned into darkness,
And the moon into blood,
Before the coming of the great and awesome day
        of the LORD.
And it shall come to pass
That whoever calls on the name of the LORD
Shall be saved.
For in Mount Zion and in Jerusalem there shall be
        deliverance,

As the Lord has said,
Among the remnant whom the Lord calls.
JOEL 2:28-32

This description by the prophet Joel is of the 144,000 who, by the power of the Holy Spirit, will speak prophesies, see visions, and participate in miracles during the Tribulation.

### They Are Separated unto God

These are the ones who were not defiled with women, for they are virgins.
REVELATION 14:4

This verse has caused a great deal of confusion among commentators. Many scholars interpret "were not defiled with women" to mean they do not commit *spiritual* adultery (2 Corinthians 11:2; James 4:4). I once held this interpretation myself. While that remains a possibility, it seems more reasonable to assume that these sealed servants of the Most High God are male celibates.

When we understand the pressures of the Tribulation period, it's easy to comprehend why these 144,000 preachers would have a very difficult married life. Paul sets the precedent in his discussion of singleness in 1 Corinthians 7: "Brethren, the time is short, so that from now on even those who have wives should be as though they had none. . . . I want you to be without care. He who is unmarried cares for the things of the Lord—how he may please the Lord. But he who is married cares about the things of the world—how he may please his wife. . . . And this I say for your own profit, not that I may put a leash on you, but . . . that you may serve the Lord without distraction" (verses 29, 32-33, 35).

If there will ever be a time when serving God without distraction is called for, it will surely be the Tribulation period!

### They Are Strong in Their Faith

> These are the ones who follow the Lamb wherever He
> goes. . . . And in their mouth was found no deceit, for they
> are without fault before the throne of God.
>
> REVELATION 14:4-5

The Jewish witnesses possess tremendous strength of character, and their example will bring revival to Israel during the Tribulation period. Because of the witnesses' loyal and truthful declaration of the gospel, millions will come to Christ during this time of distress.

This should not come as a surprise. Think of the spiritual power that would be harnessed by 144,000 evangelists who are unspotted by the world and pure in their thoughts and words!

### They Are Spared from Coming Judgment

> After these things I saw four angels standing at the four
> corners of the earth, holding the four winds of the earth,
> that the wind should not blow on the earth, on the sea, or
> on any tree. Then I saw another angel ascending from the
> east, having the seal of the living God. And he cried with
> a loud voice to the four angels to whom it was granted to
> harm the earth and the sea, saying, "Do not harm the earth,
> the sea, or the trees till we have sealed the servants of our
> God on their foreheads."
>
> REVELATION 7:1-3

The last verse in Revelation 6 makes an announcement and asks an important question: "The great day of His wrath has come, and who is able to stand?" (verse 17).

Chapter 7 responds to the announcement and answers the question through what John's vision reveals next. He sees four angels "standing at the four corners of the earth," holding back the terrible winds of God's judgments like a hunter restraining fierce dogs. The term "four corners" does not indicate a square earth; rather, it reflects the four quadrants of the compass. John reports that these destructive winds, straining to blast the earth from all four directions, are being held back. The apostle then watches as a fifth angel comes from the east and instructs the four angels to rein in the winds a little longer: "Do not harm the earth, the sea, or the trees till we have sealed the servants of our God on their foreheads" (verse 3).

Like the sun that rises from the east to sustain and preserve life on earth, this angel of divine protection keeps the faithful 144,000 preachers safe from the judgment of God.

### They Are Secure in the Midst of the Tribulation

> I looked, and behold, a Lamb standing on Mount Zion, and with Him one hundred and forty-four thousand, having His Father's name written on their foreheads.
>
> REVELATION 14:1

Just as the three young Hebrew men were kept alive in King Nebuchadnezzar's fiery furnace, so these 144,000 sealed Hebrews will be protected from Satan and the Antichrist throughout the entire Tribulation period. Mark Hitchcock paints this triumphant picture: "In Revelation 14:1-5, John sees the 144,000 at the end of the Tribulation standing triumphantly on Mount Zion—the city of Jerusalem. Notice he doesn't see 143,999. All 144,000 have been divinely preserved by the Lord. Not one has been overlooked."[2]

### They Are Successful in Their Ministry

> After these things I looked, and behold, a great multitude which no one could number, of all nations, tribes, peoples,

and tongues, standing before the throne and before the
Lamb, clothed with white robes, with palm branches in
their hands.

REVELATION 7:9

Perhaps, like me, you have heard people talk about the great revival
that will take place on this earth before Jesus returns to take His church
to heaven. I only wish this were true. Instead, as we discover from
2 Thessalonians 2, there will be a great "falling away" from the faith
(verse 3).

The massive revival coming in the future will take place *after* the
Rapture, during the Tribulation. And these 144,000 sealed Jewish evangelists will lead it. They will be empowered to preach the gospel to the
world, and the result will be a revival like the world has never seen.
Helped by the impact of the two witnesses (Revelation 11) and the
sobering effects of international calamities, the 144,000 Jewish evangelists will cover the earth with the gospel of Jesus Christ, and millions
will be saved.

John describes these newly saved as "a great multitude which no
one could number" (Revelation 7:9). He also makes it clear that these
people will hail from "every tribe and tongue and people and nation"
(5:9; see also 11:9; 13:7; and 14:6). This vast evangelistic enterprise
will fulfill the words of Jesus in His Olivet discourse: "This gospel of
the kingdom will be preached in all the world as a witness to all the
nations, and then the end will come" (Matthew 24:14).

### They Are Set Apart for the Kingdom

These are the ones who come out of the great tribulation,
and washed their robes and made them white in the blood
of the Lamb.

REVELATION 7:14

The 144,000 Jewish evangelists will be specially preserved all through the seven years of the Tribulation so that they will be alive when the Millennium begins. At that time they will enter the Kingdom and reign with Christ and His glorified church. This will fulfill God's promise to His people through the prophets Ezekiel and Zephaniah.

According to Ezekiel 48, each of the twelve tribes will have its own assigned geographical boundaries in the Millennium. The prophet Zephaniah pictures the set-apart remnant this way: "The remnant of Israel shall do no unrighteousness and speak no lies, nor shall a deceitful tongue be found in their mouth; for they shall feed their flocks and lie down, and no one shall make them afraid" (Zephaniah 3:13).

### They Are Singing a New Song in Heaven

I looked, and behold, a Lamb standing on Mount Zion, and
with Him one hundred and forty-four thousand, having
His Father's name written on their foreheads. And I heard
a voice from heaven, like the voice of many waters, and like
the voice of loud thunder. And I heard the sound of harpists
playing their harps. They sang as it were a new song before
the throne, before the four living creatures, and the elders;
and no one could learn that song except the hundred and
forty-four thousand who were redeemed from the earth.

REVELATION 14:1-3

Throughout history, God's people have written songs of celebration to commemorate the triumph of their God.

Moses penned the first recorded song of praise when the Lord led Israel out of slavery and defeated the Egyptians on the shores of the Red Sea. With great joy, Moses led the children of Israel in singing, "I will sing to the LORD, for He has triumphed gloriously! The horse and its rider He has thrown into the sea!" (Exodus 15:1). There is also the song of Deborah recorded in Judges 5, and King David's song of victory in 2 Samuel 22 and Psalm 18. In these songs of triumph, the writers celebrate God's victories on their behalf.

As John views the Lamb standing on Mount Zion in triumph, he hears a voice from heaven along with the sound of harpists, playing and singing a new song before the throne. This is a different choir from the one John saw earlier, which consisted of far more than 144,000: "The number of them was ten thousand times ten thousand, and thousands of thousands, saying with a loud voice: 'Worthy is the Lamb who was slain to receive power and riches and wisdom, and strength and honor and glory and blessing!'" (Revelation 5:11-12).

Now John sees this smaller choir (if a choir of 144,000 can be called small), and they're singing a song that no one else can learn—because no one else has experienced what these witnesses have been through. They are the ones who suffered through the bloodshed of the Tribulation, witnessing great carnage and destruction. But they also saw many people come to Christ through their ministry. Because of their unique experience, they possess a unique song of praise.

One of my most memorable experiences as a student at Dallas Seminary was the first day I went to chapel. I will never forget entering Chafer Chapel and hearing the chaplain say, "Gentlemen, let's stand to sing." When five hundred men began singing praise to God at the tops of their voices, I cried. If I was emotional over the sound of five hundred men, I cannot imagine what it would be like to hear 144,000 voices singing praise to the Lamb.

The American Grammy Award–winning composer Eric Whitacre gives us a taste of what this choir may sound like. Whitacre is best known for his Virtual Choir, in which people from around the world record their voices singing one or more parts of a song. He then merges the best tracks into one astonishingly beautiful choir and posts the results on YouTube.

Whitacre's Virtual Choir 1.0 featured 185 singers from twelve different countries. His most recent effort, Virtual Choir 3.0, combined 3,746 submissions from 73 countries and was released in April 2012. The choir has been dubbed "the choir as big as the Internet" and "the world's most beautiful choir." But Revelation describes a choir that will dwarf Whitacre's. The choir John saw is made up of twelve thousand voices from each of the twelve tribes of Israel.

Notice that the 144,000 singers are accompanied by harps. Did you know that harps are mentioned some fifty times in the Old Testament? In each instance, they are associated with joy. A harp is never played during a time of mourning or sadness. When Israel was in captivity, the psalmist described their experience this way: "By the rivers of Babylon, there we sat down, yea, we wept when we remembered Zion. We hung our harps upon the willows in the midst of it" (Psalm 137:1-2).

A new song, accompanied by the harp, is the time-honored tribute that God's people offer Him when He has come to their rescue: "I will sing a new song to You, O God; on a harp of ten strings I will sing praises to You, the One who gives salvation to kings, who delivers David His servant from the deadly sword" (Psalm 144:9-10).

As God's people recognize the ways God has delivered them, they respond with lively and joyous songs of praise. This has often been a mark of spiritual revival. During the First Great Awakening, Jonathan Edwards noted how profoundly revival had affected the worship of his congregation in Northampton, Massachusetts: "Our public praises were greatly enlivened, and God was served in our psalmody as in the beauties of holiness. There was scarce any part of divine worship wherein God's saints among us had grace so drawn forth, and their hearts so lifted up, as in singing the praises of God."[3]

As Jonathan Edwards reported, there is tremendous emotional

power in music. In a talk entitled "The Sense of an Ending," Professor Jeremy Begbie tells of preaching in a poor South African church:

> I was told, immediately before the service, that a house just around the corner from the church had just been burned to the ground because the man who lived there was a suspected thief. A week before that, a tornado had cut through the township, ripping apart fifty homes; five people were killed. And then I was told that the very night before, a gang hounded down a fourteen-year-old, a member of the church's Sunday school and stabbed him to death.
>
> The pastor began his opening prayer: "Lord, you are the Creator and the Sovereign, but why did the wind come like a snake and tear our roofs off? Why did a mob cut short the life of one of our own children, when he had everything to live for? Over and over again, Lord, we are in the midst of death."
>
> As he spoke, the congregation responded with a dreadful sighing and groaning. And then, once he finished his prayer, very slowly, the whole congregation began to sing, at first very quietly, then louder. They sang and they sang, song after song of praise—praise to a God who in Jesus had plunged the very worst to give us a promise of an ending beyond all imagination. The singing gave that congregation a foretaste of the end.[4]

As devastating as the Tribulation period will be, it is clear God never removes His hand from the earth. The 144,000 sealed Jewish evangelists are proof that God is still sovereign, still orchestrating events according to His plan of ultimate victory, and still inspiring His people to sing songs of praise to His great name.

## chapter four

# THE TWO WITNESSES

Israel's Prime Minister Yehudi Abrams smiled as he posed with Prime Minister Judas Christopher of Britain. The crowd in Tel Aviv applauded as the two men stepped up to the podium in front of a cluster of microphones and TV cameras.

"My dear citizens of Israel." Abrams's voice was buoyant. "I am happy to announce the signing of an unprecedented treaty in which Prime Minister Christopher has guaranteed peace between Israel and our Islamic neighbors—as well as defense from any other aggressor nation—for seven years. He will immediately station British troops throughout Israel to enforce the terms of the agreement. Furthermore . . ." Abrams paused, his voice cracking with emotion. "Prime Minister Christopher has generously promised to provide funds and military protection as we rebuild our holy Temple on its ancient historical site."

Cheers and applause erupted as Christopher stepped up to the microphones. "On behalf of my country, I would like to express how happy we are to be the agents that have finally brought peace to the Middle East. Please be assured that Great Britain, which spearheaded the establishment of your nation in 1948, will always be your staunch friend and ally."

Moshe Mendel, mayor of Jerusalem, watched the televised press conference from his office. "Thank the Lord God of Israel," he murmured, clasping his hands together.

For years, Jerusalem had been a target for terrorist attacks by Israel's many enemies. Now with peace assured, Jerusalem and the rest of Israel could dismantle expensive military installations that continually depleted the nation's economic resources.

\* \* \*

In the months following the treaty, Israel directed its attention and funds away from military endeavors and poured its efforts into domestic expenditures. Seemingly overnight, the nation's prosperity exploded. But with this new reality came some unexpected cultural changes as well. Following the pattern of the Western world, the Israeli people began to descend deeper into a quagmire of self-indulgence and pleasure seeking. This shift alarmed Mayor Mendel.

In a meeting with Yehudi Abrams, the mayor shoved a six-inch stack of papers across the prime minister's desk.

"What is all this?" Abrams asked.

"Look at them." Mendel's voice was tense. "Just take a look, Mr. Prime Minister."

Abrams shuffled through several pages. "These are merely applications for new-business licenses. Why are you bringing them to me?"

"Do you not see what kind of businesses are represented here?"

"Well, yes. Here's one for a casino, another for a tavern, and one for a strip club. We've had these establishments in Israel for decades. What's the problem?"

"What's the problem? Can't you see that our nation is becoming a moral cesspool? We have always exercised restraint in granting such licenses, but each of these applications is backed by citizens' petitions. If I grant them all, we'll have a strip club on every corner. We must reject these applications if we are to maintain any semblance of national morality."

"Well, if this is what the people want, who are we to deny them?" Abrams shrugged his shoulders. "Israel is, after all, a democracy."

Feeling he had no choice, Mendel issued the licenses. Once he was back in his office, he put his head in his hands, trying to shake the feeling that his country was slipping into an era of unprecedented depravity.

\* \* \*

Aaron and his live-in girlfriend, Sephora, always ate their evening meal early. They frequented an upscale restaurant in Jerusalem, and they liked the privacy before the dinner rush arrived. One night they had just begun eating when the voice of the maître d' drew their attention to the front of the restaurant.

"Yes, I know you see many empty tables," he was saying to two men who had just entered. "But . . . well, they are all reserved for the evening. You might try David's Diner two blocks down the street."

"Oh, how disgusting!" Sephora said. "Just look at them! I'm glad Lazar is turning them away."

The spurned patrons were dressed completely in black, but their suits were now faded and blotched with permanent stains. The knees and elbows were threadbare, and frayed threads rimmed the cuffs of their coats. Both men wore hats—one a grease-smudged black fedora and the other a British Ascot cap, also black. The men themselves, however, appeared to be clean, and their beards were trimmed and neat.

"Very well," the taller man said. "We thank you for your recommendation." They touched the brims of their hats and left.

Aaron and Sephora finished their dinner and took a walk, as they often did, toward Sacher Park. It was more than an hour until sundown, and the park teemed with joggers, teenagers playing basketball, and families cooking on portable grills while their children played tag. On the perimeter of the grassy expanse, a sizable cluster of onlookers stood gathered around one of the park benches.

Aaron pointed in the direction of the crowd. "What's happening over there?" Curious, they drew closer.

"Hey, it's one of the seedy men we saw at the restaurant," Sephora said.

They reached the edge of the crowd, where the words of the taller stranger rang out clear and strong: "Men and women of Israel, you have the exalted honor of being a special people chosen out of all nations to bring God's holy One to the earth. But you killed Him—the Messiah who came to save you. Other nations recognized and accepted what you rejected, and out of reverence they call this city holy."

His tone became even more serious. "But I tell you that you are not holy. Evil abounds throughout your land. Your depravity would make Sodom blush. I tell you that the Messiah whom you spurned will soon return to ascend His rightful throne and rule over you. Unless you repent of your evil, His judgment will descend like an executioner's ax, and you will perish forever."

A voice shouted from the crowd. "So this man you say we killed is going to crawl out of His grave and do us in? What is He, a zombie?" Laughter rippled through the crowd.

"Mock me if you will, but I urge you to heed our warning."

"Just who are you to tell us we are depraved and doomed?"

The speaker's companion stepped up on the bench. "We are God's witnesses sent here to call you, His people, back to the holy standards of the Law and the Prophets before it's too late."

"Two witnesses?" another voice cried. "Don't you mean two *witlesses*?" The crowd howled with laughter.

After several more exchanges, Aaron grabbed Sephora's hand and pulled her toward the walking path. "Why are we standing here listening to these kooks?" he said.

"But what if their warnings are true? What if we really did kill God's Messiah and He's coming back to judge us?"

"Oh, stop it, Sephora! Even if there was a God, do you really think He would yank a zombie from a tomb and make him king? I've had enough of this nonsense. Let's get out of here."

Sephora followed, glancing back over her shoulder. But unlike Lot's wife, she couldn't help but wonder if she was plunging into Sodom rather than leaving it.

* * *

In the next several months, the two witnesses appeared daily all over Jerusalem—in parks, in public squares, on street corners, at markets—anywhere people were around to hear. In the evenings they sometimes rented assembly halls, where they drew considerable crowds, until the police escorted them out.

As the notoriety of the two witnesses spread, they quickly became media targets. Networks broadcast clips of their speeches all over the world, and commentators used their words to mock the absurdity of Christian belief. The two men also provided fodder for late-night talk shows and political cartoonists.

But it wasn't long before the entertainment value of the two witnesses grew thin and people became intolerant of their continued demands for repentance. They were denied access to public buildings. They were run off street corners. Vendors refused to serve them because their prophetic zeal irritated customers. And at their favorite venue—public parks—people now pelted them with eggs and rotting food. Yet the two witnesses were undeterred.

One evening Aaron and Sephora stopped to get groceries after dinner. Upon leaving the store, they passed a construction site and happened upon the two witnesses addressing a jeering crowd.

Aaron stopped. "Sephora, let's go have a little fun." He tugged her toward the crowd.

"Please don't," she said. "I don't want you to ridicule those men. They scare me."

"I'm not going to ridicule them. I just want to ask a couple of perfectly reasonable questions. Come on."

Sephora reluctantly followed.

Aaron edged toward the front and then called out to the one speaking, this time the shorter of the two. "Sir, you have warned us about our impending doom. If these warnings are true, we should certainly take them seriously."

A few onlookers turned and glared at Aaron.

Ignoring them, he continued, "We will believe you if you will just give us a sign proving that you are indeed God's prophets." Aaron pointed toward a gutter, filled with water after the rain from earlier in the evening. "Sir, if you will simply part that puddle as Moses parted the Red Sea, we will believe."

The crowd snickered. The two witnesses stood impassively, gazing at Aaron.

"Very well," Aaron said. "Perhaps my test is too difficult. Let me pose an easier one. I've heard that the ancient prophet Elijah caused a widow's jar of oil to remain full no matter how much she used." He reached into Sephora's shopping bag, took out a small bottle of olive oil, and poured the contents onto the ground. Then he held the empty bottle high. "If you will just refill this bottle as Elijah filled the widow's jar, we will believe."

The witness replied, "You want a sign? Very well, I will give you a sign—a sign like that which Elijah gave to the wicked King Ahab: today's rain was the last you will see in this nation for three and a half years."

The taller witness stepped forward. "I, too, will give you a sign. Just as Moses turned the Nile into blood, tomorrow morning when you rise, your own water sources will yield contaminated water as red as blood. You will drink it because you have no option. And you will suffer all manner of diseases, much like the plagues inflicted on ancient Egypt. Your own stubbornness has brought these woes upon you so that you may see the power of God and turn to Him before worse ills descend on you."

Shouts of anger spewed from the mob, and this time the barrage they hurled at the two witnesses consisted not of rotting food but of stones. Yet their targets stood unharmed. Rocks of all sizes whizzed past them. The mob pushed in so they could attack at even closer range, to no avail.

Furious that none of the stones were hitting their mark, Aaron picked up a rock the size of a baseball.

"No!" Sephora grabbed Aaron's arm. "What if they're right? We will know soon enough. Please, let them be."

The next morning Sephora rose early and, still half asleep, turned on the kitchen tap to make coffee. When she looked at the pot, she screamed and let it slip out of her hands. The pot shattered, and brownish-red liquid splattered across the floor.

\* \* \*

The water throughout Israel remained putrid and red as the rainy season came and went with no precipitation. The water levels on the Sea of Galilee plummeted. Springs dried up, the aquifers drained, and the Jordan River slowed to a trickle, no longer reaching the Dead Sea. Crops failed; vineyards shriveled; sheep and cattle died. A constant caravan of trucks, trains, and ships brought water into Israel, but it wasn't enough. Hospitals and mortuaries were filled to capacity.

One day when Sephora was too sick to work, she lay in bed half dozing, half listening to the drone of a newsman: "And since these catastrophes coincidentally followed the predictions of the two mysterious prophets, their notoriety has exploded across the globe. Yesterday they added fuel to the controversy, as you will see in this clip."

Sephora reached for the remote and punched up the volume. The faces of the two witnesses flashed on the screen. The taller one was speaking: "People of Israel and the world, please hear me. The disasters you are now enduring are God's warnings, mercifully sent in advance of His judgment to call you to repentance. But you have not repented. You still wallow in the filth of your depravity."

Sephora flushed as she thought of her relationship with Aaron. *I know that living together isn't the most moral option, but surely what we're doing isn't nearly as bad as the sins he's talking about.*

The witness continued: "You have turned away from the God who called you to be a holy people. Worse, you have placed your trust in a man who will soon inflict more evil on the Jewish nation than Pharaoh, Nebuchadnezzar, Antiochus, Herod, the emperor Titus, Hitler, or any other despot who has yet lived. If you do not turn from your evil, be sure that the disasters that afflict you today are mere pinpricks compared to what will come."

A reporter in the crowd spoke up. "Who is this evil one you're so roundly denouncing?"

"Do you not know? He is none other than Prime Minister Judas Christopher. Hear my warning, and hear it well. This man will soon betray you. He will blaspheme God, and he will demand your unconditional worship and obedience. Reject him while there is still time, and turn back to the God who loves you."

The scene switched back to the network host. "We now have with us the prominent pollster Reuben Cohen to tell us how people are responding to this latest salvo."

Cohen's face flashed on the screen. "Our immediate straw poll shows that few people believe that the drought, the water contamination, and the gastronomical plagues are really God's judgments. Most are angry that the witnesses are using these coincidental natural disasters to reinforce their platform. Jews in particular are outraged that the two witnesses have denounced Judas Christopher—the hero who brought them peace."

"Where do you think all this will end?" the host asked.

"Frankly, I fear violence," Cohen said. "People are clamoring for these two troublemakers to be destroyed."

Sephora clicked off the TV and sat trembling. The witnesses' warning rang in her head. *More judgments are coming if we don't repent.*

* * *

As the two witnesses gained more public exposure, Mayor Mendel faced increasing pressure to take action against them. His office had been flooded by demands from people all around the world insisting that he put a stop to their outrageous threats. Yet as Mendel continually pointed out, the witnesses were doing nothing illegal.

Finally, Jerusalem's police chief took matters into his own hands. Knowing he would have overwhelming public support, he sent a squadron of officers to the park to arrest the two witnesses. As the police officers advanced toward the two men, they drew in a deep breath and then exhaled. A wave of intense heat met the officers. They forced themselves forward toward the invisible flame but soon fell to the ground, writhing and screaming in the throes of death.

The chief dispatched a second squad with orders to shoot and kill the witnesses. The two prophets stood impassively as the police officers aimed their weapons. All at once, staccato blasts resounded throughout the park. When the firing ceased, the witnesses stood rooted like mighty oaks, unfazed and unflinching. The taller one said, "You cannot harm us until we have finished the task God has called us to perform."

\* \* \*

As the two witnesses' verbal pronouncements against Judas Christopher intensified, so did his fury. They were attracting too much attention, and this wasn't the kind of publicity he was looking for. Mayor Mendel was clearly unable to deal with them; it was time to take matters into his own hands.

Christopher put in a call to Prime Minister Abrams. "You and that weak-kneed mayor have let these two gnats bite us long enough. Tomorrow morning a contingent of my troops stationed in Israel will move in and exterminate them once and for all."

"But, sir," Abrams replied, "Jerusalem's police have tried to kill them several times. They seem to be invincible."

"Nonsense!" Christopher shot back. "No one is invincible." *At least not yet,* he added to himself.

Just after sunrise the next day, the two witnesses lay dead in the street, brought down by the first rounds fired by the British squad. No one understood why these troops were successful when all previous attempts had failed. But Christopher didn't care; he was just relieved that this insidious cancer had finally been eradicated.

Live footage of the assassination was broadcast around the globe, and Christopher ordered the corpses displayed publicly so the entire world could see their humiliating end. "Leave them exposed for three and a half days," he commanded. "One day for every year their vitriol has poisoned our lives."

In the wake of the news, Israel celebrated with an orgy of indulgence. The death of the witnesses was the cover story for every news outlet and talk show around the world. Tour guides even ran excursions into Jerusalem to view the unburied corpses.

As noon approached on the fourth day of the celebrating, Prime Minister Abrams stood on a specially constructed platform overlooking the public square in the government district. Behind him sat Israel's highest political and religious officials, and the square in front of him brimmed with a sea of people. The bullet-riddled bodies of the two witnesses were sprawled before the prime minister on muslin tarps in a ghoulish parody of a funeral. The corpses were ashen except for the mottled purple blotches where blood had pooled.

Abrams addressed the crowd. "Today you see before you the bodies of two instigators who have been the bane of our existence for three and a half years. For three and a half days we have celebrated their deaths, marking the end of the horrendous devastation their mythology brought us. These agitators repeatedly called us to turn to their Christ. But now their deaths show the futility of belief in a god who cannot even protect his own. Their deaths prove that there is no God—and no need for one. Man is fully capable of ruling himself."

A rousing cheer erupted from the crowd.

"These vile carcasses do not deserve burial," Abrams continued. "Instead, we will discard them as the refuse they are. In ancient Israel, garbage was dumped over the Jerusalem wall into the Valley of Hinnom to decay and be burned. We will consign these two bodies to the same fate. As the world watches, they will be taken to the dump to rot in the sun."

At the prime minister's signal, the driver of a waiting front-end loader started the engine, and the vehicle rumbled forward. It stopped in front of the two corpses, its bucket lowered to scoop them up.

At that moment the two witnesses stirred and rose to their feet. A healthy color spread over their skin, and as the crowd watched, their wounds disappeared entirely. Suddenly there was a deafening sound like a rushing wind above the square. The terrified onlookers gazed upward to see a bright, swirling cloud coming down from the sky. It enveloped the two witnesses like a blanket and then ascended again. After the cloud lifted, the witnesses were nowhere to be seen.

The crowd went silent, and the terror in the square was almost palpable. News reporters stood with microphones in hand but unable to speak.

Then, without warning, the ground began to shake. The tremors were mild at first, but soon the quaking grew violent. Panic set in, and people started running in all directions. The platform collapsed, killing most of the dignitaries on it. The city hall behind them shook until it toppled, crushing hundreds of people in the square and hundreds more inside. Other government buildings collapsed into rubble. Gas lines broke. Fires erupted, consuming scores of victims. Fissures as deep as canyons split the ground, swallowing hundreds of people. The prime minister and his entire cabinet perished, along with more than half of Parliament.

Sephora stared at the TV as the horrific events played out before her eyes. She could barely take it all in. Although it was hard to tell for certain, it seemed that 10 percent of Jerusalem had been obliterated in a matter of moments. But she found herself strangely elated at the resurrection and ascension of the two witnesses.

Feeling convicted and shamed over her own sin, she bowed her head. The tears flowed as she prayed, "Please forgive me, Lord. I promise to put away my immorality and follow Your Christ, whatever the cost."

She spent the rest of the day boxing up her belongings. She called a cab, wrote Aaron a farewell note, and left his apartment. She knew she would never see him again.

\* \* \*

# THE SCRIPTURE BEHIND THE STORY

The coming of the two witnesses marks the beginning of God's program for witnessing to the world during the Tribulation period. Although some scholars place their appearing at the middle of the Tribulation, I believe it is more likely that their ministry will occur at the beginning.[1]

The Rapture, of course, takes all Christians out of the world at once, leaving only unbelievers to cope with the impending Tribulation. We might wonder whether God has merely written these people off, leaving them without any means to turn them toward Him. But God's love never ceases, and He never leaves Himself without a witness. The fictional Sephora in our story is an example of how these two prophets might influence some people to move toward God in the terrible times to come.

Revelation 11 offers descriptions of these two witnesses based on several categories: their personalities, their prophecies, their power, their persecution, and their preservation.

## Their Personalities

> I will give power to my two witnesses, and they will
> prophesy one thousand two hundred and sixty days, clothed
> in sackcloth.
>
> REVELATION 11:3

The two witnesses are not symbols of the law and the gospel; neither do they represent the Old and New Testaments. They are real people who will be both heeded and hated. They will speak and perform miracles. They will die as only real people do.

Scripture describes them as "the two olive trees and the two lampstands standing before the God of the earth" (Revelation 11:4). To John's readers, these metaphors would have been a clear and familiar tie to the prophecy of Zechariah. In Zechariah's vision, he saw a golden candlestick with seven lamps flanked by two olive trees yielding golden oil for the lamps (Zechariah 4:1-13). It was then revealed to the prophet that the olive trees were "the two anointed ones, who stand beside the Lord of the whole earth" (verse 14).

Zechariah was talking about two faithful men who lived in his day—Joshua the high priest and Zerubbabel, the governor who was spearheading the restoration of the Temple. Both men were testimonies to the truth that God does His work "not by might nor by power, but by My Spirit" (Zechariah 4:6).

The book of Revelation references the lampstand and the olive trees as a nod to Joshua and Zerubbabel, the two witnesses in Zechariah 4. Like the lampstand, they burned brightly. And like the olive tree, they provided fuel for the candelabra. This is a metaphor for the fact that these two witnesses in Revelation will shine in the darkness of the Tribulation and that they will be fueled by God's Spirit.[2]

So who exactly are these witnesses? Jesus called these two witnesses "*my* two witnesses," which means they had a special relationship to Him that was not shared with other witnesses (Revelation 11:3, emphasis added). But while prophecy students agree that these individuals play a unique role in the end times narrative, they have long debated the identity of each.

Most believe that one of the witnesses is Elijah the prophet. Here are their reasons:

1. Malachi the prophet predicted that Elijah would come before the Second Advent to prepare the way for the Messiah: "Behold, I [the Lord] will send you Elijah the prophet before the coming of the great and dreadful day of the LORD. And he will turn the hearts of the fathers to the children, and the hearts of the children to their fathers, lest I come and strike the earth with a curse" (Malachi 4:5-6).

   Some think that John the Baptist completely fulfilled Malachi's prophecy. But although John came in the "spirit and power" of Elijah (Luke 1:17)—meaning that the Spirit that filled and enabled Elijah also filled and enabled John the Baptist—John was not a reincarnation of the Old

Testament prophet. In fact, a group of Jews investigating John specifically asked him if he was Elijah. His response was an emphatic "I am not!" (John 1:21). Thus John was not the fulfillment of Malachi's prophecy.

2. Elijah was miraculously taken up into heaven (2 Kings 2:9-11), just as the two witnesses will be (Revelation 11:12).

3. The witnesses will have the same power to withhold rain as Elijah did (1 Kings 17:1; Revelation 11:6).

4. Elijah called down fire from heaven (2 Kings 1:10), as will the two witnesses (Revelation 11:5).

5. The duration of both the drought in Elijah's day (1 Kings 17:1; Luke 4:25; James 5:17-18) and the ministry of the two witnesses (Revelation 11:3, 6) is three years and six months.

Some scholars think the second witness is Enoch, but I believe Moses is the more likely conclusion, for the following reasons:

1. Moses appeared with Elijah at the transfiguration of Christ (Matthew 17:3).

2. God gave Moses the ability to turn the water into blood (Exodus 7:19-20), and the witnesses will be given that same power (Revelation 11:6).

3. God preserved Moses' body so that he might be restored (Deuteronomy 34:5-7); the bodies of the witnesses will be restored as well (Revelation 11:11).

4. Satan contended with Michael the archangel for the body of Moses (Jude 1:9). It's possible that in doing so he was trying to hinder God's plan for the last days.

5. Moses and Elijah stand for the Law and the Prophets. Since the ministry of the witnesses will occur within the Jewish nation, it makes sense that representatives of the Law (Moses) and the Prophets (Elijah) would appear to the Jews.

Timothy Demy and John Whitcomb make a strong case for why Elijah and Moses are the witnesses described in Revelation 11:

No two men in Israel's entire history would receive greater respect and appreciation than Moses and Elijah. Moses was God's great deliverer and lawgiver for Israel (Deuteronomy 34:10-12). First-century Jews actually thought that Moses had given them the manna in the wilderness (John 6:32). And God raised up Elijah to confront Israel in a time of great national apostasy. God vindicated him by sending fire from heaven and "a chariot of fire and horses of fire" to escort him out of this world. So highly did the Jews of Jesus' day think of Elijah that when they saw Jesus' miracles, some people concluded that Elijah had returned (Matthew 16:14).[3]

### Their Prophecies

I will give power to my two witnesses, and they will prophesy one thousand two hundred and sixty days, clothed in sackcloth.

REVELATION 11:3

These two witnesses are true prophets, speaking by divine revelation under the authority of Christ. The duration of their prophetic testimony has been set at 1,260 days. This is equal to forty-two months, or three and a half years.

We get an idea of the nature of their prophecy by the description of their clothing. The witnesses are seen wearing mohair sackcloth, which is consistently presented in Scripture as an outward expression of mourning or repentance. Jacob put on sackcloth when he heard about Joseph's presumed death (Genesis 37:34). David put on sackcloth when he heard about Abner's murder (2 Samuel 3:31). Note that the dramatization at the beginning of this chapter takes the liberty of depicting the two witnesses in black suits, the present-day equivalent of mourning clothing.

The prophecy of these witnesses is given to both the Jews and the Gentiles. Some believe that this is the reason for two witnesses. The content of their prophecy is judgment: first on the Jews, and then on the Gentiles. According to Revelation, they will preach their message of judgment every day for the entire three and a half years of their ministry.

In keeping with the requirements of the Jewish law, their testimony is established because there are two of them: "Whoever is deserving of death shall be put to death on the testimony of two or three witnesses; he shall not be put to death on the testimony of one witness" (Deuteronomy 17:6). The testimony of one witness could be subjective, corrupted, or incomplete. But two witnesses who agree corroborate each other's testimony and thus confirm the truth of the matter.

In biblical times, God often used two witnesses to validate a truth. Two angels testified to the resurrection of the Savior. Two men in white testified to His ascension. God often dispatches His people in twos as well. Think of Moses and Aaron, Joshua and Caleb, Zerubbabel and Joshua, Peter and John, Paul and Silas, Timothy and Titus. The disciples were sent out two by two, and the seventy were also told to travel in pairs. These two witnesses will follow that pattern as they proclaim one of the most important calls to repentance of all time.

### Their Power

> I will give power to my two witnesses, and they will
> prophesy one thousand two hundred and sixty days, clothed
> in sackcloth.
>
> REVELATION 11:3

The Spirit of God will empower both the words and deeds of the two witnesses in order to convict their hearers to repent and turn to God.

#### THE POWER OF THEIR PREACHING

Let's take a look at the message the Spirit will give these prophets to see why they will generate such hatred. William R. Newell has captured the essence of their preaching agenda and their powerful presence in Jerusalem:

> Day after day the excitement will increase as these witnesses give their testimony. And what will that testimony be?
>
> 1. They will say that the Lord Jesus Christ, who has been rejected, is the "Lord of all the earth." They will say . . . , "As Jehovah, the God of Israel, liveth, before whom I stand, there shall not be dew nor rain these years, but according to my word." . . .
>
> 2. They will testify unsparingly of human wickedness to men's very faces. You have probably never heard a preacher that told you to your face just how bad you were. . . . These

witnesses will tell to the teeth of a horrid godlessness which is ready to worship the Devil, just what they are *before God*!

3. They will testify of the character of the judgments just past . . . as having been directly from God, and warn of coming judgments infinitely more terrible. . . .

4. They will decry the blasphemous claims the wild beast will shortly be making . . . , that man is to be deified! They will denounce all the goodness of man as *a lie*!

5. They will testify that Jerusalem, although the holy city in God's purposes, is spiritually "Sodom and Egypt," and will announce coming judgments upon the city and people. They will tell the Jews that they "killed the Lord Jesus" (1 Thessalonians 2:15-16), and that He will yet be the King over all the earth.

Now such witnessing as this *brings out men's wickedness*. People fairly *rave* to destroy these witnesses![4]

Unbelievers resist truth because it brings to the surface their God-instilled knowledge of right and wrong, which they've buried in order to pursue their ungodly behavior without the annoyance of conscience (Romans 1:18-21). That's why the people will demand that the two witnesses be killed. They will be convinced that shooting the messengers will shut off the message.

### THE POWER OF THEIR PLAGUES

The two witnesses will inflict plagues upon the unbelieving people to bring them to belief and repentance. These plagues will come in three forms:

1. **The plague of death:** Like the 144,000 Israelite witnesses (Revelation 7:3; 9:4), these two witnesses will be utterly protected during the three and a half years of their

testimony. They will be given the power to defend themselves by annihilating those who would hurt them: "If anyone wants to harm them, fire proceeds from their mouth and devours their enemies" (11:5).

In the past, Elijah called down fire from heaven (1 Kings 18:37-38; 2 Kings 1:10-12). This time, the fire will come out of the prophets' mouths.

Even though they are the targets of the entire world, the witnesses cannot be slain until they complete the Lord's mission. They will encounter fierce opposition like no human servant of God has ever faced, but they will be invincible until their work is done.

2. **The plague of drought:** Scripture describes these witnesses as having "power to shut heaven, so that no rain falls in the days of their prophecy" (Revelation 11:6). This drought in Israel, lasting three and a half years, will be a reminder of a similar Old Testament event: "Elijah was a man with a nature like ours, and he prayed earnestly that it would not rain; and it did not rain on the land for three years and six months" (James 5:17; see also 1 Kings 17–18).

The years of the drought seem to coincide with the first three and a half years of the Tribulation period. Both the preaching of the witnesses and their miracle-working power seem to keep the Antichrist from taking full control of the earth. Only when they are swept out of his way will he be able to undertake his quest for world dominion.

3. **The plague of disease:** Just as Moses did during his confrontation with Pharaoh in Egypt, the two witnesses will "have power . . . over waters to turn them to blood" (Revelation 11:6). This corresponds with the second

trumpet of Revelation 8: "The second angel sounded: And something like a great mountain burning with fire was thrown into the sea, and a third of the sea became blood. And a third of the living creatures in the sea died, and a third of the ships were destroyed" (verses 8-9). The witnesses will also have power "to strike the earth with all plagues, as often as they desire" (11:6).

Again, we must remember that these two witnesses will not perform these miracles out of spite or vindictiveness. Their intent will be to awaken the people to their sinfulness and move them to repentance and belief. In our story, the character Sephora shows how effective this tactic can be in a heart that is open to truth.

### Their Persecution

> When they finish their testimony, the beast that ascends out of the bottomless pit will make war against them, overcome them, and kill them.
>
> REVELATION 11:7

The earthly end of the witnesses will be dramatic, and it will come at the hands of the Beast (also called the Antichrist).

#### THE DEATH OF THE WITNESSES

Revelation 11:7 speaks of "the beast that ascends out of the bottomless pit." This is the first of thirty-six references to the Beast in the book of Revelation. It is not, however, the beginning of the Beast's career. For three and a half years, empowered by Satan, he will have been working behind the scenes—consolidating governments and forging a peace treaty with Israel.

At the midpoint of the Tribulation period, when the two witnesses have completed God's mission, the Beast will break his treaty with Israel and assassinate the witnesses. Their murder will be his first celebrated act and will gain him a large following.

### THE DISPLAY OF THEIR BODIES

In ancient times, even the worst of criminals were buried on the day of their death (Deuteronomy 21:22-23). But Scripture says of the witnesses: "Their dead bodies will lie in the street of the great city which spiritually is called Sodom and Egypt, where also our Lord was crucified" (Revelation 11:8).

That "great city" spoken of in this verse is Jerusalem, which Henry Morris describes as both "the holy city, the city of peace" and "the city where God's prophets die." It is in Jerusalem that the armies of the Beast "will apprehend and slay [the witnesses] and leave their bodies unburied in the street for all their enemies to see."[5]

In spite of Jerusalem's religious trappings, John describes the Holy City in insidious terms, likening it to two of the wicked-est places in history: Sodom, known for its sexual perversion; and Egypt, famous for its persecution of the Jewish nation. Jerusalem's degeneracy will arise in the wake of her miraculous deliverance at the hand of God from the armies of Gog. All of this will happen even as the Tribulation Temple is being constructed on its historic site and the ancient Jewish sacrifices are being restored. Outwardly Jerusalem will seem better than ever, but inwardly it will reek with rottenness and death, much like Sodom and Egypt.

Revelation 11 goes on to say, "Those from the peoples, tribes, tongues, and nations will see their dead bodies three-and-a-half days, and not allow their dead bodies to be put into graves" (verse 9). Years ago critics ridiculed this verse and its "impossible" predic-tion. But today, with the advance of the Internet, social media, and satellite television, no one snickers at the possibility of a worldwide viewing audience. Tim LaHaye writes, "Ours is the first generation that can literally see the fulfillment of 11:9 in allowing the people of the entire world to see such an awesome spectacle. This is one more indication that we are coming closer to the end of the age, because it would have been humanly impossible just a few years ago for the entire world to see these two witnesses in the streets at a given moment of time."[6]

## THE DELIGHT OF THEIR ENEMIES

As if the mocking display of the witnesses' bodies weren't enough, the masses will turn their death into a holiday: "Those who dwell on the earth will rejoice over them, make merry, and send gifts to one another, because these two prophets tormented those who dwell on the earth" (Revelation 11:10).

This is the only mention of any kind of rejoicing on earth during the entire Tribulation period. One writer describes it this way: "Now comes the real revelation of the heart of man: glee, horrid, insane, inhuman, hellish, ghoulish glee! There is actual delight at the death of God's witnesses—utter unbounded *delight!* . . . A regular Christmastime-of-Hell ensues."[7]

### Their Preservation

> After the three-and-a-half days the breath of life from God entered them, and they stood on their feet, and great fear fell on those who saw them.
>
> REVELATION 11:11

The witnesses' deaths and the public humiliation of their exposed corpses will not be the end of the story. Three and a half days after their assassinations, two miracles will occur before a watching world.

### THEIR RESURRECTION

First, the "breath of life from God" will enter into them. This is the same breath, or Spirit, that brought back Jesus from the dead.

Just as the whole earth will witness the deaths of these prophets, the whole earth will also witness their return to life. As you can imagine, this shocking event will generate indescribable fear and dread. This is one miracle the Beast will not be able to counterfeit.

### THEIR RAPTURE

Once the witnesses are resurrected, "a loud voice from heaven" will call them to "come up here." And they will ascend to heaven in a cloud while their dumbfounded enemies watch (Revelation 11:12). This is nothing less than the rapture of the two witnesses.

However, there is one major difference between the Rapture of the church and the rapture of these two prophets. Paul describes the Rapture of the church as occurring "in a moment, in the twinkling of an eye, at the last trumpet" (1 Corinthians 15:52). Believers will be snatched away too suddenly for anyone to see them depart. The rapture of the two witnesses, on the other hand, will be viewed by the entire world—including their enemies (Revelation 11:12).

Henry Morris describes the terror the enemies of God will experience when they observe the ascent of the two witnesses:

> All [the witnesses'] enemies, all those who had rejected their
> word and rejoiced when they died, especially the beast who
> had hunted them to death . . . will gaze transfixed as they
> watch them ascend far up into the heavens and into the
> presence of their Lord. The word for "beheld" (Greek *theoreo)*
> is a strong word, implying a transfixed stare. The sight will be
> enough to strike terror into the hearts of the most arrogantly
> rebellious of their enemies. A moment before, such men
> were rejoicing in supreme confidence that Christ was finally

defeated and Satan's man was on the victor's throne. But now
Christ had triumphed again. The ascent of the prophets into
heaven was a dire prediction that even greater judgments
were about to descend from heaven. The three-and-a-half-day
festivities were about to be followed by another three-and-a-
half years of judgments more severe than ever.[8]

## THEIR REVENGE

As all of Jerusalem watches the rapture of the two witnesses, a great
earthquake will shake the city so that one-tenth of it falls in ruins.
This will be a literal earthquake that visits God's judgment upon
the earth and results in seven thousand fatalities in Jerusalem alone
(Revelation 11:13). J. A. Seiss poignantly remarks, "They would not
allow burial to the slain Witnesses, and now they themselves are
buried alive in the ruins of their own houses, and in hell forever."[9]

The language describing the death of the seven thousand is worth
noting. The original text actually reads "men of name" instead of
"people." As the dramatization at the beginning of this chapter shows,
these seven thousand men may be leaders or well-known individuals.

The great joy that the world expresses at the death of the two
witnesses will become smothered by great fear. As Revelation 11:13
tells us, those remaining "were afraid and gave glory to the God of
heaven." We must not think of this fearful response as faith or as
a turning to God in repentance, but rather as a temporary state of
terror that evokes no true change of heart.

John Phillips offers a vivid description of the rapture of the two
witnesses:

Picture the scene—the sun-drenched streets of Jerusalem,
the holiday crowds flown in from the ends of the earth for
a firsthand look at the corpses of these detested men, the
troops in the Beast's uniform, the temple police. There they

are, devilish men from every kingdom under heaven, come to dance and feast at the triumph of the Beast. And then it happens! As the crowds strain at the police cordon to peer curiously at the two dead bodies, there comes a sudden change. Their color changes from cadaverous hue to the blooming, rosy glow of youth. Those stiff, stark limbs—they bend, they move! Oh, what a sight! They rise! The crowds fall back, break, and form again.[10]

The ministry of the two witnesses reflects the love and mercy of God even on hardened unbelievers, though apparently only a few will heed their message of redemption. The resurrection and rapture of these prophets will be one of the most dramatic moments that planet Earth will ever experience. And it will signal the beginning of the end for all the enemies of God.

*chapter five*

# THE DRAGON

GOLDEN LIGHT danced around the angels as they gathered in the second heaven. The vast assembly waited expectantly as Lucifer, the greatest and most beautiful of the archangels, made his way to the front. In moments he would take his seat at the head of the great angelic congress to report God's latest instructions to them.

But instead of mounting the steps to the marble dais, Lucifer took aside his closest aide, Michael, an archangel like himself.

"The congress will have to wait," Lucifer said. "Dismiss the assembly. We must speak immediately."

Michael made the announcement and the gathering dispersed, leaving the two archangels standing alone. Michael could see by Lucifer's dark countenance that he was not here to discuss a light matter.

"You are troubled, Lucifer. What has happened?"

"As you know, I have just returned from the high heaven, where God is enthroned. He has revealed to me His most recent project—a vast and daring one. He has created a new physical world beneath the lowest heaven. It is utterly glorious—perhaps the most beautiful thing He has ever made aside from ourselves. He is populating this world with a new race of creatures, and He has modeled them after Himself, granting them intelligence, free will, and creativity. He will charge them with the rule and care of His new world and infuse them with His own Spirit."

"Lucifer, you baffle me. Why is this not good news? Why does it disturb you?"

"Why does it disturb me? I'll tell you why!" Lucifer shouted. "God wants us, His angels, to minister to these new creatures. We are to be messengers to them, protecting and assisting them in their little endeavors. How can He expect us, the highest order of creatures in all of the universe, to stoop so low as to become errand runners and servants to inferior beings? We should be *ruling* them, not serving them. I tell you, Michael, this is not to be tolerated!"

A short time later, Lucifer reconvened the great council of all the angels. When they were assembled, he mounted the steps to the dais and addressed the legions of mighty beings before him. He first explained the new assignment God had charged them with, and then, to their amazement, he spewed out his disdain: "We run God's errands. We watch over and protect His creation. Why should we be required to forever submit to His will and stifle our own? I tell you, my oppressed comrades, we must not accept this degradation any longer. Hear me, and hear me well: we possess the power to seize the throne of God."

Michael, positioned in the first tier beneath the dais, stepped forward immediately. "My dear captain, think about what you are saying. Have you forgotten who we are? Like these newly formed earth beings, we, too, are God's creation. He gave us a vital role in His universal Kingdom and made us to find joy in serving Him. Who are we to defy our Creator?"

As the debate between the two mighty archangels escalated, so did Lucifer's rage. His rising anger began to infect some of the angels in the assembly, and as he ranted on, the rebels' cries swelled until a great chorus of voices echoed their leader's outrage. Such vocal support bolstered Lucifer's belief that he had won the unwavering loyalty of the other angels. At last, he raised his hand, and the entire host fell silent.

"Your affirmation confirms that you are with me. Therefore I call all of you to battle," he commanded. "We will depose that arrogant tyrant who humiliates and oppresses us. We will take His throne, and we will make His high heaven our dwelling place. Are you with me?"

His words were met by a roar of assent.

Lucifer, however, had miscalculated his support. The angels who had cheered him on were merely the most vocal ones, numbering only about one-third of the whole. But Lucifer remained undeterred, assembling his army and leading the march forward. He immediately found his way barred by Michael, who had rallied the rest of the angels against him.

The two armies clashed in a titanic supernatural battle. Michael's army drove the rebels back and hurled them from the second heaven.

The fallen leader heard the voice of Michael speak from high above him: "Lucifer, you have been my friend, and it grieves me deeply that you have severed our unity. You have chosen hatred over love, pride over humility, evil over good, and darkness over light. Therefore, God has decreed that your name shall no longer be Lucifer, the bearer of light. From this day forward you shall be called Satan, the adversary. No longer will you be a creature of love and beauty. You will be a dragon—a hated, loathsome creature whose utterances and deceptions will deliver those who heed you into eternal fire."

In an instant, a smoldering Satan sat brooding beside a stream on the newly created planet. One thought obsessed him: *How can I spite*

*God and regain power?* After a great deal of scheming, he arose and called his lieutenants to him. He presented a detailed plan by which they could wrest from God the new world He had made, annihilate its inhabitants, and make it their own domain.

"While it is much too small a kingdom for a being of my stature," he bragged, "it will serve as a power base from which we can launch subsequent attacks until we have wrenched the entire universe from the hand of God."

"But how can we do this?" one of his minions asked. "You told us that God has placed His own Spirit within the two humans. That gives them power we cannot overcome."

Satan smirked. "When God explained this new creation to me, He said that if the human couple ever disobeyed Him, His Spirit would depart and they would die. Our task, then, is to get the man and woman to disobey God. I will deceive them into thinking He is not their benefactor but a selfish tyrant."

Satan left his lieutenants and disguised himself as one of the more cunning earthly creatures. And using a mix of lies and half-truths, he seduced the couple into rejecting their Creator. But to his consternation, they did not immediately die. God confronted them with their disobedience and revealed the pain, sorrow, and eventual death that would come as a result. But He also promised something their seducer had never anticipated—that one of their future descendants would restore all they had lost and would crush Satan's head.

When Satan heard this prophecy, new outrage boiled in his heart. He charged a full battalion of his fiercest demons to conduct a guerrilla war to prevent the promised Redeemer from coming. Throughout the centuries, they attacked the family, the kings, and the nation charged with bringing God's promise to fruition. But neither Satan nor his legions could keep the promised Child from being born.

* * *

It was in the reign of the Roman emperor Tiberius when Satan's battalion leader came to him with news that a man named Jesus had just been baptized in the Jordan River.

"What makes you think He is the One?" Satan asked, already knowing the answer.

"When He emerged from the water, a voice from heaven proclaimed Him to be God's own Son. For thirty years He was known simply as Jesus of Nazareth, but His true identity has now been revealed. This Jesus is the One we have been fearfully awaiting."

The devil immediately transported himself to the Jordan River. He arrived to see Jesus walking alone into the barren wilderness between Jerusalem and the Dead Sea. Satan followed Him until He stopped on a desolate plain where no vegetation grew. For forty days he watched as Jesus fasted and prayed. The adversary thought to himself, *Now that He is weak and hungry, He will grasp at anything I offer.*

To Satan's surprise, Jesus offered no resistance as he approached. "They say You are the Son of God. Why should I believe it? If it's true, it should be easy for You to prove. You are famished with hunger. Merely turn one of these stones into a loaf of bread, and I will believe You."

"It is written," Jesus told His tempter, "'Man shall not live by bread alone, but by every word that proceeds from the mouth of God.'"

Satan then took Jesus to the pinnacle of the Temple. "Since You are the Son of God, throw Yourself down. Surely Your angels will save You. Look at all the people in the courtyard below. If they saw such a miracle, think how quickly they would believe in You."

Once again, Jesus refused.

Finally, Satan took Him to a high mountain, where he conjured up a panoramic vista revealing all the great kingdoms of the world. As he swept his arm over the magnificent view that lay below them, he said, "All this is Yours to rule if You will but fall down right now and worship me."

Then, in a voice charged with power and authority, Jesus said, "Away with you, Satan! For it is written, 'You shall worship the Lord your God, and Him only you shall serve.'"

When Satan returned and sat before his council, no one dared ask if his attack had been successful. The fury on his face told them everything.

The council sat silent and wary until their leader addressed them. "There is no doubt that this Jesus is indeed the Son of God. If we do not get rid of Him—and soon—every plot we have devised since our exile will come to nothing. Worse, if this Christ comes to power, He will seek to drive us from this world as we were driven from heaven."

A voice from among the gathered demons moaned, "Everything we've tried has failed. What else can we do?"

"We can change our tactics," Satan replied. "Since we cannot prevail against Jesus directly, we must work covertly. We know from God's prophecy to Adam and Eve and others that Jesus is the Messiah sent to save humanity from the death we inflicted on them. If we can deceive the Jews about His purpose and make them doubt that He is their promised Messiah, they will turn against Him."

"But how will we do that?" one of Satan's henchmen asked.

"We must use the national and religious pride of their leaders—especially the Pharisees—so that they perceive Jesus not as the Messiah but as a fraud out to undermine their power. No doubt He will try to gain their support with wise words and miracles. So we must blind their eyes to the good He does and make them envy His growing popularity. Nothing infuriates a Pharisee so much as the thought of someone usurping his influence."

* * *

The Jewish leaders were indeed easy to manipulate. A spark of jealousy over Jesus' growing influence had already ignited in their hearts, and for the next three years Satan and his followers fanned that flame into a burning passion for Jesus' death. The devil saw victory looming on the horizon. Determined not to let it slip from his fingers, he entered the fray himself, inciting the avarice of one of Christ's closest companions.

It was the night of the Jewish Passover feast when the Dragon made his move. As Jesus arrived at Mount Olivet with three of His disciples to pray, the very atmosphere felt ominous. Satan could see legions upon legions of angels hovering low over the mountain.

While Jesus prayed, Satan persuaded Judas to lead an armed band of Jewish officials to Mount Olivet. Once there, he was to identify his Master with a kiss of greeting. Satan had found nothing to celebrate since his fall, but the irony of using a kiss—an expression of love—as an act of betrayal was the closest he'd come yet.

Jesus was arrested on the spot and taken directly to Annas, the high priest, for trial. At Satan's prompting, the high priest put Jesus through a sham of a trial, using false witnesses and trumped-up charges. Then Annas sent Him for final judgment to the Roman governor, Pontius Pilate.

The following morning Jesus was brought before Pilate on the steps of the Roman garrison, the Antonia Fortress. A restless mob of Jews had already assembled to watch the proceedings. Satan knew that Pilate was weak—he was afraid of offending the emperor and losing his position, and equally afraid of offending the Jews and causing a riot. It soon became apparent that he did not want to execute Jesus. Instead, he attempted to appease the bloodlust of the Jewish leaders by having Jesus scourged and then released.

Satan sounded the alarm to his troops: "Quick! Descend en masse into that mob. Stir them into a frenzy of hate. I want them so enraged that the governor fears an outright insurrection!"

The demons did their job. Soon the air rang with furious voices shouting for blood. As their master expected, Pilate yielded to the pressure and gave Jesus over to the Jews to be crucified.

As Jesus writhed on the cross, Satan gloated in triumph. When he heard God's own Son cry, "My God, My God, why have You forsaken Me?" and finally watched His tortured body emit a last rasping breath, Satan's exultation knew no bounds.

Satan gloried in the finality of it all. He had succeeded in thwarting God's plan. Humanity would not be redeemed; their Champion had been destroyed. The earth was ripe for the taking. Satan burst into a spasm of laughter that rang long and loud throughout the halls of hell.

Three days later, while Satan was conducting a mass assembly for his fallen angels, a sharp noise like a fierce wind interrupted his words. Its volume increased until it became almost unbearable. A blinding blur of light rushed over them and exploded through the massive gates, scattering shards of stone and splinters of mighty beams. All that was left of the gates of hell was a gaping hole that was now belching black smoke.

The force of the impact knocked all the demons to the ground. Shrieks of terror filled the hall as they lay there cowering, too afraid to rise.

"Cease your howling and pull yourselves together!" Satan bellowed. "Jesus has escaped, and death, our most potent weapon, has been wrested from us. We could not hold the Master of Life. He has broken the chains of death, and you can be sure that He will now reunite with His body and break out of the tomb in the same way."

"What can we do?" one of the demons cried.

"First, we must face reality." Satan's voice was grim. "We cannot win against God. Even if we slaughtered the humans and flung their rotting carcasses all over the globe, Jesus would simply resurrect them as He has been resurrected. Our doom is sealed.

"But here is what we can do." Satan's voice grew louder. "We may go down in the end, but we will leave a wound on God by taking down as many of His precious humans as possible. We can still make their lives miserable. We can still fill them with disease, grief, pain, and conflict—and for some, eternal death. We must stifle all thought of our inevitable end and redouble our efforts to spite the God we hate."

\* \* \*

In the succeeding centuries, Satan and his rebels enjoyed spectacular successes. Yet his frustration grew. Whether he persecuted Christians outright or misled and deceived them, he could not destroy them. The truly dedicated ones wore supernatural armor that his evil could not penetrate. Furthermore, these Christians prayed—an activity the adversary could not bear. It seemed that God always responded to their pleas for help, whether in the manner they expected or in some more glorious way.

"Even when we kill them, they defeat us," one of them complained. "When we separate them from their bodies, God's angels snatch them away and escort them to safety."

In desperation, Satan abandoned all caution and began to set the stage for his last hurrah—a global persecution of God's people. Sensing that his end was drawing near, his craving for adoration and worship welled up again, even stronger this time. If he was to satisfy that original lust, it must be done soon.

Blinded by his belief that he was God's equal, Satan did not realize that everything he did was actually an imitation—a grotesquely distorted replication of God's works. His whole strategy was nothing but a counterfeit of his rival.

This pattern of imitation finally led Satan to manifest himself in human form. He knew it would be impossible to reenact the wonder of the Incarnation, however. Instead of becoming a baby, he identified a rising political leader of power and influence who had demonstrated his loyalty by ruthless tyranny, and he offered him what he had offered Jesus: dominion over all the kingdoms of the world. The man eagerly accepted.

Satan provided him with an accomplice—a false prophet whom he endowed with demonic powers that enabled him to function as an evil caricature of God's Holy Spirit. Now Satan, too, was a trinity—a diabolical trinity made up of the devil, the Antichrist, and the unholy spirit.

Satan's influence in the world grew to an unprecedented scope as his two human accomplices deceived the masses with their spectacular success. Soon they overtook entire nations and, by deception or force, led the people of the earth to worship Satan. They imposed severe penalties on anyone who refused.

With such power now in hand, Satan moved his two agents to abandon all subterfuge and openly inflict persecution on God's people. He released the full power of his demonic horde, and they indulged their hate in a rampage of slaughter and destruction.

Satan, now heady with success, began to rethink the inevitability of his doom. He boasted to his closest accomplices, "God's people are now a mere remnant, and ours include the leaders of all the civilized nations. With the surviving believers cowering in caves and remote jungles, the only people God's favor remains upon are the Jews. We have the strength to wipe their malodorous little nation off the globe and secure forever our grip on this earth."

Acting on this grandiose vision, Satan moved the Antichrist to amass the largest army in human history and march against Israel. What he didn't know was that he was marching to his defeat.

* * *

# THE SCRIPTURE BEHIND THE STORY

In the great drama of the end times, Satan's role is that of the antagonist. There would be no end-times drama—indeed, no end times at all—had Satan not rebelled against God and corrupted His perfect creation. The end-times role of this diabolical agent of the Apocalypse is detailed in just one place in the Bible: the twelfth chapter of the book of Revelation. This chapter presents significant truths about Satan's nemesis, his nature, his vendetta, and his end. Each of these is introduced by the word *great*:

1. A "great sign"—a woman (Revelation 12:1)
2. A "great, fiery red dragon" (verse 3)
3. A "great wrath" (verse 12)
4. Two wings of a "great eagle" (verse 14)

As we explore these truths, we will discover the foundations that support our dramatization about this creature who is the source of all evil.

### The Great Sign of a Woman

A great sign appeared in heaven: a woman clothed with the sun, with the moon under her feet, and on her head a garland of twelve stars. Then being with child, she cried out in labor and in pain to give birth.

REVELATION 12:1-2

The picture of this woman is startling. She is clothed with the sun, standing on the moon, and wearing a crown of twelve stars. Perhaps most significantly, she is in the throes of childbirth. There are numerous ideas about the meaning of this woman, but only one is consistent with the teaching of the entire Word of God: she represents the nation of Israel, and she makes her entrance into the drama as the targeted victim of Satan's malevolence.

Throughout the Old Testament, Israel is often portrayed as a woman in travail. For example, the prophet Isaiah writes, "As a woman with child is in pain and cries out in her pangs, when she draws near the time of her delivery, so have we been in Your sight, O LORD. We have been with child, we have been in pain; we have, as it were, brought forth wind; we have not accomplished any deliverance in the earth" (Isaiah 26:17-18; see also 66:7-8; Micah 4:10; 5:3).

Isaiah's image of a woman in labor failing to give birth to a child describes the failure of the Jewish people to bring about hope and salvation for humanity. And yet, after hundreds of years of disappointed hopes, the Jewish people had the privilege of bringing the Deliverer into this world: "She bore a male Child who was to rule all nations with a rod of iron. And her Child was caught up to God and His throne" (Revelation 12:5).

This remarkable statement captures three of the most significant events in Christ's life:

1. His Incarnation: "She bore a male Child."
2. His Ascension: "Her Child was caught up to God and His throne."
3. His Second Coming: "[He] was to rule all nations with a rod of iron."

The final fulfillment of Revelation 12:5 is recorded for us near the end of the book of Revelation: "Out of His mouth goes a sharp sword, that with it He should strike the nations. And He Himself will rule them with a rod of iron. He Himself treads the winepress of the fierceness and wrath of Almighty God" (Revelation 19:15).

So the first great sign in Revelation 12 is a woman, Israel. Her child is Satan's ultimate nemesis: Christ Himself, the grand hero of the end-times drama.

## *The Great Dragon*

> Another sign appeared in heaven: behold, a great, fiery
> red dragon having seven heads and ten horns, and seven
> diadems on his heads. His tail drew a third of the stars of
> heaven and threw them to the earth. And the dragon stood
> before the woman who was ready to give birth, to devour
> her Child as soon as it was born. . . . So the great dragon was
> cast out, that serpent of old, called the Devil and Satan, who
> deceives the whole world; he was cast to the earth, and his
> angels were cast out with him.
>
> REVELATION 12:3-4, 9

Satan's path is ever downward. From heaven to earth . . . from
earth to the bottomless pit . . . from the bottomless pit to the lake
of fire. Here Revelation 12 pulls the curtain aside and lets us view
Satan's expulsion from heaven. Verse 9 gives us perhaps a more complete description of Satan than any other passage in the Bible. He
is called the great dragon, the old serpent, the devil, Satan, and the
deceiver of the whole world. Not a very pretty picture.

It is important to recognize that these descriptors are not about
his physical appearance; they show what his nature is like. It is not
correct to assume that Satan is ugly like a dragon. Actually, he is
bright like the sun and glorious in appearance. Paul says that Satan
"transforms himself into an angel of light" (2 Corinthians 11:14). In
fact, his original name, Lucifer, means "star of the morning."

Satan's activity mimics his nature: he deceives by hiding the hideous
nature of sin under a facade of attractiveness. He is vicious, vile, and
ferocious. His color is red, for his path has always been stained with
blood and death. In calling Satan a serpent, this passage reminds us
of his cunning and deception in the Garden of Eden. From the very

beginning, Satan has opposed God and plotted the death of humanity. Our Lord said, "He was a murderer from the beginning" (John 8:44).

It is generally understood that "Satan" is the Old Testament name for this evil being, and "the devil" is the New Testament name. The name *Satan* means "adversary." Satan is the adversary of God and of every one of God's children. He is the roaring lion who "walks about . . . seeking whom he may devour" (1 Peter 5:8).

The Greek word for "devil" is *diabolos*. Literally, the term means "slanderer." That's the label used in Revelation 12:10 when Satan is described as "the accuser of our brethren." When Satan steps into the courtroom of heaven, his only motive is to defame those who believe in Christ. Like a corrupt prosecuting attorney, he tries to condemn us and destroy our reputation before the Judge.

Lastly, the devil is described as the one "who deceives the whole world" (Revelation 12:9). The devil's purpose in the past was to keep Christ away from the world. Having failed that goal, the only option left to him is to keep the world away from Christ. He does so by sprinkling lies with truths and half-truths to create doubt in our minds about the faithfulness and glory of God. Paul exposed this strategy in his letter to the Corinthians, saying that Satan has blinded people's minds, "lest the light of the gospel of the glory of Christ, who is the image of God, should shine on them" (2 Corinthians 4:4).

After describing Satan's nature, Revelation 12 goes on to describe his power, his partners, and his purpose.

### SATAN'S POWER

The fiery red dragon of Revelation 12:3 has "seven heads and ten horns, and seven diadems on his heads." Biblically speaking, the number seven usually symbolizes totality, and the head conveys the idea of intelligence. The horns are a symbol of strength. So for the Dragon to have seven heads and ten horns speaks of Satan's distinct intelligence and cunning.

| Satan's Counterfeit Strategy | |
| --- | --- |
| **Jesus Christ** | **Satan** |
| **Light** of the World (John 9:5) | Transforms himself into an angel of **light** (2 Corinthians 11:14) |
| **King** of Kings (1 Timothy 6:15) | **King** over the children of pride (Job 41:34) |
| **Prince** of Peace (Isaiah 9:6) | **Prince** of the power of the air (Ephesians 2:2) |
| Lord my **God** (Zechariah 14:5) | **God** of this age (2 Corinthians 4:4) |
| **Lion** of the tribe of Judah (Revelation 5:5) | Roaring **lion**, seeking whom he may devour (1 Peter 5:8) |

The crowns or diadems on his head are in keeping with the portrait of Satan throughout the Bible: he is a crowned monarch. In Matthew 12:25-26, Jesus refers to Satan as a king with a kingdom. Elsewhere he is described as the ruler of this age (Ephesians 6:12). Three times in the book of John, Satan is referred to as "the prince of this world" (12:31; 14:30; 16:11, KJV). In 2 Corinthians 4:4, Paul refers to Satan as "the god of this age," and in Ephesians 2:2, he's called "the prince of the power of the air."

As "the prince of this world," Satan has subjects: evil men and women. And as "the prince of the power of the air," he has subjects: evil spirits. He is the ruling spirit over those bent on disobedience and the architect of evil in the world. In 1 John 5:19 we are told that "the whole world lies under the sway of the wicked one."

God did not give Satan the world to rule; Satan wrested it from the hands of Adam and Eve. God had charged them to "fill the earth and subdue it" and to "have dominion over . . . every living thing . . . on the earth" (Genesis 1:28). When the primeval couple fell from that God-given throne, Satan filled it himself.

### SATAN'S PARTNERS

Revelation 12:4 says that Lucifer's tail "drew a third of the stars of heaven and threw them to the earth." Here the stars represent angels, just as they are called when they sang together at the creation of the world (Job 38:7). When Lucifer fell in pride and arrogance against God, he took one-third of the angels with him.

Some people struggle with the idea of Satan having angels, based on their presumption that all angels are good. Yet later in the twelfth chapter of Revelation, we are told that Michael led a host of angels against the Dragon and his angels. In Jesus' address at the Mount of Olives, He affirmed that Satan has angels: "[God] will also say to those on the left hand, 'Depart from Me, you cursed, into the everlasting fire prepared for the devil and his angels'" (Matthew 25:41).

In 2 Peter 2:4 and Jude 1:6, we read that some of the fallen angels are imprisoned and that those who are not work as Satan's accomplices. These fallen angels have lost all semblance of what was once good in them. They have been organized by their master to influence human activity and world events behind the scenes for evil. "We do not wrestle against flesh and blood," Paul writes, "but against principalities, against powers, against the rulers of the darkness of this age, against spiritual hosts of wickedness in the heavenly places" (Ephesians 6:12).

Clearly, these evil angels, like their master, also have great freedom in the universe. Lucifer was allowed to creep into the Garden of Eden, and he has restricted access to the presence of God, where he accuses the brethren constantly (Job 1; Revelation 12:10). Satan's servants are likewise at work in the world, executing his diabolical strategy.

### SATAN'S PURPOSE

From the very beginning, Satan's purpose has been to destroy the Child of the woman: "The dragon stood before the woman who was ready to give birth, to devour her Child as soon as it was born" (Revelation 12:4). When God told Satan in the Garden of Eden that the seed of the woman "shall bruise your head" (Genesis 3:15), Satan began his campaign to eradicate that promised seed. Knowing from prophecy that the Promised One would spring from Israel, the adversary did everything he could to keep that nation from being formed. He incited Esau to attempt to kill his brother, Jacob, who would father the twelve tribes of Israel. When that failed, he incited Pharaoh to murder all the Jewish baby boys in Egypt. Had either Jacob or Moses not survived, the nation of Israel would never have existed.

At one point in Israel's history, Satan almost succeeded. The promised Redeemer was to come through the royal line of David. After David's descendant King Jehoshaphat died, a series of intrigues and murders eliminated the entire Davidic line except King Ahaziah and his family. Ahaziah was also murdered, and the queen mother usurped the crown and killed all of his children, finally ending the royal line— or so she thought. But the high priest's wife managed to hide Ahaziah's youngest son, Joash, until he could be crowned. In that little boy— that lone male survivor of Israel's royalty—resided the promised seed and the ultimate purpose of God (2 Chronicles 22:10-12).

Thwarted but undaunted, Satan incited the wicked Haman to plot the extermination of all the Jews. But God raised up Esther "for such a time as this" to expose Haman's scheme, and the promised seed was spared (Esther 4:14).

When the prophesied Child was finally born, Satan instilled fear and hatred in King Herod, who had all the babies in Bethlehem murdered. He thought that surely the promised seed would be slain in this insidious act of infanticide (Matthew 2:16). But the sovereign hand of God intervened and directed Joseph to flee with his family to Egypt, thus sparing Jesus' life.

Immediately after Jesus' baptism, Satan confronted Him in the wilderness with the three famous temptations portrayed in our dramatization. But Jesus rendered His adversary powerless with the sword of the Spirit—the Word of God.

After this failure, the devil made two attempts to murder Jesus by proxy. He tried to coerce the people of Nazareth to throw Jesus off the top of a hill (Luke 4:29), and then he fanned the hatred of the scribes and Pharisees until they tried to stone Him to death (John 8:59). But each time Jesus miraculously escaped unharmed.

Finally, on a Friday afternoon at three o'clock, Satan saw the fruition of his centuries-long campaign when the Son of God, the promised seed, succumbed to a bloody death on a cross. When Christ's mangled body was wrapped in linen, embalmed in spices, and sealed in a sepulchre, Satan thought he had won. But God had purposed for this promised Child to rescue and rule the nations, and God never changes His purposes. On the third day, He raised Jesus from the dead, thwarting Satan's purpose.[1]

### The Great War

War broke out in heaven: Michael and his angels fought
with the dragon; and the dragon and his angels fought,
but they did not prevail, nor was a place found for them in
heaven any longer.

REVELATION 12:7-8

These verses refer not just to a single battle but to a war with many battles on many fronts. These include the battle between Michael and Satan, the battle between Satan-led angels and God-led angels, and the battle between Satan-led people and God-led people. The book of Revelation tells us that a final battle between these fierce enemies is to occur eventually.

It is important to remember that there is no such thing as abstract evil. Evil always originates in an intelligent, self-aware personality—either Satan himself or one or more of the angelic creatures delegated to perform his will. The passage in the Bible that most clearly demonstrates this truth—and the angelic conflict that results—is Daniel 10.

Daniel had been in prayer for twenty-one days when an angel, probably Gabriel, visited him in a vision. The angel reported that Daniel's prayer had been heard from its first utterance, but as Gabriel was flying to deliver the answer, the prince of Persia attacked him. Only when Michael was dispatched from heaven to assist him was Gabriel able to come to Daniel. It is evident that the prince of Persia was a fallen angel under Satan's control. This passage isn't referring to an earthly prince, because no human could successfully resist an angelic messenger of God.

That the opponent is identified as the "prince of Persia" shows how Satan has organized his angelic troops: he has assigned a fallen angel to every country and province. This prince was responsible for Persia, which held the Jewish nation in captivity. Michael and Gabriel managed to destroy this evil angel's influence over the Persian king and establish their own influence on behalf of God's people. It is in complete harmony with the Word of God to believe that the prince of Persia who opposed Daniel was the devil's own angel.

These scenes of angelic conflict in Revelation and Daniel show us that the war between the forces of evil and the forces of good rages throughout the invisible regions of heaven as well as here on earth.

Perhaps you are thinking, *But hasn't Satan already been judged?* That is correct; he was judged at the cross. John 16:8, 11 says, "When [the Holy Spirit] has come, He will convict the world of sin, and of righteousness, and of judgment . . . because the ruler of this world is judged." Hebrews 2:14 echoes this idea: "Inasmuch then as the children have partaken of flesh and blood, [Christ] Himself likewise shared in the same, that through death He might destroy him who had the power of death, that is, the devil."

Since Satan has been judged by Christ's work at the cross, why, then, does the enemy seem to be winning?

The answer is that, legally, Calvary was Satan's complete undoing—all his hopes disintegrated into ashes when the Lord Jesus died and rose again. Like any legal action, however, the decision must be enforced. In our nation's courts, convicted murderers are seldom executed until years after their conviction. The ultimate victory has been won, but it won't be totally implemented until some point in the future.

In the meantime, it is heartening to know that Christ's victory over Satan can be enforced now by means of prayer. Daniel prayed for twenty-one days, and finally the angel of Satan was defeated. Earthly victories depend on heavenly victories, and vice versa. We who battle evil on the earth are fellow warriors with the angels who battle evil in the invisible realms, and our prayers form a network of power and communication that work in tandem on both fronts. This means the praying church actually wields a strong hand in determining the outcome of human events. As someone has said, "It is not the mayors that make the world go 'round; it is the pray-ers."

Satan can still wreak havoc, as our dramatization shows, but he cannot win against the Christian who claims the victory of Christ as his or her own. God's servants may encounter all kinds of persecutions or even death, but their ultimate victory is guaranteed. This divine assurance gives us the courage to fight on, knowing we are protected from any weapon Satan can throw at us. "The weapons of our warfare are not carnal but mighty in God for pulling down strongholds, casting down arguments and every high thing that exalts itself against the knowledge of God, bringing every thought into captivity to the obedience of Christ" (2 Corinthians 10:4-5).

### The Great Wrath

Rejoice, O heavens, and you who dwell in them! Woe to the inhabitants of the earth and the sea! For the devil has come

down to you, having great wrath, because he knows that he
has a short time.
REVELATION 12:12

At the end of time, when believers arrive in heaven, they will
have been made perfect in holiness, and there will be nothing Satan
can say or do about it. His role as the accuser will be finished! His
presence in heaven will be abruptly concluded as he is thrown one
last time to the earth. But heaven's purification will mean the earth's
pollution as Satan's fury explodes in an attempt to defy God and
destroy His people.

The book of Revelation describes the wrath that the earth will
experience at the hands of Satan in the last days.

### AN AGGRAVATED ASSAULT

Revelation 12:12 gives this warning: "Woe to the inhabitants of the
earth and the sea! For the devil has come down to you, having great
wrath, because he knows that he has a short time." The word used
for wrath here means "strong passion or emotion." Donald Grey
Barnhouse compares it to a caged animal: "The animal that was
dangerous enough when he roamed through the whole forest is now
limited to a stockade, where, mad with the restrictions which he sees
around him, and raging because he feels the end near, he throws the
insane strength of the death struggle into all his movements."[2] Satan's
assault against God's people will be marked by the desecration of the
Temple, the installation of the image of the Beast in the Temple, and
the all-out persecution of the Jewish people.

### AN ANTI-SEMITIC ASSAULT

The book of Revelation foretells the last wave of anti-Semitism that
will roll over the world: "When the dragon saw that he had been cast
to the earth, he persecuted the woman who gave birth to the male

Child. . . . So the serpent spewed water out of his mouth like a flood after the woman, that he might cause her to be carried away by the flood" (Revelation 12:13, 15).

The devil hates Israel because, from a biological perspective, Christ came from this nation. Satan wants to destroy Israel, denying its people a home when the Messiah returns to earth and establishes His promised Kingdom.

The evil one is like a spiteful child who destroys a friend's toy: if he can't have it, he doesn't want anyone else to have it either. So, as Revelation 12 tells us, Satan casts a flood of water out of his mouth to carry the woman (Israel) away. Some take this to mean that he will loose a literal flood that will sweep Israel down the Jordan Valley. Others see it as symbolic of Satan's total effort to exterminate the nation. Whatever the "water like a flood" may mean, it is certain that there will be an aggressive, organized effort to attack and destroy the Jewish people.

### AN ANGRY ASSAULT

The last verse in Revelation 12 states that the dragon is "enraged" to the point of making war with those within the nation of Israel who "keep the commandments of God and have the testimony of Jesus Christ" (verse 17). This is a reference not to Jews in general but to Jewish believers. I agree with the many students of prophecy who identify this group with the 144,000 Jewish witnesses of Revelation 7. These sealed preachers certainly fulfill the description of obedience and outward witness. Satan will be angry with these faithful followers for one reason: they have aligned themselves with his greatest enemy.

### *The Great Wings*

> The woman was given two wings of a great eagle, that
> she might fly into the wilderness to her place, where she

is nourished for a time and times and half a time, from
the presence of the serpent. . . . But the earth helped the
woman, and the earth opened its mouth and swallowed up
the flood which the dragon had spewed out of his mouth.

REVELATION 12:14, 16

To ancient Israel, the "two wings of a great eagle" would have
recalled the grace of God as He delivered them from Egypt: "You
have seen what I did to the Egyptians, and how I bore you on
eagles' wings and brought you to Myself" (Exodus 19:4; see also
Deuteronomy 32:11-12).

Revelation 12 makes it clear that Israel will one day be removed
to some special place of protection in the land. Some have considered this a reference to Petra, a well-fortified ancient city carved deep
within protective cliffs southeast of the Dead Sea. The phrase in
verse 14 seems to indicate that the Jews will experience supernatural
provision, as did Elijah at the Brook Cherith and the Israelites in the
wilderness of Sinai. Whatever means God uses, we can be certain that
He will preserve a godly remnant of His people.

Carolyn Arends tells a story that helps us understand how Satan
can continue to inflict so much trouble on people when he has
already been judged at the cross:

> As a kid, I loved Mission Sundays, when missionaries on
> furlough brought special reports in place of a sermon. . . .
>
> There is one visit I've never forgotten. The missionaries
> were a married couple stationed in what appeared to be a
> particularly steamy jungle. . . .
>
> One day, they told us, an enormous snake—much longer
> than a man—slithered its way right through their front door
> and into the kitchen of their simple home. Terrified, they
> ran outside and searched frantically for a local who might

know what to do. A machete-wielding neighbor came to the rescue, calmly marching into their house and decapitating the snake with one clean chop.

The neighbor reemerged triumphant and assured the missionaries that the reptile had been defeated. But there was a catch, he warned: It was going to take a while for the snake to realize it was dead.

A snake's neurology and blood flow are such that it can take considerable time for it to stop moving even after decapitation. For the next several hours, the missionaries were forced to wait outside while the snake thrashed about, smashing furniture and flailing against walls and windows, wreaking havoc until its body finally understood that it no longer had a head. . . .

At some point in their waiting, [the missionaries] told us, they had a mutual epiphany. . . .

"Do you see it?" asked the husband. "Satan is a lot like that big old snake. He's already been defeated. He just doesn't know it yet. In the meantime, he's going to do some damage. But never forget that he's a goner."

Arends concludes by reminding us that one day all of Satan's thrashing and flailing will stop: "The story haunts me because I have come to believe it is an accurate picture of the universe. We are in the thrashing time, a season characterized by our pervasive capacity to do violence to each other and ourselves. The temptation is to despair. We have to remember, though, that it won't last forever. Jesus has already crushed the serpent's head."[3]

*chapter six*

# THE BEAST FROM THE SEA

"Cabinet Member Ends Crippling Strike." The headline blared across the front page of the *Times*.

The walkout had triggered a severe national crisis, virtually shutting down Britain for more than five weeks.

The trouble had been building for decades. Several trade unions had merged, and this "union of unions," as the amalgamation had been dubbed, gained a stranglehold on Britain's economy, making increasingly outlandish demands on behalf of the railroad workers, truckers, factory laborers, and petroleum refiners it represented. Production had dropped drastically while employers' costs rose, which forced them to increase prices, lay off workers, and go into substantial debt. Many businesses declared bankruptcy, while others teetered on the brink.

When the union of unions demanded a 12 percent pay hike, six-hour workdays, and free child care, the manufacturers finally balked, and a nationwide strike resulted. Truck and rail deliveries stopped.

Petrol tanks dried up. Riots and looting erupted. Britain spiraled into chaos.

On the day the crisis ended, the resolution was the top story on BBC News. The news anchor recounted the prime minister's attempt to intervene, ordering the strikers back to work and imposing stiff fines if they refused. When that failed, he mobilized the home guard to stop the rioting and restore order. The resulting deaths and injuries triggered widespread public resentment toward the prime minister.

"When a solution seemed impossible," the anchor said, "an unknown junior cabinet officer, Judas Christopher, undersecretary of the Board of Trade, requested permission to meet with the heads of the unions and businesses." Within three days, he had hammered out what both sides called a win-win deal.

"We've just learned that Judas Christopher is about to emerge from the negotiating conference," the anchor continued. "We will go now to our reporter on the scene, Allison Lancaster."

Allison's face appeared on the screen. Crowds at the Palace of Westminster milled about behind her. "Thanks, Kent. Undersecretary Christopher's aide has promised us a brief interview. In fact, here he comes now."

A tall, striking man in his early thirties walked toward the camera, flashing an engaging smile. He greeted Allison and the crowd warmly.

"Secretary Christopher," she said, "what can you tell us about the agreement you have so miraculously negotiated over the past three days?"

"Well, I can't go into all the details, but I can say that the heart of it involves no raises or shortened hours." Christopher's voice was golden, his articulation precise. "Instead," he continued, "we have tied wages to production. The business owners have guaranteed generous bonuses to every employee who increases his or her output."

After Christopher flashed another winning smile and made his exit, Allison turned back to the camera. "Though little is known about this junior cabinet officer, it seems that he is presently more popular than the prime minister himself. Back to you, Kent."

\* \* \*

Christopher's stunning success soon won him a widespread following. Not long afterward, he accused the prime minister of incompetency and hinted at an illicit affair. It was only a matter of time before the prime minister's government fell and Parliament elected Christopher prime minister by a landslide.

A few days after his election, Judas Christopher addressed the nation from his office at Number 10 Downing Street, offering bold, unprecedented solutions to the severe inflation that had been spawned by the strike and by runaway welfare policies. A follow-up poll showed overwhelming approval for both Christopher and his plan.

"I've never seen anything like it," his aide said. "You've got the British lion by the tail."

Sure enough, Prime Minister Christopher's policies turned the country's economy around, solidifying his position as Britain's savior. Other leaders throughout Europe, caught in the same downward spiral, began to duplicate his policies, and soon their economies rebounded as well.

But everything came crashing down when, in an instant, millions of people around the globe disappeared. The cars they'd been driving collided with other vehicles or spun off the road. Pilots vanished and their planes crashed, resulting in thousands of fatalities. Assembly lines clogged when factory machines were left unmanned. Two nuclear power plants exploded when operators vanished.

Further chaos ensued. Retailers, manufacturers, law-enforcement offices, and government agencies were paralyzed, with one-third of their employees missing. Hospital and nursing-home patients died for lack of services and medical assistance. Without delivery personnel, store shelves were bare. Crime became rampant as starving people took matters into their own hands.

The remaining citizens soon realized that it was only the Christians who had disappeared. "This is terrible!" Christopher's aide lamented. "No sooner do you solve one catastrophe than another piles on top of it."

"No, it's an opportunity." Christopher almost sounded excited. "We must never let a crisis go to waste. Get me on TV immediately."

That evening, he outlined his solution to all of Britain. Declaring a national emergency, he drafted able-bodied citizens for one-year terms to fill vacated positions, reorganize businesses, protect property, and make repairs. Christopher immediately became the go-to man for other European leaders who were confronting similar challenges.

\* \* \*

On the heels of the mass disappearance, Israel was threatened by surrounding Islamic nations. With the Western nations in turmoil, most people assumed no one would come to Israel's defense. A major Middle Eastern war seemed inevitable, and pundits were convinced that Israel would not survive.

Prime Minister Christopher called a meeting of his cabinet. "We cannot allow the Middle East powder keg to explode. This war is sure to spread to other nations and unravel our success. The Jewish problem has plagued the earth since 1948, and every American president has tried to resolve it. It's time to defuse this volatile nation once and for all."

Christopher flew to Jerusalem, and after conferences with both Israel and the surrounding Muslim countries, he announced the successful negotiation of a seven-year peace treaty guaranteeing protection to the Jews. There was much speculation about the secret deal he had arranged to pacify the Islamic states.

During a lull in the negotiations, one TV newsman's mic caught Christopher saying privately to the Palestinian leader, "Just sit tight for three years or so, and I'll see that you get your wish." Christopher's security agents immediately seized the reporter and confiscated his recording device. He was never seen again.

Overnight, Judas Christopher became a hero to the Israelis. He solidified that position by declaring support for the rebuilding of the Jewish Temple near the site of the recently destroyed Dome of the Rock. An astounded world lavished praise on him for yet another spectacular success.

As a result of the treaty, the Jews immediately diverted defense funds toward the reconstruction of a Temple that would eclipse the glory of Solomon's Temple. In less than four years, they completed the masterpiece and restored the ancient Jewish worship practices.

Four months after construction was complete, Clive Nelson, head of Britain's Secret Intelligence Service, sat across the desk from Judas Christopher.

"As you know, Mr. Prime Minister, for some time now we have been monitoring a buildup of troops and weapons in both Russia and Egypt. We've just learned that these nations intend to invade Israel within the month."

"Are other nations involved?" Christopher asked.

"Yes. Syria, Ethiopia, and Libya will join Egypt from the south, and several allies will join Russia from the north. Israel has relaxed its military diligence since the treaty, and these nations are taking advantage of it."

"Does Israel know of this?"

"Yes, we have informed them so they can prepare."

"You should have consulted me first!" Christopher slammed his fist on the table. "I have no intention of honoring that treaty. It served my purpose at the time, but I will not risk my influence in the West in a war that offers us no advantage. In fact, keeping out of this war will play into our hands."

"I am very sorry, sir. I had no idea—"

"Which is exactly why you must always check with me before you release information to other countries. Let the Russians and Muslims destroy Israel. It will save me the trouble of peeling that scab from the earth."

The following day, the Secret Intelligence Service chief's car exploded when he turned the key in the ignition.

\* \* \*

As predicted, Russian and Muslim armies soon invaded Israel. They marched toward Jerusalem, prepared to crush the city. But before they could accomplish their goal, a massive earthquake struck. Sulfuric fires and boulder-sized hailstones rained down, decimating the invading troops. The troops who survived, blinded by the billowing smoke and dust, began firing on each other until only a straggling remnant was left standing. Israel, though severely ravaged, was saved.

Judas Christopher wasted no time. The moment the battle ended, he marched into Libya, Ethiopia, and Egypt—three nations whose armies had been decimated—on the pretense of punishing them for violating the seven-year treaty. While he was still in North Africa, the Secret Intelligence Service informed him that the Israelis, angered by his failure to defend them, were rising up in insurrection. Christopher immediately turned his armies northward and made a move that caught the world by surprise: he marched into Israel and put down the uprising, torturing and killing thousands of Jews.

The day after the battle, the Israeli prime minister stood stiffly before Christopher, refusing the offered seat at the negotiating table. "You have defeated us through betrayal. Please state your terms." He made no attempt to hide the contempt in his voice.

"My terms?" Christopher replied. "I offer no terms but total surrender. I intend to rule you with a rod of iron. You troublesome Jews will never again contaminate the world with your arrogance or flaunt your claim to be God's chosen people. My troops will occupy your nation, and you will concede all power to me."

Christopher returned to England, leaving the people of Israel angry but firmly in his grip. With his growing influence in Europe and his control of the Middle East, he was starting to be viewed as the de facto leader of the world—a role that had once been held by the president of the declining United States.

But mere influence was not enough. Christopher's quest for outright power had only just begun.

* * *

Prime Minister Christopher stared unseeing into the blazing fireplace. He rested his chin in his hands, pondering his next move.

Slowly the room darkened until the flames, flickering like the tongues of serpents, were the only source of light. The blaze shot higher, and soon Christopher could make out an image within it—a vague but undeniable form of a man, towering over him like a smoldering goliath. The form and face were as beautiful as an angel, but its features were twisted with agony. Christopher broke into a cold sweat.

"I know what you want, Judas Christopher." The voice spoke, deep and low. "You want power. More and more power until you rule all the civilized nations of the world. And I can give it to you."

"Who are you? Why are you offering this to me?" Christopher's voice quaked.

"I am the true prince of this world. All the kingdoms of the earth are mine, unwittingly forfeited to me by your primeval parents. You have long been my faithful servant, though you did not know it was I whom you served. What I now hold out to you I have offered to only One other in the history of this planet. He refused, and He paid the price. But you can succeed where He failed."

"I know who you are talking about," Christopher said. "Yes, you made Him pay the price. But they say He was resurrected."

"And just as His Master resurrected Him, I can resurrect you."

"How can you promise that?" Christopher's fear refused to ebb, yet a craving welled up in his heart.

"I can assure you because I will be with you—indeed, I will be *in* you. Acknowledge me as your lord, and I will fill your entire being with myself. I will be yours, and you will be mine."

"I accept." The words came quietly but fervently. The choice came easily. To refuse the one desire of his heart would be unthinkable.

"It is done," the presence said.

Within moments the flame subsided, the darkness lifted, and Christopher found himself alone once more.

*　*　*

When the European nations held their next annual congress, Christopher was the keynote speaker. His speech was magnificent, and the delegates responded with a standing ovation. Only minutes later, he stood on a balcony to address a huge crowd assembled at the pavilion outside the building. He smiled and waved expansively, and when the adulation subsided, he publicly renewed his commitment to the well-being and protection of Europe, calling for the European Union to merge as one united power and expand their armed forces to ensure mutual prosperity and security.

At that moment, six rapid rifle shots rang out. Christopher's head jerked backward, and he fell to the ground. Sirens blared, and in moments, medics were rushing him to the nearest hospital.

A half hour later, BBC reporter Allison Lancaster addressed a worldwide TV audience. "According to doctors attending Judas Christopher, he has sustained a mortal wound. Recovery is impossible."

Later that evening Allison Lancaster again faced the TV cameras. For the first time in her career, her voice faltered on the air.

"Those of you who witnessed the shooting of Prime Minister Judas Christopher this afternoon will find what I am about to report difficult to believe." She gripped the microphone in both hands, trying to hold it steady. "The world watched him go down when shots were fired earlier today. But a little after five o'clock, the prime minister opened his eyes, got out of his bed, and walked out of the hospital of his own accord. I have with me Dr. Nigel Anderson, one of the physicians who attended the prime minister."

"Dr. Anderson, how is recovery from such a wound possible?"

"It is not possible. And yet it happened," the doctor said, shaking his head. "A bullet went all the way through the prime minister's head, and yet he is alive. There is no rational explanation for it."

The congress of the European Union was still in session, and the day after Christopher's recovery, the leaders of the member nations met in secret. They forged a single dominion divided into ten provinces and nominated Judas Christopher as their president. His rivals—heads of three of the nations represented—resisted vigorously. But their delegations overrode them, and Christopher won the election by a wide margin. Within a few weeks, one of the three resisting premiers died of food poisoning. Another was killed in a car accident. The third was found at the bottom of a hotel pool.

Judas Christopher, now president-elect of the powerful ten-nation empire of Europe, returned to his London office and called Archbishop Damon Detherow. Detherow was a high-ranking church leader who was widely known for his work to unite all the world's religions.

Christopher got right to the point. "We have before us a golden opportunity, and the time is now. With your widespread religious influence and my political skills, we can work together to accomplish great things."

"I'm listening."

"The natural disasters over the past few years—the earthquakes, floods, famines, volcanic eruptions, sulfuric rain, hailstones, and meteor strikes, not to mention the disappearance of Christians—have shaken Western confidence in materialism and spurred people to reconsider religion. People are now wondering whether there's some kind of spiritual influence that could be the cause of these disasters. And, like ancient primitive societies, they are beginning to think these spirits may need to be appeased."

"What exactly do you have in mind?"

"People need a worldwide government, and I can provide it. They are also ready for a worldwide religion, and you can provide that. Their need for gods to assuage their fear gives us a perfect opportunity to combine our efforts. Together we can create an irresistible force by which we can unite all people of the world as one."

Nothing stood in Detherow's way. He was now in the clutches of Judas Christopher's dark master.

* * *

In the coming weeks, the archbishop formulated his plans, which were designed to ultimately redirect the world's worship toward President Christopher.

First, the archbishop built a massive altar in Jerusalem and, like the prophet Elijah of old, called down fire from heaven to ignite the sacrifice laid upon it. Next, he created an enormous statue of Judas Christopher and placed it in the Jewish Temple. With thousands of people watching on-site and billions more observing online and on TV, he called for the image to speak in Christopher's voice and demand that all of humanity worship him alone.

In response to these miracles, countless people around the globe turned to Christopher as their new god. Those who refused were hunted down and executed.

Because the unrelenting disasters—both natural and man-made—had severely weakened every nation, Christopher knew the time was right to bring the rest of the planet under his control.

Christopher's forces—a trans-European army consisting of legions of well-equipped, highly trained troops—invaded Russia first, where they met only token resistance from the country's ravaged armies. His conquest of China and India also proved surprisingly easy, and with these major Eastern powers defeated, the mere threat of invasion brought the rest of Asia under his flag.

Christopher's takeover of the Americas was met with even less resistance. The United States, still weak from decades of crushing debt and unsustainable government largesse, actually voted to place itself under Christopher's leadership and impeach its own president. The Central and South Americas, equally plagued by internal turmoil, followed suit.

With his worldwide conquest complete, President Christopher called Archbishop Detherow into his office. "All the nations we've taken over are in economic chaos," he said. "The world's most pressing needs are for financial stability and food. This is another crisis I don't intend to waste; we must exploit the situation to our advantage. I know you've been working on a plan to solve the economic crisis while at the same time secure the people's absolute religious loyalty. Let's hear it."

"Well," Detherow began, "we cannot solve the economic problem unless we manage all the world's resources. That means we must track all trade to enforce equitable redistribution. We can accomplish this by assigning to every person an individual number that enables him or her to participate in commerce of any kind. This means everything from international manufacturing and shipping to buying a loaf of bread at the local market."

"That may address the economic problem, but what about the religious component?"

"A condition for receiving the number will be a signed pledge to worship you and you only. We will devise a way to use the number to monitor their adherence to the pledge."

"And what happens to those who refuse the number?" Christopher asked.

Damon Detherow chuckled. "To paraphrase Thomas Hobbes, their lives will be nasty, brutal, and short."

*  *  *

Archbishop Detherow's plan was a sweeping success. The only resisters were a few scattered Orthodox Jews and Christians, whom Christopher decimated with a reign of terror that eclipsed the French Revolution, the Sudanese Civil War, and the Rwandan genocide in brutality. Christopher quickly expanded his despotism beyond just Christians, and soon all the nations began to feel the weight of his cruelty.

When the world realized that Christopher's promises meant nothing, his treaties were worthless, and their economic problems were actually multiplying, talk of rebellion fomented around the globe, and several nations began to assemble their armies to move against the dictator. Christopher dismissed the threats as idle talk and turned his attention to a project he had longed to accomplish since he came to power: the complete annihilation of the Jewish state. His hatred of the Jews had swollen like a malignant tumor until it consumed his every thought.

Believing himself to be invincible, he assembled his massive armies and led them into Israel himself, intending to enjoy firsthand the slaughter of every Jew in the nation. But just as he positioned his forces for the attack, a coalition of North African forces led by Egypt attacked him from the south and fired the first salvos of rebellion. No sooner had he turned his armies toward the south than a coalition of Russian-led troops attacked from the north.

Christopher repulsed the southern forces and was starting to drive back the northern attackers when yet another army of more than a million Chinese troops advanced on him from the east. Christopher's forces met the rebel armies on Israel's plain of Megiddo. Blood flowed in torrents as millions of troops perished. It was a battle of unprecedented scope and destruction.

When the carnage began to subside, Christopher refocused his efforts on Israel. Leaving the Megiddo front to his generals, he marched a large contingent to Jerusalem. Upon reaching the city, he stood on Mount Olivet overlooking the object of his hatred. He delighted in the irony that this mountain was the very place where his master had inflicted unspeakable agony on his archenemy. Christopher raised his hand to signal the attack. At that moment a thunderous noise erupted above him, and he looked up to see the cause of it.

His day of reckoning was at hand.

* * *

# THE SCRIPTURE BEHIND THE STORY

Paul-Henri Spaak, the prime minister of Belgium in the 1930s and 1940s, reportedly made the following statement:

> The truth is that the method of international committees has failed. What we need is a person, someone of the highest order or great experience, of great authority, of wide influence, of great energy. Let him come and let him come quickly. Either a civilian or a military man, no matter what his nationality, who will cut all the red tape, shove out . . . all the committees, wake up all the people and galvanize all governments into action.[1]

When the Antichrist ascends the global stage, the world will be waiting to receive him in precisely this way.

So who exactly is the Antichrist? While there are more than one hundred passages of Scripture that describe him, the title *antichrist* is mentioned in only five verses in the New Testament—each time by the apostle John. Four of the five occurrences refer to opponents of Christ and His work in John's day (1 John 2:18, 22; 4:3; 2 John 7). Only once does this term refer to the individual who is the focus of this chapter: "Little children, it is the last hour; and as you have heard that the Antichrist is coming, even now many antichrists have come, by which we know that it is the last hour" (1 John 2:18).

Here John contrasts the many antichrists (lowercase *a*) with *the* Antichrist (capital *A*). The spirit of the antichrist, which is at work in our world today, will one day be concentrated in one being.

The prefix *anti* can mean both "against" and "instead of." Both meanings apply to this coming world leader. He will overtly oppose Christ and at the same time will try to insert himself in the place of Christ.

There are more than twenty-five different titles given to the Antichrist, all of which help to paint a picture of the most despicable man who will ever walk the earth. In the book of Revelation, he is referred to as the rider on the white horse (6:2), "the beast" (11:7), and the "beast rising up out of the sea" (13:1). Some people think he is Satan incarnate. We know for certain that Satan gives him his power, his throne, and his authority.

Here are some of the Antichrist's other aliases:

- The little horn (Daniel 7:8)
- The king of fierce features (Daniel 8:23)
- The one who understands sinister schemes (Daniel 8:23)
- The prince who is to come (Daniel 9:26)
- The one who makes desolate (Daniel 9:27)
- The willful king (Daniel 11:36)
- The man of sin (2 Thessalonians 2:3)

| The Counterfeit Christ | |
|---|---|
| **Christ** | **Antichrist** |
| Son of God (John 1:34) | Son of perdition (2 Thessalonians 2:3) |
| Holy One (Mark 1:24) | Lawless one (2 Thessalonians 2:8) |
| Came down from heaven (John 3:13) | Came up from the bottomless pit (Revelation 11:7) |
| Energized by the Holy Spirit (Luke 4:14) | Energized by Satan (Revelation 13:4) |
| Does the Father's will (John 6:38) | Does his own will (Daniel 11:36) |
| Cleansed the Temple (John 2:14-16) | Defiles the Temple (Matthew 24) |
| Man of Sorrows (Isaiah 53:3) | Man of sin (2 Thessalonians 2:3) |
| Humbled Himself (Philippians 2:8) | Exalts himself (Daniel 11:37) |
| Called "the Lamb" (John 1:36) | Called "the Beast" (Revelation 11:7) |
| Received up to heaven (Luke 24:51) | Sent to the lake of fire (Revelation 19:20) |

- The son of perdition (2 Thessalonians 2:3)
- The lawless one (2 Thessalonians 2:8)

It is not possible to know the precise identity of this future world ruler. In the dramatization he is given a name and a country of origin, but these details are fictional. He will, however, have a name, and he will likely come from some European nation (Daniel 2, 7). And we know what kind of man he will be, for the Bible gives us a wealth of information about him. Let's explore what facts we can know.

### His Preparation

In the latter time of their kingdom, when the transgressors have reached their fullness, a king shall arise, having fierce

features, who understands sinister schemes. His power
shall be mighty, but not by his own power; he shall destroy
fearfully, and shall prosper and thrive; he shall destroy the
mighty, and also the holy people.

DANIEL 8:23-24

This Scripture passage says that this world leader will rise to power
in the earth's last days. Whenever we read the words "the latter time"
or "the last time" in Scripture, they refer almost exclusively to the
Tribulation period.

At the beginning of this period, an ominous personality will
arise—inconspicuously at first—from among the masses. John says,
"I saw a beast rising up out of the sea, having seven heads and ten
horns, and on his horns ten crowns, and on his heads a blasphemous
name" (Revelation 13:1).

The word *sea*, when used symbolically in the book of Revelation,
refers not to a vast body of water but to the restless nations of the
earth—and more specifically, the Gentile nations. This interpretation is confirmed in Revelation 17, when John records Jesus' words
to him: "The waters which you saw, where the harlot sits, are peoples,
multitudes, nations, and tongues" (verse 15).

Since the Antichrist will make a covenant with the Jewish nation,
many people assume that he himself must be a Jew. But there are
several reasons why this assumption seems improbable:

1. Daniel prophesied that the prince, or the Antichrist,
   would come from the people who would destroy the city
   of Jerusalem and the sanctuary (Daniel 9:26). Those were
   the Romans who, under Titus, decimated Jerusalem and
   Herod's Temple in AD 70. Therefore, "the prince who is to
   come" must be a Roman prince. In other words, he will be
   a European Gentile.

2. Daniel also saw the Antichrist as the "little horn" that arose out of the ten horns on the head of the fourth beast (Daniel 7:7-8, 19-26). This fourth beast represents the Roman Empire, which followed Greece, Medo-Persia, and Babylon in their conquest of the Jewish people.

3. The Antichrist is described as history's most vicious and wicked persecutor of the Jewish people. Typically speaking, Gentiles persecute Jews; Jews do not!

## His Presentation

> Let no one deceive you by any means; for that Day will not come unless the falling away comes first, and the man of sin is revealed, the son of perdition, who opposes and exalts himself above all that is called God or that is worshiped, so that he sits as God in the temple of God, showing himself that he is God. . . . For the mystery of lawlessness is already at work; only He who now restrains will do so until He is taken out of the way. And then the lawless one will be revealed.
>
> 2 THESSALONIANS 2:3-4, 7-8

According to Paul, "that Day"—a term for the seven-year Tribulation period during which the Antichrist will be revealed—cannot happen until there is first a "falling away." The Greek word for "falling away" is *apostasia*, which appears only one other time in the New Testament. There it is translated "forsake" (Acts 21:21). Paul is telling us that before the Antichrist can be revealed, there will be a falling away, a forsaking, on the part of professing believers. This will not be a time when just a few people abandon their doctrinal beliefs; it will mark a period of major, widespread departure from the faith.

In His Olivet discourse, Jesus predicted such a time: "Many will be offended, will betray one another, and will hate one another. Then many false prophets will rise up and deceive many. And because lawlessness will abound, the love of many will grow cold" (Matthew 24:10-12). The apostle Paul describes this period in further detail: "The Spirit expressly says that in latter times some will depart from the faith" (1 Timothy 4:1). "The time will come when they will not endure sound doctrine, but according to their own desires . . . they will heap up for themselves teachers; and they will turn their ears away from the truth, and be turned aside to fables" (2 Timothy 4:3-4).

Contrary to what many people think, this present age will end not in a time of revival but in a time of apostasy. The Antichrist cannot be revealed before the great apostasy occurs, for it is this descent into chaos and rampant immorality that will set the stage for his arrival.

Up to this point, one thing has restrained the Antichrist from coming: he cannot appear until "He who now restrains" (the Holy Spirit) is removed (2 Thessalonians 2:7). When the church is raptured, the restraining work of the Holy Spirit, who is now holding back the man of sin and keeping the world from utter lawlessness, will be removed, and the earth will be subject to the full effects of sin. After the falling away and the Rapture, it will be time for the Antichrist to be revealed.

### His Personality

He was given a mouth speaking great things and blasphemies.
REVELATION 13:5

According to the prophet Daniel, the Antichrist shall "speak pompous words against the Most High" (Daniel 7:25; see also 7:7-8; 11:36). The NIV translates Daniel's word *pompous* as "boastfully."

According to biblical scholar A. W. Pink, the Antichrist "will have a perfect command and flow of language. His oratory will not only gain attention but command respect. Revelation 13:2 declares that his mouth is 'as the mouth of a lion' which is a symbolic expression telling of the majesty and awe-producing effects of his voice."[2] Just as the voice of a lion surpasses that of all other beasts, so the Antichrist will outrival orators both ancient and modern.

According to the prophet Daniel, the Antichrist will also be physically impressive. His "appearance was greater than his fellows" (Daniel 7:20). The expression "was greater" here means "abundant in size, in rank." In the Bible, this term often refers to a captain or chief or lord—a man of high rank or impressive appearance, like Saul in the Old Testament (1 Samuel 9:2), who was head and shoulders above his peers. When this man walks into the presence of others, he will immediately capture their attention.

He will also be a man of great intellect. Daniel describes him as one who "understands sinister schemes" and "through his cunning . . . shall cause deceit to prosper under his rule" (Daniel 8:23, 25).

When the events of the Tribulation have begun and people are devoid of hope, this man will rise up. People will flock to him like desperate sheep, ready to do whatever he says.

### His Plan

> Through his cunning, he shall cause deceit to prosper under his rule.
>
> DANIEL 8:25

> He shall come in peaceably, and seize the kingdom by intrigue.
>
> DANIEL 11:21

Daniel was given a picture of this world leader in his famous dream: "I was considering the horns, and there was another horn, a little one, coming up among them, before whom three of the first horns were plucked out by the roots" (Daniel 7:8). "Plucked out by the roots" literally means "to squeeze out, to push out by subterfuge, to come in and cleverly replace." Daniel goes on to explain: "The ten horns are ten kings who shall arise from this kingdom. And another shall rise after them; he shall be different from the first ones, and shall subdue three kings" (verse 24).

The little horn that Daniel sees rising would be the eleventh horn—a leader who subdues three of the ten kings, one by one. He will do so not by war but by clever political manipulation, and then he will claim their power for himself.

The Antichrist will begin as one of many minor political leaders, attracting little attention at first, but gradually grasping more and more power. His plan is to defeat all other world leaders and eventually take over the world through whatever means necessary—first by deceit and intrigue, and later by force.

### His Pride

He opened his mouth in blasphemy against God, to blaspheme His name, His tabernacle, and those who dwell in heaven.

REVELATION 13:6

Dr. Henry Morris describes what will motivate the Antichrist's evil actions:

Not content to merely rail against God, the dragon-inspired beast must utter diatribes and obscenities against all He stands for (His name), defaming His holiness, His love, His law, His grace. He curses the heavens (the dragon has recently been expelled from heaven) where God dwells. Those who dwell with God in heaven, including not only the holy angels but also all the raptured saints, share in his vilifications. This continual barrage of slander must now take place on earth, since the Devil no longer has access to heaven where he used to accuse the brethren.[3]

This man will even despise false gods—an extreme demonstration of the Antichrist's pride: "The king shall do according to his own will: he shall exalt and magnify himself above every god, shall speak blasphemies against the God of gods. . . . He shall regard neither the God of his fathers nor . . . any god. . . . But in their place he shall honor a god of fortresses; and a god which his fathers did not know" (Daniel 11:36-38). "A god of fortresses" refers to his pride in his own military might.

The Antichrist will acknowledge no religion at all other than the worship of himself and Satan. In his attempt to wipe the thought of God from the world's collective mind, he will try to change the moral and natural laws of the universe (Daniel 7:25). He will create his own morality, saying, "Forget about God's restrictive laws. Here's a new set of guidelines." He will do away with religious feast days. Some think he may try to replace the seven-day week, which is God-ordained time, with a ten-day week, as Napoleon sought to do during the French Revolution.

The Antichrist will strip away anything that has to do with religious structure, history, or stability. In starting his own religion, he will endeavor to obliterate God.

### His Peace Treaty

He shall confirm a covenant with many for one week.

DANIEL 9:27

In Daniel's prophecy, the reference to "one week" is not a literal seven-day period but a description of seven years (Daniel 9:24-27).

The Antichrist will make a seven-year covenant with Israel at the beginning of the Tribulation period, promising to protect the Jews from their many enemies. Mark Hitchcock writes,

> [The Antichrist] will be the consummate unifier and diplomat. He will acquire power using the stealth of diplomacy. His platform will be peace and prosperity. Emerging with an olive branch in his hand, he will weld together opposing forces with ease. The dreams of the United Nations will be realized in his political policies. He will even temporarily solve the Middle Eastern political situation, which may well earn him accolades such as the Nobel Prize or being anointed *TIME* magazine's man of the year. He will bring such peace to the Middle East that the Temple Mount area in Jerusalem will be returned to Jewish sovereignty (Daniel 9:27). He will undoubtedly be hailed as the greatest peacemaker the world has ever seen.[4]

Because of this treaty, Israel will let down its guard and redirect military expenses toward agriculture, cultural improvements, and the rebuilding of the Jewish Temple. However, halfway through the seven-year Tribulation period—after three and a half years—the Antichrist will break his covenant and turn against Israel: "In the middle of the week, he shall bring an end to sacrifice and offering. And on the wing of abominations shall be one who makes desolate" (Daniel 9:27).

### His Persecutions

> It was granted to [the Antichrist] to make war with the saints and to overcome them. And authority was given him over every tribe, tongue, and nation.
>
> REVELATION 13:7

When the peace treaty with Israel is broken, all hell will break loose on the earth. This ushers in the second half of the Tribulation period, often referred to as "the Great Tribulation." Daniel describes it this way: "I was watching; and the same horn was making war against the saints, and prevailing against them" (Daniel 7:21). He goes on to describe the persecution the Antichrist will enact: He "shall persecute the saints of the Most High" (verse 25), and "He shall destroy fearfully, and shall prosper and thrive; he shall destroy the mighty, and also the holy people" (8:24).

The Hebrew word translated "persecute" literally means "to wear out." The Antichrist will wear out the saints (those who become Christians during the Tribulation) the way an abusive driver wears out an automobile tire. The Antichrist won't just harass these believers; he will seek to snuff them out—probably through economic pressure and public seizure of goods when they refuse to take the mark of the Beast (Revelation 13:16-17). He will no doubt force many of them to starve to death.

In His Olivet discourse, Jesus described this terrible time: "There will be great tribulation, such as has not been since the beginning of the world until this time, no, nor ever shall be. And unless those days were shortened, no flesh would be saved; but for the elect's sake those days will be shortened" (Matthew 24:21-22). How short? John tells us in Revelation 13:4-5 that "the beast," or the Antichrist, will be "given authority to continue for forty-two months."

Antiochus Epiphanes, who prefigured the Antichrist, was "the first person in history to persecute a people exclusively for their religious faith."[5] On one occasion, Antiochus caught a group of Jews observing the Sabbath in a cave. He had the mouth of the cave sealed and fires set inside to suffocate them. That's just one example of how the Antichrist may persecute believers.

*His Power*

> The coming of the lawless one is according to the working
> of Satan, with all power, signs, and lying wonders.
>
> 2 THESSALONIANS 2:9

*Power*, *signs*, and *wonders* are all words that describe the genuine miracles of Christ. However, Paul adds the word *lying* to this description of the Antichrist to discredit his so-called miracles. Satan will empower him to perform certain counterfeit signs and lying wonders, which will dupe the world into gushing, "Who is like the beast?" (Revelation 13:4).

The Antichrist's deception will be so sweeping that eventually people will be unable to believe the truth. As Paul explains it, the work of Satan through the Antichrist will bring about "all unrighteous deception among those who perish, because they did not receive the love of the truth, that they might be saved. And for this reason God will send them strong delusion, that they should believe the lie" (2 Thessalonians 2:10-11).

Two events will take place almost simultaneously with the breaking of the Antichrist's treaty with Israel. First of all, the Antichrist will kill the two witnesses: "When they finish their testimony, the beast that ascends out of the bottomless pit will make war against them, overcome them, and kill them" (Revelation 11:7). Then the Antichrist will enact his most sensational feat. It will appear that he has been killed, and then, to the astonishment of the whole world, he will be raised back to life by the power of Satan in a grotesque counterfeit of the resurrection of Jesus Christ: "I saw one of his heads as if it had been mortally wounded, and his deadly wound was healed. And all the world marveled and followed the beast" (13:3).

Satan cannot create anything new. In his efforts to deceive, he can only counterfeit what the real Creator has accomplished. So to echo Christ's death and resurrection, the Antichrist will fake his death and then "rise again." And just as Christ's resurrection sparked rapid growth in the church, the so-called resurrection of the Antichrist will cause the world to follow him (with the exception of those who accept Christ during the Tribulation).

Satan is the great deceiver and the great destroyer. He does not have the power to give life. He can imitate God, but he will never have the power to duplicate Him.

### His Profaneness

> They worshiped the dragon who gave authority to the beast;
> and they worshiped the beast, saying, "Who is like the beast?
> Who is able to make war with him?"
> REVELATION 13:4

When the Antichrist breaks his treaty with Israel, he will surround Jerusalem with his troops and seize the newly constructed Temple. And then, as one last mockery of God, Satan will install his man of sin as a god in the Temple. At that point, "all who dwell on the earth will worship him, whose names have not been written in the Book of Life of the Lamb slain from the foundation of the world" (Revelation 13:8).

The false prophet will erect an animated image of the Antichrist in the Jewish Temple and enable it to speak (Revelation 13:14-15). He will then command the world to worship the image, ultimately fulfilling Daniel's prophecy: "'When you see the "abomination of desolation," spoken of by Daniel the prophet, standing where it ought not' (let the reader understand), 'then let those who are in Judea flee to the mountains'" (Mark 13:14; see also Matthew 24:15-16).

*His Punishment*

> He shall even rise against the Prince of princes; but he shall
> be broken without human means.
>
> DANIEL 8:25

One writer has described the Antichrist this way: "Take all of the sin of the world; compress it into one human mold; and out will come this wicked one. That is why Paul called him *the man of sin and the son of perdition*."[6]

What kind of punishment . . . what kind of end does such a person deserve? Daniel gives us the answer: "He shall be broken without human means" (Daniel 8:25). John paints the scene for the Antichrist's destruction: "I saw the beast, the kings of the earth, and their armies, gathered together to make war against Him who sat on the horse and against His army" (Revelation 19:19; see also Zechariah 12:1-9; 14:1-3; Revelation 16:16). And when the Beast comes face-to-face with Christ, he will meet a swift end: "The lawless one will be revealed, whom the Lord will consume with the breath of His mouth and destroy with the brightness of His coming" (2 Thessalonians 2:8). As these writers tell us, when the Antichrist dares to defy the second coming of Jesus Christ after the Great Tribulation, he will be finished.

A. W. Pink captures the unique punishment the Antichrist will face:

> Scripture has solemnly recorded the end of various . . .
> evil personages. Some were overwhelmed by waters; some
> devoured by flames; some engulfed in the jaws of the earth;
> some stricken by a loathsome disease; some ignominiously
> slaughtered; some hanged; some eaten up of dogs; some
> consumed by worms. But to no sinful dweller on earth, save
> the Man of Sin . . . has been appointed the terrible distinction

| The Career of the Antichrist | | |
|---|---|---|
| The Tribulation Period | | |
| **The Beginning of Sorrows**<br>**(3½ years)** | | **The Great Tribulation**<br>**(3½ years)** |
| Appears in last days<br>(Daniel 8:23-24) | | Mortally wounded<br>(Revelation 13:3) |
| Born in obscurity (Revelation 13:1) | | Miraculously recovers<br>(Revelation 13:3) |
| Born a Roman prince (Daniel 9:26) | | Speaks blasphemies for forty-two<br>months (Revelation 13:5) |
| Restrained by the Holy Spirit<br>(2 Thessalonians 2:6-7) | | Persecutes saints<br>(Revelation 13:7) |
| Blasphemes God<br>(Revelation 13:5-6) | | Given authority over the world<br>(Revelation 13:7) |
| Subdues three kings (Daniel 7:8) | The Antichrist breaks the treaty with Israel. | Worshiped by all the earth<br>(Revelation 13:8) |
| Seizes kingdom by intrigue<br>(Daniel 8:25) | | Energizes the false prophet<br>(Revelation 13:12) |
| Energized by Satan<br>(Revelation 13:2-5) | | Makes war against Christ<br>(Revelation 19:19) |
| Tries to change time and law<br>(Daniel 7:25) | | Defeated by Christ<br>(2 Thessalonians 2:8) |
| Makes seven-year treaty with Israel<br>(Daniel 9:27) | | Cast alive into a lake of fire<br>(Revelation 20:10) |
| Kills the two witnesses<br>(Revelation 11:7) | | Tormented forever<br>(Revelation 20:10) |

of being consumed by the brightness of the personal appearing of the Lord Jesus Himself. Such shall be his unprecedented doom, an end that shall fittingly climax his ignoble origin, his amazing career, and his unparalleled wickedness.[7]

Christ's return will officially end the career of the Antichrist. But it will not be the end of him. When we are told that he will be destroyed, this does not mean that he will be annihilated but rather that he will be utterly defeated and rendered powerless. He and his evil partner, the false prophet, will be apprehended and will become the first two humans cast into the lake of fire for all eternity: "The beast was captured, and with him the false prophet who worked signs in his presence, by which he deceived those who received the mark of the beast and those who worshiped his image. These two were cast alive into the lake of fire burning with brimstone" (Revelation 19:20).

One thousand years after their incarceration in the lake of fire (at the end of the Millennium), the beast and the false prophet will still be alive and in torment. At that point they will have company: "The devil, who deceived them, was cast into the lake of fire and brimstone where the beast and the false prophet are. And they will be tormented day and night forever and ever" (Revelation 20:10). Thus will end the ignominious reign of the unholy trinity.

As we see the signs of the end times increasing and intensifying today, the world is being prepared for the coming of this evil one. As Christians, we must keep our lamps trimmed so we will be among those the Lord removes before this man's terrible career begins.

*chapter seven*

# THE BEAST FROM THE EARTH

THE TV CAMERAS were trained on the trim, middle-aged man who sat ready on the interview set. The director's fingers signaled the last five seconds of the countdown, and the program host began. "Welcome, ladies and gentlemen, to America's number one Sunday-morning opinion show. I'm your host, Timothy Martin, and today I am honored to have as my guest a man who is undoubtedly the most talked-about religious leader in the world today. Would you please welcome Archbishop Damon Detherow, recently appointed head of the United Council of World Religions."

Martin stood, and Detherow entered, a warm smile spreading across his face as he waved at the studio audience. He shook hands with the host and beamed at the crowd until the applause subsided.

"Archbishop Detherow," Martin said, "I'm sure everyone in our network audience knows about all you've accomplished in your illustrious career, but let me summarize. You were originally the pastor of an evangelical megachurch, and you gained a wide following through your mesmerizing oratory, your religious insights, and your uncommon desire to unify people of all faiths. With unity as your focus, you built your church into the largest religious gathering in the world. And then, after twenty years, you left your pastorate at the peak of your success. Can you tell us why?"

"Thank you for your kind words, Tim. Believe me, I deserve none of the credit; it has all been the Lord's doing. I left my congregation because it became clear that God was calling me to a much broader ministry—one that reaches out to people of other faiths as well."

"By 'other faiths,' I presume you mean all Christian denominations," Martin said. "Baptists, Presbyterians, Methodists, Catholics?"

"Yes, I do mean Christians of any stripe," the pastor replied. "But God is calling me to reach out even further. His tent is much larger than we think. He has revealed to me that all people who worship a higher power are actually worshiping Him, whether they know it or not."

"Are you saying that Hindus, Buddhists, Muslims, and Christians all worship the same God?"

Detherow beamed his trademark smile. "God is so big, so universal, so inscrutable, that no one should presume to understand the ways He reveals Himself. That the Buddhists or Hindus or Muslims may not see God with the same eyes you or I do does not mean they are not connected to Him or that their religion is not authentic. The truth they see is illumined by their own light within."

"Yet we've long heard Christians claim that the only way to God is through Christ. Doesn't this divide them from the devoted practitioners of other religions?"

"Yes, it does." Detherow sighed, shaking his head. "And it is so sad that they cannot see we are all worshiping the Universal One, whether we call Him Jehovah, Jesus, Allah, the Great Spirit, or whatever. Christianity has been too exclusive to see this broader truth. I feel God's hand upon me to change that."

"You have initiated practices within Christianity that will lead to this change, have you not?"

"Yes, but I can't claim exclusive credit for that. Many other respected church leaders and writers have encouraged Christians to borrow mystic practices from other religions in order to sweep away the roadblock of rational thinking and open themselves to real faith. You see, true spirituality transcends rationality. So those who embrace these practices find themselves in touch with God and at one with the universe. They come to realize that they are part of God themselves. This is what will unite the religions of the West and the East."

"But surely you don't mean to welcome satanic or occult religions into your inclusive tent?"

"Once we understand the ultimate goodness of God, we see that He works on two fronts. On the one hand, He draws us with His love; on the other, He goads us forward through pain and suffering. When we truly understand the benevolent intentions of God, we realize that God is merely the name we give to the drawing force before us, and Satan is the name we give to the prodding force behind us. But at heart, they are one and the same. The goal of both is to bring us into the universal oneness of all being."

"Pastor, what is your ultimate hope as archbishop of the United Council of World Religions?"

"My hope is, with God's help, to bring about unity among all religions. Christ Himself called His church to an undivided oneness. This is what I dream of fostering."

"In other words," Martin said, "you hope to achieve a one-world religion."

\* \* \*

Among those watching the interview was Judas Christopher. Now that his position as the prime minister of England was secure, he had his sights set on Europe. As the interview progressed, his pleasure grew.

When the program ended, Christopher called his aide. "Chambers, have Archbishop Detherow flown here immediately. I must meet with him."

The next day, a dazed Archbishop Detherow sat in a plush chair by the fireside at Number 10 Downing Street facing Prime Minister Christopher, who was now the de facto leader of the Western world. With little prelude, the prime minister got right to the point.

"You made it clear in yesterday's interview that your goal is to unite all the religions of the world. I have long admired your remarkable success in breaking down the walls between religions, and especially in moving Christians in America away from their attitude of exclusivity."

"It has been easier than I could have predicted, Mr. Prime Minister. The Western collapse of critical thinking has helped immensely, virtually obliterating the concept of absolute truth and leading people to rely more on emotion than on reason. The demand for rational proof for their beliefs has virtually gone out the window. Then, with American affluence thrown into the mix, you end up with people who are bent on indulging their desires—people who think they are entitled to a life of ease. With this mind-set, they are easily led away from sacrificial religious concepts to those that promise feel-good spirituality and prosperity."

The prime minister nodded, and Detherow went on. "Values-free education and a media that bombards people with 24-7 entertainment have also had an impact. People no longer rely on the Bible as either their standard for living or their source of truth. In fact, few people even bother to read it anymore."

Christopher let Detherow's words hang in the air for a moment before breaking the silence. "How quickly do you think you could achieve your goal of a one-world religion if you had the power of the state behind you?"

Detherow felt his heartbeat quicken. "What are you thinking, sir?"

"Consolidation. Just as the time is right for a one-world religion, it is also right for a one-world government."

"You have my attention, Mr. Prime Minister."

"Historically, government and religion have been the primary ruling forces in people's lives," Christopher explained. "Political states in the past have consolidated their power by merging these forces into one. Think of the Islamic states today, the Catholic-state fusion of medieval Europe, Israel under David and Solomon, and the ancient Medo-Persians. Since your goal in the religious realm is the same as mine in the political arena, I propose that you and I form a liaison and unite our purposes."

"I—I hardly know what to say. I am humbled that you would think to include me."

Christopher rose to his feet. "Well, I would love to keep discussing this, but it will have to be at another time. I have an important event to attend tomorrow, and I must prepare."

"Of course, Mr. Prime Minister. It's been in the news for weeks. You're addressing the assembled congress of the European Nations at the Great Hall in Rome, are you not?"

"Yes. And then from the balcony overlooking the square, I will address an assembly of the people." Christopher looked straight at Detherow. "Remain here in London. Think on my suggestion, and we'll meet again the day after tomorrow, once I return."

*  *  *

The next day Detherow rose early, still heady over the opportunity before him. His mission in life was about to be combined with the authority of the state, headed by the most influential leader in the world.

All morning he sat in his hotel room, tapping out proposals on his laptop to present to the prime minister. Just before noon, he took a break for lunch. He flipped on the TV, and immediately a newsflash interrupted the regular programming.

"Ladies and gentlemen, we have just learned that Prime Minister Judas Christopher has been shot in the head while delivering his speech in Rome. According to the attending physicians, he has sustained a mortal wound and will not survive."

Detherow fell back into his chair, stunned. His hope of heading the first consolidated world religion had risen to soaring heights, only to plunge like Icarus into a black sea of vast disappointment. He stared at the screen as reporters regurgitated the horrific details over and over.

The phone rang, startling Detherow out of his daze. "Archbishop Detherow," a commanding voice said, "I am the head of the prime minister's Secret Intelligence detail. You must fly to Rome immediately; the doctors say the prime minister's body will not last the night. It would please the people to know that during his last minutes, a man of God was with him. Your flight to Rome has been booked, and a limousine is already on the way to take you to Heathrow Airport."

Four hours later, Detherow entered the ICU in Rome's Salvator Mundi International Hospital. The Secret Intelligence agent met him at the door. "We want you to say a prayer over the prime minister before he dies," the agent whispered. "A cameraman is here to record the prayer so it can be broadcast around the world."

Detherow was ushered through a cluster of dignitaries to Christopher's body, which lay still amid a tangle of tubes and wires.

Detherow stepped up to the bed and began to pray, still trying to absorb this turn of events.

Suddenly everyone in the room began murmuring, and one of the nurses shrieked. Detherow opened his eyes and jumped back. The prime minister was sitting up, looking strong and healthy—as if nothing had happened.

"Somebody unhook me from these tubes. And remove this bandage from my head!" Christopher demanded.

A nurse quickly attended to him. Gasps filled the room as the onlookers caught a glimpse of his head: there was no evidence that Judas Christopher had even been wounded.

"What are you staring at?" he asked his stunned audience. "If you will please step out, I will get dressed."

As the dignitaries filed out in stunned silence, Christopher called out, "Detherow, I want to see you in my office in two days. We have plans to make."

Then the prime minister got up, put on his suit, and marched out of the room.

Within the span of twenty-four hours, the congress of the European Nations reconvened, with Christopher present, and elected him president of their newly formed ten-nation coalition.

The next morning, Archbishop Detherow again sat in Judas Christopher's office. This time, the atmosphere was eerily different. He felt a sickening chill creep up his spine the moment Christopher entered the room. It was as if some invisible evil presence accompanied him. But since Detherow didn't believe in the concept of evil, he dismissed the feeling as superstition.

"Mr. President," Detherow blurted out, "like the rest of the world, I am still reeling from your miraculous recovery. There is no way you should be alive, and yet here you sit, strong and healthy without even a trace of your encounter with death. Can you explain this?"

"Deep down, I think you know who I am. And I think you know who you are."

\* \* \*

Archbishop Detherow did know who President Christopher was. As he looked back on his quest to unite all religions, he now realized that from the very beginning, he had actually been in the service of a dark master—the archenemy of God. His quest for religious unity had merely been a prelude to his real mission, which was to lead the world to worship a being of immense power—one who was determined to wrest the world from God's hands.

The archbishop threw himself wholeheartedly into Judas Christopher's quest to clinch political power by fusing it with the universal impulse to worship. And Detherow knew just what needed to be done: they must redirect worship from the world's multiple gods to one godlike being. If they could capture people's spirits, their minds and bodies would soon follow.

Two plans came to Detherow immediately, as if they'd been thrust into his mind by some outside force. The first mimicked the ancient prophet Elijah's miracle of calling down fire from heaven. Detherow had a massive altar built in the Temple, and he called people to come to Jerusalem to witness the return to the traditional Jewish sacrificial system. With a large crowd gathered around, he proclaimed, "This is a day to celebrate, regardless of what religion you subscribe to. As a symbol of our solidarity, let fire come and ignite this offering!" Sure enough, the offering went up in flames, and the event was the talk of every synagogue, church, and mosque around the world.

Now Detherow knew it was time to prepare for the second miracle. This event, he was certain, would tip the balance and convince the world that the powers of the heavens were fully aligned with Judas Christopher.

Detherow conscripted a group of the most talented sculptors in the world to carve an intricate statue of a man. More than thirty feet tall, the statue was of heroic proportions, in the classic Greek style. The face was an exact likeness of Judas Christopher. No seams or imperfections were visible; everything had been overlaid with bronze to polished perfection.

Christopher made plans for Detherow to return to Jerusalem to initiate their one-world religion in the newly reconstructed Temple. "The Jewish leaders think you are coming merely to dedicate the new

Temple. But you know what to do. I have arranged for the event to be broadcast throughout the world."

The appointed day came, and the Temple's court of Gentiles teemed with thousands of spectators. Both Jews and non-Jews had flocked to Jerusalem to witness the historic occasion. Electronic screens the size of billboards had been erected throughout the Temple court, assuring everyone a clear view of the proceedings. As government officials and dignitaries arrived in limousines, they were ushered to their designated chairs on a specially constructed platform.

When the clock struck noon, everyone on the platform rose as a soloist sang the international anthem. When the final notes died away, Archbishop Damon Detherow stepped up to the podium.

"Ladies, gentlemen, and noted guests, I welcome you to this historic occasion. Today I have the honor of dedicating this Temple as the central place of worship for the entire world. Today we will affirm that heaven has now come down and vested itself in the lives of humankind. No longer will your God be distant; no longer will belief in Him be optional. Today you will witness a phenomenon that will remove all doubt that He is among us."

The high priest, Asa Zechariah, wondered at the meaning of Detherow's enigmatic words, but he said nothing.

"As you know," the archbishop continued, "only priests can enter the Temple's Holy Place. So at this time, I will ask High Priest Zechariah to enter the sanctum with twelve attending priests as you watch the proceedings on the screens."

As the high priest entered the room, he stopped short. Two men stood before the curtain that covered the most sacred place in the Temple: the Holy of Holies.

"What are you doing here?" the priest demanded.

Without answering, the two men gripped the edges of the massive curtains and parted them.

The twelve priests gasped and turned their faces away. Only the high priest dared to look up. His eyes widened as he cried out in anguish, "The Ark of the Covenant is gone! And in its place . . ." His words were swallowed up in a wail of anguish.

The other priests followed his gaze into the sacred place, and what they saw filled them with horror. In place of the Ark of the Covenant, there was now a thirty-foot bronze image of Judas Christopher. The priests fell to the floor, tearing their robes in grief. The masses in the court stared at the screens, not yet comprehending what they were seeing.

As they watched, the image raised its arms. The people gaped as it opened its mouth to speak.

"Citizens of our world, hear me," the image said. The resonant voice was unmistakably that of Judas Christopher. The lips and jaws moved in perfect sync with the words, and somehow the bronze surface moved as fluidly as human skin. Even the muscles of the torso and arms contracted naturally with each gesture the image made.

"Today I announce that I am not only your political ruler; I am also your one true god, and you must have no other. Serve me and you will prosper and live long on the earth. Continue to serve your little gods and spirits, and you will surely die. Let those who have ears hear and obey."

When the statue's mouth ceased moving, the image returned to its original position. The crowd sat in stunned silence as Archbishop Detherow again stepped up to the podium. "Ladies, gentlemen, and citizens watching around the world, the miracle you have witnessed today has been performed so that you may believe. It is the work of the most powerful spirit of the invisible realm—a spirit that is guiding our president and his servants. That same spirit will guide you as well, if you will but believe and submit. Today I call on you to make that choice."

The archbishop paused and looked at the crowd before continuing. "I now call for a moment of silence during which all of us in this assembly and beyond will fall to our knees and bow to the image as a sign of our allegiance and devotion."

Nearly every person in the massive crowd responded immediately. Only about a hundred remained seated. Half of the dissenters bolted from the court. Those who refused to bow and those who ran were seized and escorted away by armed troops, never to be seen again.

* * *

Using both intimidation and military conquest, President Christopher soon extended his rule throughout the civilized world. But the widespread wars, in addition to unprecedented natural disasters, left the planet in economic chaos. The countries under Christopher's leadership demanded that he solve the problem. He used the crisis to his advantage, bringing both the global economy and the world's religious practices under his unchecked control.

Detherow took over all the networks to deliver an address to every nation on earth.

"Citizens of the world, listen as I declare to you a new law that President Christopher has issued by executive decree. To put an end to the current economic crisis and correct the historical imbalance between those in poverty and those with plenty, he has devised a system to ensure that food and goods are evenly distributed throughout the world. Every person on earth shall be given a number enabling him or her to buy and sell the food, goods, and services necessary to function in society. There will be no exceptions; every individual must carry his or her assigned number as a license to participate in commerce, either as a supplier or a consumer.

"By accepting this number, you will agree to discontinue worshiping any god of any religion, whether you are Buddhist, Hindu, Muslim, Jew, Christian, or any other faith. Peace and plenty will come only when religious divisions are obliterated. All people must unite in worshiping the undisputed master of our world, Judas Christopher, who is the physical manifestation of the power of the air, anointed to bring this planet into a new era of peace and goodwill."

Over the next several weeks, the process of assigning the numbers proceeded in earnest. Notices were placed on the Internet, TV, and radio; letters were sent to every person with a known address; and government workers called on homes in remote areas around the globe.

The recipients of the numbers were given three options: they could have their number encoded electronically on an existing credit card, they could receive a new encoded card, or they could have a microchip implanted beneath the skin of their hands or foreheads. These chips would be scanned as authorization for any type of commercial transaction.

In time, every known person on the planet bore a number, with the exception of a few primitive jungle tribes that had no communication with the civilized world, and pockets of Christians in several countries. Many of these Christians, it was believed, had escaped to remote areas where they lived in isolated communities, fed by sympathetic friends and family members. Many of them simply starved.

One evening, as President Christopher and his sidekick, Archbishop Detherow, sat together by the fireplace in the presidential palace, an aide entered and announced that the numbering was complete. The president said nothing at first, but after a moment he began to chuckle. The chuckle soon swelled into a laugh so contagious that Detherow couldn't help but join in. Their laughter grew higher and louder.

Soon the two men were laughing uncontrollably. Their time had come.

\* \* \*

# THE SCRIPTURE BEHIND THE STORY

We can't know for sure how the false prophet will be introduced to the world or what his path to notoriety will be. But it may well be something like what has been imagined in the opening story. We also don't know the identity of this coming world religious leader, but we do know what he will be like, what he will do, and what will happen to him in the end.

All of this information is given to us in the Word of God, especially in Revelation 13. Here we learn about the false prophet's profile, purpose, power, program, and ultimately, his punishment.

*His Profile*

> I saw another beast coming up out of the earth, and he had
> two horns like a lamb and spoke like a dragon.
> REVELATION 13:11

John describes this religious leader as a "beast coming up out of the earth," which is obviously a metaphor to describe his predatory nature. He is a man, and he is called "the false prophet" three times in the book of Revelation (16:13; 19:20; 20:10).

John profiles the false prophet as a composite of two opposite types of animals: a lamb and a dragon. As a lamb, he will appear meek and mild—a counterfeit of the true gentleness of Jesus. Notice that early in our dramatization, he seems humble and self-effacing. Jesus warned His followers of such deceivers: "Beware of false prophets, who come to you in sheep's clothing, but inwardly they are ravenous wolves" (Matthew 7:15; see also Matthew 24:11, 24; Mark 13:22; 1 John 4:1).

As a dragon, the false prophet will manipulate and deceive the masses. "The dynamic appeal of the false prophet will lie in his skill in combining political expediency with religious passion, self-interest with benevolent philanthropy, lofty sentiment with blatant sophistry, moral platitude with unbridled self-indulgence. His arguments will be subtle, convincing, and appealing. His oratory will be hypnotic, for he will be able to move the masses to tears or whip them into a frenzy. . . . His deadly appeal will lie in the fact that what he says will sound so right, so sensible, so exactly what unregenerate men have always wanted to hear."[1]

His lamb-like appearance and his dragon-like speech suggest a strong relationship with the devil and his evil cohort, the Antichrist. Because of their cruel and vicious ways, all three are described as beasts in the book of Revelation. And all three are characterized by their eloquent but deceptive speech.

It is important to understand why Satan has recruited these two evil cohorts: the three of them form an unholy trinity. Just as God is a trinity, so Satan has a trinity. Donald Grey Barnhouse says, "The devil is making his last and greatest effort, a furious effort, to gain power and establish his kingdom upon the earth. He knows nothing better than to imitate God. Since God has succeeded by means of an incarnation and then by means of the work of the Holy Spirit, the devil will work by means of an incarnation in Antichrist and by an unholy spirit."[2]

Satan counterfeits God the Father; the Antichrist counterfeits God the Son; the false prophet counterfeits God the Holy Spirit. So the beast from the earth, or the false prophet, is the third person in the unholy trinity.

## His Purpose

He exercises all the authority of the first beast in his presence, and causes the earth and those who dwell in it to worship the first beast, whose deadly wound was healed.

REVELATION 13:12

| The Two Trinities | | |
|---|---|---|
| **Person** | **Holy Trinity** | **Unholy Trinity** |
| First | Father | Satan |
| Second | Son | Antichrist |
| Third | Holy Spirit | False Prophet |

Just as the Holy Spirit has one main objective—to glorify the Son—so the false prophet has one objective: to cause people to worship the Antichrist. "As Christ received authority from the Father (Matthew 11:27), so Antichrist receives authority from the dragon (Revelation 13:4), and as the Holy Spirit glorifies Christ (John 16:14), so the false prophet glorifies the Antichrist (Revelation 13:12)."[3]

The false prophet will be a religious figure, but his religion will be demonic. His goal will be to unite the world around the Antichrist. At first, all religious ideas will be encouraged because a multiplicity of religions will dilute the influence of Christianity. But at some point, Satan will attempt to force all worship to coalesce around himself.

It may seem strange that a religious leader would be so central in all that will happen in the Tribulation, but we should not be surprised. This has been the pattern throughout history. Religion and political power are the two forces that exercise the most control over human life. One acts as an authority that forces, and the other acts as an attraction that draws. Combine the two, and the result is virtually absolute power.

W. A. Criswell writes, "I do not suppose that in the history of mankind, it has ever been possible to rule without religious approbation and devotion. . . . In the days of Pharaoh, when Moses and Aaron stood before the sovereign of Egypt, he called in Jannis and Jambres, the magicians, the religionists of his day, to oppose Jehovah. When Balak, the king of Moab, sought to destroy Israel, he hired the services of Baalim to curse Israel. . . . Ahab and Jezebel were able to do what they did in Israel, in the debauchery of the kingdom, because they were abetted and assisted by the prophets of Baal."[4]

At the end of the age, religion will be one of the tools that Satan uses to unite the world under the leadership of the Antichrist, which is why the false prophet will be so essential to his success.

### His Power

> He performs great signs . . . in the sight of men. And he
> deceives those who dwell on the earth by those signs which
> he was granted to do in the sight of the beast.
>
> REVELATION 13:13-14

The power of the false prophet will not be his own. It will be given to him by the Antichrist, who himself is empowered by the Dragon, or Satan. Scripture documents this fact clearly, telling us five times in Revelation 13:2-8 that the power of the Antichrist comes from the devil himself. And then, three times in Revelation 13:12-15, we are told that the Antichrist gives his power to the false prophet: "He exercises all the authority of the first beast in his presence. . . . He deceives those who dwell on the earth by those signs which he was granted to do in the sight of the beast. . . . He was granted power to give breath to the image of the beast."

These statements make it clear that the power of the Antichrist and the power of the false prophet originate with the Dragon, Satan. All the false prophet's power will be demonic. And if there's any doubt left about his ability to perform miracles, let's consider these words from Jesus: "False christs and false prophets will rise and show great signs and wonders to deceive, if possible, even the elect. See, I have told you beforehand" (Matthew 24:24-25).

John draws our attention to three ways the false prophet will enact miracles through the power of Satan.

### CALLING DOWN FIRE FROM HEAVEN

The first of the false prophet's miracles will be to call down fire upon the earth: "He performs great signs, so that he even makes fire come down from heaven on the earth in the sight of men" (Revelation 13:13). God has often revealed Himself and His judgment through fire. He called down fire upon Sodom and Gomorrah as a result of the people's wickedness (Genesis 19:24). Fire came down from heaven and consumed Nadab and Abihu for their carelessness in the Tabernacle (Leviticus 10:1-2). And the end of Revelation records that one day God will destroy Satan's army with fire from heaven (Revelation 20:7-9).

When the false prophet calls down fire, he is attempting to mimic God. But I believe there is even more to his action. The false prophet is also claiming to be the fulfillment of the prophecy of Malachi: "Behold, I will send you Elijah the prophet before the coming of the great and dreadful day of the LORD" (Malachi 4:5).

Hundreds of years before Malachi wrote his prophecy, Elijah called down fire from heaven on Mount Carmel in front of the 450 prophets of Baal, and that fire consumed the water-soaked sacrifice as a testimony to the power of Elijah's God (1 Kings 18:19, 38). Elijah was the only Old Testament prophet to bring down fire, but Malachi declared that God would send another Elijah before the coming of the Messiah. The false prophet will attempt to convince people he is Elijah—the forerunner of the Lord. It is a deceitful attempt to give an air of legitimacy to his presence.

New Testament scholar Craig Keener reminds us that signs and miracles alone are not foolproof marks of a true prophet: "Signs by themselves can be positive or negative; what enables us to discern true prophets from false ones is . . . to evaluate them by their moral character. The point is that we know them by their message and their fruit, not by their gifts (Deuteronomy 13:1-5; Matthew 7:15-23)."[5]

### COMMANDING THAT AN IMAGE BE BUILT

The false prophet's miracles, performed through the great occult power granted him, will achieve their intended effect by luring the masses into idolatry and convincing people to build a giant statue in honor of the Antichrist—what John describes as "an image to the beast who was wounded by the sword and lived" (Revelation 13:14). This idol will become the center of false worship until the end of the Tribulation.

The image is mentioned four times in Revelation 13: once in verse 14 and three times in verse 15. It is mentioned six more times in the rest of the book (14:9, 11; 15:2; 16:2; 19:20; 20:4).

The image of the Beast marks the final stage of apostasy and idolatry that has always characterized false religion. Nineteenth-century theologian J. A. Seiss made this observation about how the world will come to worship the image of the Beast one day:

> [It is not] difficult to trace what sort of arguments will be brought to bear for the making of this image. In the ages of great worldly glory and dominion statues were raised to the honor of the great of every class, but who of all the great ones of the earth is so great as the Antichrist! Statues have ever been common for the commemoration of great events; but what greater event and marvel has ever occurred than that in the history of this man, in that he was wounded to death, and yet is restored to life and activity, with far sublimer qualities than he possessed in his first life? . . . And who will there be among the proud sons of earth to stand against such arguments?[6]

The image of the Beast is evidently what the Lord Jesus had in mind when He gave His Olivet discourse: "When you see the 'abomination of desolation,' spoken of by Daniel the prophet, standing in the holy place . . . then let those who are in Judea flee to the mountains. . . . For then there will be great tribulation, such as has not been since the beginning of the world until this time, no, nor ever shall be" (Matthew 24:15-16, 21).

In his second letter to the Thessalonians, Paul also describes this moment: "Let no one deceive you by any means; for that Day will not come unless the falling away comes first, and the man of sin is revealed, the son of perdition, who opposes and exalts himself above all that is called God or that is worshiped, so that he sits as God in the temple of God, showing himself that he is God" (2 Thessalonians 2:3-4). When that day comes, the diabolical trinity of Satan, the Antichrist, and the false prophet will have accomplished their goal of becoming the objects of worldwide worship.

### CAUSING THE IMAGE TO BREATHE AND SPEAK

After the false prophet erects the statue of the Antichrist in the most sacred area of the newly constructed Jewish Temple, he will then "give breath to the image . . . that the image of the beast should . . . speak" (Revelation 13:15). Some people think this will be done through some form of ventriloquism or electronic voice reproduction. But commentator Dr. Henry Morris has another explanation that I find very plausible:

> This image is more than a mere robot with a computer voice. That would be no great marvel today, with all the accomplishments of automation and kinemetronics (or audio-animatronics). Millions of people have observed an image of Abraham Lincoln move and "speak" at Disneyland, but they were hardly moved to bow down in worship of his image.

The image of the man of sin will speak intelligibly
and his words will not be preprogrammed. He will issue
commands, among them the command to slay all who
do not worship him. Those who observe this remarkable
phenomenon, whether in person at Jerusalem or on another
side of the world by television, will be convinced the image
is really speaking of its own volition.[7]

Dr. Morris goes on to explain: "The false prophet is enabled (by
his own master, Satan) to impart a spirit to the image, but that spirit
is one of Satan's unclean spirits, probably a highly placed demon in
the satanic hierarchy. This is a striking case of demon possession,
with the demon possessing the body of the image rather than that of
a man or woman."[8]

There is no magic here—this is raw demonic power at work.
Through Satan, the false prophet will possess the ability to make an
inanimate object appear to come to life. It is another example of the
dark power that will characterize the Tribulation period and allow
Satan to gain credibility in the world's eyes so he can carry out his
evil program and deceive many in the final days.

### His Program

He causes all, both small and great, rich and poor, free
and slave to receive a mark on their right hand or on their
foreheads, and that no one may buy or sell except one who
has the mark or the name of the beast, or the number of his
name.

REVELATION 13:16-17

The false prophet will wear two hats. Not only will he be the world's
religious leader, but he will also become the Antichrist's economic czar.

After displaying his power through the image of the Beast, he will move to set up a comprehensive economic program. He will demand that everyone accept the mark of the Beast or be banned from all business transactions.

This mark is just one more form of counterfeit. In Revelation 7:3, the 144,000 Jewish evangelists are sealed on their foreheads and set apart for God. Now we see the false prophet marking his followers on the forehead in an attempt to seal his people to the unholy trinity.

The differences between the two marks are significant: "The counterfeit mark of Satan will have no power over those who bear the authentic mark of God. God's seal will protect His witnesses from harm, whereas Satan's seal will subject his people to harm. Another difference is that the seal of God will be given only to a select few—the 144,000 Jewish witnesses. But the seal of the Antichrist will be required of everyone."[9]

No one will be exempt from the requirement of the mark. From millionaire to pauper, CEO to hired hand, all will be compelled to receive it—or to suffer greatly if they do not. "No one will be able to shop at the mall, eat at a restaurant, fill up at gas stations, pay utility bills, buy groceries, get prescriptions filled, pay to get the lawn mowed, or pay the mortgage without the mark of the Beast. It's the Tribulation trademark."[10]

The word for "mark" in Greek is *charagma*, and it is used eight times in the book of Revelation in reference to the mark of the Beast. In antiquity, this symbol was connected with an emperor and often contained not only the emperor's name but also his effigy and the year of his reign. The charagma was necessary for buying and selling, and it was required on all kinds of documents as proof of their validity. In the same way, the mark of the Beast allows its bearers to conduct their affairs. It also indicates that the one wearing it is a worshiper of the Beast who submits to his rule.

The cooperation between government and religion will leave no place of refuge for any who rebel. "What is portrayed is a tremendous union in which capital and labor are both subject to the control and direction of one man. Anyone who is outside that vast combination will be ruthlessly boycotted: no one will work for him or employ him; no one will purchase his produce or sell goods to him. . . . Bankruptcy and starvation face such a man."[11]

During World War II, money alone was not enough to buy sugar and certain other staples in the United States; people also had to use their food stamps or have a card that allowed them to purchase various items. Certain commodities were rationed and could not be bought without authorization. That is only a shadow of how it will be in the Tribulation. When people go to buy food, they will be asked to show their cards or perhaps present their right hands or foreheads to be scanned. Only then will they be permitted to purchase what they need.

While no one can say for certain what the mark of the Beast will be, Revelation 13:18 gives us an enigmatic clue: "Here is wisdom. Let him who has understanding calculate the number of the beast, for it is the number of a man: His number is 666."

There have been countless theories about the meaning of the number 666 over the centuries. People have scoured Scripture for clues, trying to find significance in merely coincidental facts. For instance, the number appears in the eighteenth verse of Revelation 13. Eighteen is six plus six plus six. One of the largest men who ever lived was Goliath. He was six cubits tall, the head of his spear weighed six hundred shekels, and he had six pieces of armor (1 Samuel 17:4-7). Nebuchadnezzar's statue in the book of Daniel was sixty cubits tall and six cubits wide, and six musical instruments summoned the worshipers (Daniel 3:1-15, NIV). Such observations have been used to pin the label "antichrist" on almost every prominent leader from the Pope to Hitler to American presidents. If people try hard enough, they can find a way to manipulate almost any name to fit that number. Such attempts, however, are merely contrivances. They tell us nothing about the meaning of the number of the Beast. The bottom line is that no one really knows what 666 means.

Perhaps the most likely answer is that, in the Bible, six is the number for human beings. People were created on the sixth day, and they are to work six of seven days. A Hebrew could not be a slave for more than six years.

God's number, on the other hand, is seven. He created seven days in a week. There are seven colors in the visible spectrum and seven notes in a musical scale. Biblically, there are seven feasts of Jehovah (Leviticus 23); seven sayings of Jesus from the cross; and seven "secrets" in the Kingdom parables (Matthew 13). At the fall of Jericho, seven priests marched in front of the army bearing seven trumpets of rams' horns, and on the seventh day they marched around the city seven times (Joshua 6).

In the book of Revelation, which is more properly titled "the Revelation of Jesus Christ," the number seven is used more than fifty times. There are seven churches, seven Spirits, seven candlesticks, seven stars, seven lamps, seven seals, seven horns, seven eyes, seven trumpets, seven thunders, seven heads, seven crowns, seven angels, seven plagues, seven bowls, seven mountains, seven kings, seven beatitudes, seven years of judgment, seven letters to the seven churches, seven "I am" statements of Christ, and seven songs in heaven.

Seven is God's number, the number of completeness. But six is the number for humans, the number of incompleteness. Perhaps this is the meaning of 666—that human beings, even to the triple, fall short of God's perfection. On our own, we are incomplete and we long for fulfillment in the perfect completeness of God.

Donald Grey Barnhouse illustrates why the most important thing to know about the mark of the Beast is not specifically who it represents but what it should arouse in us:

The children of the great composer, Bach, found that the easiest method of awakening their father was to play a few lines of music and leave off the last note. The musician would arise immediately and go to his piano to strike the final chord. I awoke early one morning and went to the piano in our home and played the well-known carol "Silent Night." I purposely stopped just before playing the last note. I walked out into the hallway and listened to the sounds that came from upstairs. An eight year old had stopped his reading and was trying to sound the final note on his harmonica. Another child was singing the last note, lustily. An adult called down, "Did you do that purposely? What is the matter?" Our very nature demands the completion of the octave.[12]

The number 666 reminds us that there is something missing. That missing "something" is a Someone. He is a seven—the mark of perfection, the complete number.

## His Punishment

> The beast was captured, and with him the false prophet who worked signs in his presence, by which he deceived those who received the mark of the beast and those who worshiped his image. These two were cast alive into the lake of fire burning with brimstone.
>
> REVELATION 19:20

In spite of the power and control the false prophet will exercise during the Tribulation, his doom is sealed. He will be "cast alive into the lake of fire." Those who take the mark of the Beast will not fare well either. Revelation 16:1-2 details "a foul and loathsome" sore that comes upon them. Revelation 14:10-11 says they will "drink of the wine of the wrath of God" and "shall be tormented with fire and brimstone in the presence of the holy angel and in the presence of the Lamb . . . forever and ever."

While it may appear that those who take the mark of the Beast are simply doing what they have to do to protect themselves and their families, they will be judged for identifying with the satanic evil of the false prophet. But what about those who refuse to take the mark?

Their refusal will seem like a death wish, but what seems like death will in reality result in everlasting life: "I saw thrones, and they sat on them, and judgment was committed to them. Then I saw the souls of those who had been beheaded for their witness to Jesus and for the word of God, who had not worshiped the beast or his image, and had not received his mark on their foreheads or on their hands. And they lived and reigned with Christ for a thousand years" (Revelation 20:4).

What seems like foolishness to the world will prove to be wisdom, for these martyrs will have heeded the words of Jesus: "Do not fear those who kill the body but cannot kill the soul. But rather fear Him who is able to destroy both soul and body in hell" (Matthew 10:28).

The false prophet will come with power and influence, deceiving many and causing widespread destruction through his plan of economic domination. But his days are numbered. While he may taste limited success as a counterfeiter, he is no match for the original. The false prophet will be allowed to spread evil during the Tribulation, but God is merely biding His time. One day God's justice will prevail, and the false prophet will meet his fiery end.

*chapter eight*

# THE VICTOR

Judas Christopher, leader of the United World Empire, sat at the head of a long oak table with his governing council around him. The council consisted of his inner circle of advisers as well as heads of various governmental departments. Seated behind the table were representatives from the major world nations, chosen for their influence within their countries. All of them had pledged allegiance to Christopher and had accepted the universal number required to participate in the worldwide economy.

President Christopher had grown increasingly belligerent as the meeting went on, breaking into bestial rants that chilled his subordinates. Every person in the room knew the cause of his displeasure: he was smarting from the defeat of the armies he'd commanded to destroy Israel.

The primary targets of his verbal storm were the representatives from Russia, Iran, Egypt, and China—the axis of nations whose armies had failed him. The worst of it fell upon the Russian dignitary, Alexandr Ivazov, since Russia's generals had directed the campaign.

"What happened?" Christopher bellowed. "You were equipped with the most up-to-date weaponry, leading the world's largest, best-trained military force against a paltry excuse of a nation. I even paved the way for your success with the peace treaty I made with those gullible Jews. They had already disarmed—they were practically sitting ducks! How could you possibly have failed? And yet you bumbling fools managed to find a way."

Ivazov, red faced and seething, finally exploded. "Can't you see that the loss wasn't our fault? You know very well why we were defeated: we were hit with an earthquake that topped the Richter scale, and monstrous hailstones mixed with sulfurous fire. Our armies were decimated."

"So you say." Christopher's voice was cold as frost. "But it wasn't the fire or hail or earthquake that got you, was it? It was panic. Your troops lost their heads and started firing on anything that moved. And the only thing moving was their fellow soldiers, running for cover like terrified rabbits. You idiots annihilated your own armies."

"With all due respect, sir, you were not there. If you had been engulfed in choking, blinding smoke and dust, as our troops were, you would understand the confusion. They couldn't even see the sun. As if that weren't enough, a scourge of dysentery swept through, killing half of our men and immobilizing many who remained. Against human foes, we were invincible. But no army on earth has weapons against the disasters we faced."

"You may soon face even greater foes. I am ordering you and the other nations represented in this room to raise new armies. We will attack Israel again."

Silence blanketed the room. After a tense moment, the Russian representative realized that the time he'd feared had come. He must walk the plank. "Mr. President, you cannot do this to us. Do you realize how tenuous your hold on the world is? Your string of broken promises, ignored treaties, military conscription, and exorbitant taxes has angered many nations. Your tyranny is fostering poverty and disease around the world. And when incidents of rebellion are put down with brutal force, deep resentment festers like a boil."

"Mr. Ivazov." Christopher's voice was low. "If you don't stop your ranting this minute—"

"No! I will not stop! Someone in this room needs to tell you what you refuse to hear. If you demand another conscription after our recent losses, it will trigger massive revolt in the Russian coalition of states."

Christopher called for guards to enter the room. "Take this traitor out and shoot him!" He pointed straight at Ivazov. "And take his gutless minions with him," he added, gesturing at the representatives from China, Egypt, and Iran. "I will not tolerate this kind of insubordination."

The guards seized the four dissenters and escorted them out the door.

Meanwhile, Christopher continued speaking as if nothing out of the ordinary had occurred. "My dear council members, we will build a new coalition of armies and destroy Israel once and for all. This army will be invincible—larger than any military force ever assembled. Each of you will instruct your national leaders to do whatever it takes—force conscription, plunder your natural resources, nationalize your factories if you need to. Do you understand me?"

The removal of the four dissenters effectively stifled any debate. Yet the members of the council found themselves caught between two impossible options. If they presented Christopher's demands to their leaders at home, it would incite insurrection. Yet if they opposed the president, it would clearly mean death.

Archbishop Detherow read their thoughts and rose to address the group. "My esteemed council members, please allow me to apprise you of the reality of the situation. President Christopher has not made his decision in a vacuum. He and I both serve an immensely powerful master who stands invisibly above us all. He has single-handedly wrested this earth from God, and ever since the beginning, he has fought to solidify his rule over it. For the past two thousand years, his primary opposition has been Christians. Now that they have been virtually wiped off the planet, our dominance is almost complete. When we annihilate the Jews, the entire earth will belong to us."

Detherow paused and scanned the room. Every eye was on him. "Whether you know it or not, each of you also serves this master. The number you bear marks you as his. And because you serve him, you need not fear waging this war. We have powerful allies beyond anything you can imagine—an invisible army of his loyal angels. Even as we speak, they are orchestrating our moves and strategy. If we serve our master wholeheartedly, he will give us certain victory."

A tentative voice spoke from the back. "But he did not give us victory in our previous war."

"That's because we had division among us—those traitors who were just removed from our presence," Christopher said. "Their fate should remind you that there is a penalty for disloyalty."

"And that penalty can be even worse than what you just witnessed," Detherow added. "Our dark master always breaks the tools that fail him. And let me assure you, you do not want to be one of those failed tools."

\* \* \*

Judas Christopher immediately began to build his coalition army. In the months that followed, his military might grew as troops, arms, and munitions were brought in from countries around the world. However, Russia, China, and Egypt—along with some of their client states—refused to contribute troops or supplies.

When the president received the news about the dissenters, he was irate. "After we drown every Jew in the Mediterranean Sea, we will freeze every Russian in Siberia."

To make up for the absence of these forces, Christopher doubled the quota of troops and arms from the other nations. At first the overextended governments were slow to respond. But eventually they were won over through threats, intimidation, and stiff sanctions. Before the year came to a close, the president had amassed the largest army assembled in recorded history. His troops numbered in the millions, backed by a state-of-the-art arsenal and staggering fleets of armored vehicles, warplanes, and naval vessels.

The president, aware of the undercurrent of rebellion running through many nations, replaced three-quarters of the countries' native generals with leaders of his own choosing. Then he announced that he himself would be the supreme commander over the combined forces.

With the armies assembled, Christopher began to send troops and weaponry into Israel. Aircraft carriers were stationed offshore along Israel's Mediterranean coast. He landed his ground troops near the port cities of Haifa, Hadera, Netanya, Tel Aviv, and Ashdod and brought in troops, tanks, rocket launchers, and heavy artillery from the east.

Israeli troops met the invasions with little resistance. The beleaguered nation was vulnerable after the triple blows of ill-advised disarmament, the invasion by Russia and Egypt, and the cleanup efforts after the war and the simultaneous natural disasters. It had taken Israel seven months just to bury all the bodies.

Christopher quickly captured Herzliya, a coastal city just north of Tel Aviv, and set up his operational headquarters there. He was in the war room with his generals, orchestrating their march toward Jerusalem, when a loud knock rattled the door.

A marine colonel burst in. "Sir, pardon the interruption, but we just received an urgent intelligence report."

"Well, spit it out," Christopher demanded.

"Russia and Egypt have rebelled. They are—"

"That is old news, Colonel. You'd better have a better excuse than that for disrupting this meeting."

"Yes, Mr. President, there is more. Russia has been raising its own army—an enormous coalition amassed from former USSR client states. They are now marching against us from the north. Egypt and its allies have also raised coalition armies, and they are coming at us from the south."

"Where are they now?"

"Our reports confirm that the Russian axis is crossing the Golan Heights and pushing southward. The Egyptian coalition is encamped on the Sinai Peninsula, and they are moving north at a rapid pace."

Judas Christopher slammed his fist onto the table, rattling coffee cups and water glasses. "Our attack on Jerusalem will have to wait," he growled. "Cancel the air raid immediately. We need to squash these insurgents. We'll divide our armies—one to meet the Russian allies, and one to meet the Egyptian coalition. But I swear by the fires of hell, we will return to Jerusalem."

The generals and their staffs worked through the night, revising battle plans and communicating new orders to their field officers. The president paced around the room, fuming, barking orders, and countermanding his generals' tactics while cursing them for their incompetence.

The next morning, Christopher's northern armies met the Russian allies at Tel Megiddo on the Plain of Esdraelon. His southern divisions met the Egyptian coalition at the city of Be'er Sheva at the edge of the Negev desert.

With their massive air power, ground forces, and artillery, the armies could not be contained within the two narrow fronts. Soon they were clashing in scores of theaters over the entire length and breadth of Israel, from the Golan Heights in the north to the Gaza Strip in the south.

As the battles raged, Christopher and his staff generals kept their eyes locked on a floor-to-ceiling monitor in the war room. A map of Israel filled the screen, displaying all the nation's cities and topographical features. Scores of bright disks the size of checkers dotted the map from top to bottom. Green dots signified Christopher's troops; yellow dots marked the Russians; and blue dots stood for Egypt and its allies. As intelligence reports came in, the dots moved electronically from one area to another.

"Mr. President!" The colonel burst into the room again. His face was ashen and his voice urgent. "I have terrible news, sir."

"What is it?"

"We've just learned that China has also raised an army, and it's twice the size of the combined armies we're now battling."

"How many troops are there?"

"Estimates are in the millions. But that's not the worst of it." The colonel paused.

"Well, don't just stand there. Let's hear it."

"They're coming at us from the northeast. They just crossed the dry bed of the Euphrates at Ar-Raqqa. Their planes and rockets are already bombarding the Golan Heights, and their ground troops will reach the border by morning."

The veins in Christopher's neck pulsed. "Why am I just now hearing this? A force that size can hardly be hidden. You should have known about this army the moment it left China."

"But, sir, you instructed us to focus all our attention on military movements in Israel. You can hardly expect us to—"

"Enough!" Christopher bellowed. He turned to his aide. "Take this man out and have him shot. I will not tolerate this kind of incompetence in my army."

Turning his attention back to the map, Christopher saw a cluster of orange dots added to the map that pinpointed the location of the Chinese armies.

\* \* \*

For the next several months, the president and his military officials watched the colored dots cluster, disperse, and reassemble in a kaleidoscope of patterns as the four coalitions maneuvered in battle. Cities were lost and taken. Ground troops met head-on in deserts, woods, plains, and mountains across the entire country.

As the battles raged, there wasn't a single square foot in the entire nation where the sounds of war could not be heard. The atmosphere was polluted by the roar of fighter planes, the explosions of bombs and rockets, the booms of heavy artillery, and the staccato bursts of handheld weapons. The worst sounds of all were the agonized screams of the dying and wounded, both military and civilian.

The mood in Christopher's war room oscillated between euphoria and despair as Christopher and his staff watched their armies advance and retreat again and again. But slowly the advances began to outnumber the retreats, and the green dots began to dominate central Israel. The yellow, blue, and orange dots were soon relegated to the far reaches of the country.

Feeling assured of victory, Christopher called a meeting of his generals at the conference table in front of the electronic screen. "Gentlemen, look at that map. My forces now have the upper hand throughout central Israel. We have pushed the northern rebels back almost to Lake Tiberias, and the southern rebels have been forced to northern Sinai." He turned to look at the archbishop. "You know what this means, don't you, Detherow?"

"Of course. It means you can now redeploy enough troops to accomplish your original goal—the final destruction of Jerusalem."

"Precisely. Generals, listen to me. Take half the troops stationed between Netanya in the north and Hebron in the south and march them toward Jerusalem. Before they arrive, my air force and navy planes will weaken the city with bombs. When they're done, the invasion itself will be little more than a casual stroll through the city's streets."

"How do you want your forces deployed, sir?" The generals had long since learned not to devise their own strategies.

"I want half of them to take Jerusalem from the north, and half from the south. We will set up our field headquarters in Bethlehem, five miles south of the city, and launch the attack from Mount Olivet. I will direct the southern invasion myself. Once we have moved into the city, the northern forces will close in and cut off all escape routes."

On reaching Bethlehem, Christopher and his generals met in an old warehouse. They could hear continual bursts of bombshells coming from the direction of Jerusalem.

"Gentlemen," the president began, his eyes flashing with glee, "tomorrow we will launch our final campaign against Jerusalem from the very town that was once revered by Christians as the birthplace of our archenemy. Do you see the irony of it? We are about to accomplish what the ancient King Herod could not. He tried to destroy the Messiah by slaughtering all the baby boys of this city. And here we are, poised to undo everything that surviving Child did by destroying the very nation He came to save."

Damon Detherow laughed, baring his teeth in a grotesque grin.

"It will be the end of this enemy nation that our master has tried to annihilate for centuries," gloated Christopher. "After tonight's air blitz, our ground troops will march in and plunder the city the way a child gathers Easter eggs."

\* \* \*

The next morning President Christopher personally led his troops toward the undefended Jerusalem. Detherow usually stayed behind within the protected field camps, but on this day Christopher insisted that the archbishop accompany him. "I want you to witness firsthand this pivotal moment in history," he said.

The nighttime blitz had accomplished its purpose. Oily black smoke billowed in columns throughout the city. Christopher reached Mount Olivet and positioned his troops for the invasion. He stood on top of the mountain, savoring the moment, before giving the signal to attack. In seconds, he would have the satisfaction of watching the city suffer its final blow.

Suddenly a resounding trumpet blast shattered the air. Startled, Christopher looked around for its source. When he saw his troops gaping upward in terror, he followed their gaze. The sight struck him speechless. The morning sky had pulled away like drawn curtains, revealing a mighty Warrior astride a magnificent white horse. He wore a robe dipped in blood, and on His head was a crown glittering with gold and gems. He held a sword in His mouth that flashed brightly in the sun.

When Christopher managed to peel his eyes away from the Man, he saw an enormous army of men and women in the clouds behind Him. They were robed in white, and they, too, were mounted on white horses. The entire sky from east to west was filled with masses of magnificent beings—humanlike but with faces as brilliant as lightning. The entire throng hovered expectantly, as if ready to descend.

It never occurred to Christopher that his state-of-the-art armies should easily defeat the antiquated army above him. The heavenly force was mounted on horses, which ought to have been useless against his modern weaponry. Except for the sword—an utterly outdated weapon—in the mouth of their Leader, the host above was neither armed nor dressed for battle. But in that moment, Christopher could not think; he could only feel. And what he felt was abject, immobilizing fear.

All at once, an angel with all the brightness of the rising sun stepped forward. In a voice that rang through the heavens, he summoned the great birds of the earth to Israel, inviting them to a bountiful feast consisting of the flesh of the fallen enemies of God.

Vultures began to flock in such multitudes that they darkened the sky. They covered the entire land, alighting anywhere they could—fences, rooftops, trees, walls, communication towers, and billboards. From their perches, they hungrily scanned the armies occupying Israel, awaiting the coming slaughter.

With a loud shout, the magnificent Warrior and His hosts descended. Archbishop Detherow, standing beside Christopher, was the first to realize who the descending Warrior was. Unable to stand, the archbishop fell on his face, wailing in terror and covering his head with his hands.

Judas Christopher, now trembling violently, proceeded toward Jerusalem, urged onward by his hatred for the Jews and his fear of his master. None of his troops followed, though Detherow, crying and mumbling hysterically, half crawled, half slithered along behind him.

Suddenly Christopher stopped short and collapsed to his knees. Directly in his path stood the towering figure of the mighty heavenly Warrior mounted on His white steed. His eyes burned into Christopher's soul like a white-hot laser.

Christ dismounted, took the sword formed from the words of His mouth, and gazed down at Christopher. The Antichrist crumpled to the ground beside the quaking Detherow. Then the ground began to roll with a sickening movement, like that of a storm-tossed ship.

A rumble came from somewhere deep in the earth. It grew in force until Christopher, feeling as if his head would split, clapped his hands over his ears. Just when the noise became unbearable, Mount Olivet cracked apart at its peak. Then the gap opened into a crumbling chasm all the way from Jerusalem to Jericho.

In the next moment, white-clad beings seized Christopher and Detherow and hurled them, screaming, into the chasm. Their shrieks ceased abruptly when a thunderous belch issued from the pit, followed by billows of black, rancid smoke.

Christ, with sword still in hand, remounted His steed and forged into the thick of Christopher's troops, swinging His deadly weapon in sweeping arcs. As the armies fell before Him, He rode on, slashing tanks, transport vehicles, artillery, and entire military installations. In His wake, He left heaps of twisted steel, crumbled bricks, and splintered planks. He swept the sword upward, and warplanes burst into flame before crashing to the earth.

Once Christopher's armies were decimated, Christ galloped toward the other battlefronts. Before the sun set, the combatants on all the battlefields of Israel lay dead, strewn across the landscape in mammoth heaps. Blood flowed like rivers through dry gullies and formed crimson pools in low-lying fields. The horde of ravenous birds had already begun their grisly feast.

The throngs of angels ascended back into the heavens as Christ returned victorious to Mount Olivet. The joyous white-robed saints gathered around Him and lined the road before Him, paving the way from the mountain to Jerusalem's Zion Gate with a thick carpet of palm fronds. The air rang with joyful shouts as Christ made His second Triumphal Entry into His Holy City—this time mounted not on a humble donkey colt but on a great white horse. And this time, He was there not to suffer but to rule.

\* \* \*

# THE SCRIPTURE BEHIND THE STORY

In Revelation 19 we reach the moment we've been waiting for—the turning point of the entire story. Throughout the book we've seen evil run rampant, inflicting unprecedented suffering and persecution on the faithful. But at last comes the moment God's people have been waiting for since Christ ascended into heaven before His awestruck disciples: He returns!

And what a return it is. No longer can misguided people caricature Him as meek and mild and infinitely tolerant. He now comes in unrelenting power and annihilates the enemies of God in the bloodiest battle the world will ever know. It is the climax of God's judgment upon this wicked world. John introduces Christ the victor with this description: "In righteousness He judges and makes war" (Revelation 19:11).

Because of the abundant grace we experience every moment of our lives, we often forget about God's justice. Or worse, we try to turn the tables and judge God for His justice, accusing Him of being overly harsh and unloving.

This parable illustrates God's long-suffering mercy and eventual judgment, demonstrating the outrageousness of our accusation:

On the first day of class a teacher carefully explained to the one hundred college freshmen in his classroom that they would be responsible for completing three term papers within the semester. The papers would be due on the last day of September, October, and November, and there would be no extensions.

At the end of September, ninety students dutifully turned in their papers, while ten remorseful students quaked in fear. "We're so sorry," they said. "We didn't make the proper adjustments from high school to college, but we promise to do better next time." The teacher bowed to their pleas for mercy and gave them an extension but warned them not to be late next month.

The end of October rolled around, and about eighty students turned in their papers, while twenty of them showed up empty handed. "Oh, please," they begged, "it was homecoming weekend, and we ran out of time." The teacher relented once more but warned, "This is it. No excuses next time. You will get an F."

The end of November came, and only fifty students turned in their papers. The rest told the teacher, "We'll get it in soon."

"Sorry," he replied. "It's too late. You get an F."

The students howled in protest, "That's not fair!"

"Okay," the teacher replied, "you want justice, do you? Here's what's just: you'll get an F for all three papers that were late. That was the rule, right?"[1]

This is the way it will be when Christ returns to judge the world. For more than two thousand years He has mercifully waited to execute His justice. As the time draws near, Christ will pull out all the stops to help us turn to Him before Judgment Day. He will dispatch two miracle-working witnesses to warn of His coming wrath, and then He'll send an additional 144,000 witnesses to take the gospel to the whole world once more. But on that day when He leaves heaven with His saints and angels, the era of His grace will end, and the hour of His wrath will come.

For many people, the idea of a judging God is a deal breaker—an excuse to reject Christianity. N. T. Wright sums up such an attitude this way:

The word *judgment* carries negative overtones for a good many people in our liberal and post-liberal world. We need to remind ourselves that throughout the Bible . . . God's coming judgment is a good thing, something to be celebrated, longed for, yearned over. . . . In a world of systematic injustice, bullying, violence, arrogance, and oppression, the thought that there might come a day when

the wicked are firmly put in their place and the poor and
weak are given their due is the best news there can be. Faced
with a world in rebellion, a world full of exploitation and
wickedness, a good God *must* be a God of judgment.[2]

How could we call God "good" if He allowed evil to forever corrupt the world He created and pronounced to be good?

The Bible gives us some key details about the way Christ will
return to earth in judgment and justice.

### The Priority of His Return

Then will appear the sign of the Son of Man in heaven. And
then all the peoples of the earth will mourn when they see
the Son of Man coming on the clouds of heaven, with power
and great glory.

MATTHEW 24:30, NIV

Christians are familiar with the first coming of our Lord to
Bethlehem, as recorded in the Gospels. But people are often surprised to learn that references to the Second Coming outnumber
references to the first by a factor of eight to one. Scholars have
identified 1,845 biblical references to the Second Coming. In the
Old Testament, Christ's return is emphasized in no less than seven-
teen books, and New Testament authors speak of it in twenty-three
of the twenty-seven books. Seven out of every ten chapters in the
New Testament mention His return. In other words, one out of
every thirty verses in the New Testament teach us about the return
of Christ to this earth.

In 1 and 2 Thessalonians, the first two books written for the
early church, the return of Christ is taught in every single chapter.
The Lord Himself referred to His return twenty-one times. The
Second Coming is second only to salvation as the most dominant

subject in the New Testament. The fact that Christ's second coming features so prominently in Scripture is an indication that this event is important to God—and as a result, it should also be important to us.

### The Prediction of His Return

> As it is appointed for men to die once, but after this the judgment, so Christ was offered once to bear the sins of many. To those who eagerly wait for Him He will appear a second time, apart from sin, for salvation.
>
> HEBREWS 9:27-28

Though the exact expression "the second coming of Christ" is not found in the Bible, the concept is foretold in a number of places. There are seven key passages in particular, spanning from Enoch in the book of Genesis to John in the book of Revelation, that give us a preview of how this event will occur.

| The First and Second Comings of Christ | |
|---|---|
| **His First Coming** | **His Second Coming** |
| Born in obscurity (Philippians 2:5-7) | Seen by every eye (Revelation 1:7) |
| Wrapped in swaddling clothes (Luke 2:7) | Clothed in a royal robe dipped in blood (Revelation 19:13) |
| Surrounded by cattle (Luke 2:16) | Accompanied by the armies of heaven (Revelation 19:14) |
| The doors of the inn were closed (Luke 2:7) | The doors of heaven will be opened (Revelation 4:1) |
| Had the voice of a newborn baby (Luke 2:12) | Will have a voice with the sound of many waters (Revelation 1:15) |
| The Lamb bringing salvation (John 1:29) | The Lion bringing judgment (Revelation 5:5) |

### ENOCH

According to Jude, Enoch was the first to predict the second coming of Christ: "Enoch, the seventh from Adam, prophesied about these men also, saying, 'Behold, the Lord comes with ten thousands of His saints, to execute judgment on all, to convict all who are ungodly among them of all their ungodly deeds which they have committed in an ungodly way, and of all the harsh things which ungodly sinners have spoken against Him'" (Jude 14-15).

### DANIEL

Daniel was known for his prophetic dreams, both about events in his lifetime and about things that would occur in the end times. Here he describes the return of the Son of Man (Christ):

> I was watching in the night visions,
> And behold, One like the Son of Man,
> Coming with the clouds of heaven!
> He came to the Ancient of Days,
> And they brought Him near before Him.
> Then to Him was given dominion and glory and a kingdom,
> That all peoples, nations, and languages should serve Him.
> His dominion is an everlasting dominion,
> Which shall not pass away,
> And His Kingdom the one
> Which shall not be destroyed.
>
> DANIEL 7:13-14

### ZECHARIAH

The prophet Zechariah predicted the final epic battle between Christ and the Antichrist at the end of the Tribulation:

> The LORD will go forth
> And fight against those nations,

As He fights in the day of battle.
And in that day His feet will stand on the Mount of Olives,
Which faces Jerusalem on the east.
And the Mount of Olives shall be split in two,
From east to west,
Making a very large valley;
Half of the mountain shall move toward the north
And half of it toward the south.

ZECHARIAH 14:3-4

**JESUS**

In His Olivet discourse, Jesus describes the signs that will foreshadow
His second coming:

As the lightning comes from the east and flashes to the
west, so also will the coming of the Son of Man be. . . .
Immediately after the tribulation of those days the sun will
be darkened, and the moon will not give its light; the stars
will fall from heaven, and the powers of the heavens will
be shaken. Then the sign of the Son of Man will appear
in heaven, and then all the tribes of the earth will mourn,
and they will see the Son of Man coming on the clouds of
heaven with power and great glory. And He will send His
angels with a great sound of a trumpet, and they will gather
together His elect from the four winds, from one end of
heaven to the other.

MATTHEW 24:27, 29-31

**THE ANGELS**

After Jesus ascended into heaven, the angels, speaking to the disciples,
offered this promise about Jesus' return: "Men of Galilee, why do you
stand gazing up into heaven? This same Jesus, who was taken from

you into heaven, will so come in like manner as you saw Him go into heaven" (Acts 1:11).

### PAUL

In his second letter to the Thessalonians, Paul describes what the Day of Judgment will be like: "The Lord Jesus is revealed from heaven with His mighty angels, in flaming fire taking vengeance on those who do not know God, and on those who do not obey the gospel of our Lord Jesus Christ. These shall be punished with everlasting destruction from the presence of the Lord and from the glory of His power, when He comes, in that Day, to be glorified in His saints and to be admired among all those who believe" (2 Thessalonians 1:7-10).

### JOHN

In the book of Revelation, John describes his vision of Christ's return: "Behold, He is coming with clouds, and every eye will see Him, even they who pierced Him. And all the tribes of the earth will mourn because of Him" (Revelation 1:7).

### *The Place of His Return*

> In that day His feet will stand on the Mount of Olives,
> which faces Jerusalem on the east. And the Mount of Olives
> shall be split in two, from east to west, making a very large
> valley; half of the mountain shall move toward the north and
> half of it toward the south.
>
> ZECHARIAH 14:4

While we cannot know exactly when our Lord's second coming will occur, we can know, without doubt, *where* it will occur. The passage from Acts 1 leaves no room for discussion. We also have the testimony of the angels as Jesus was ascending into heaven: "'This same Jesus, who was taken up from you into heaven, will so come in like manner as you saw Him go into heaven.' Then they returned to Jerusalem from the mount called Olivet" (Acts 1:11-12).

In spite of all the evidence in the Bible that validates the return of Christ, the vast majority of people do not believe it will happen. Peter describes these people: "Scoffers will come in the last days, walking according to their own lusts, and saying, 'Where is the promise of His coming? For since the fathers fell asleep, all things continue as they were from the beginning of creation'" (2 Peter 3:3-4).

No matter what the popular majority says, Christ's coming is certain. The *time* of His coming is uncertain, known only to God the Father: "Of that day and hour no one knows, not even the angels of heaven, but My Father only" (Matthew 24:36). But when the day comes, we can be assured that all eyes will be fixed on the sky above the Mount of Olives.

### The Preparation for His Return

I saw the beast, the kings of the earth, and their armies,
gathered together to make war against Him who sat on the
horse and against His army.
REVELATION 19:19

In the final showdown, all the rebellion of the prior seven years will come to a head at the Battle of Armageddon. In this battle, the Antichrist, the kings of the earth, and the pitiful souls following them will gather together one last time to try to defeat Jesus Christ. Their army will be made up of the soldiers of the ten nations of the revived Roman Empire. The Beast (the Antichrist), with the false prophet at his side, will lead the massive army in defying Christ's authority and right to rule—the ultimate revolt against God. When Christ's return draws near, they will do everything they can to try to prepare for the battle of the ages.

## The Portrayal of His Return

> I saw heaven opened, and behold, a white horse. And
> He who sat on him was called Faithful and True, and in
> righteousness He judges and makes war.
> REVELATION 19:11

The first time He came to earth, Jesus appeared in obscurity. The second time, however, "every eye will see Him" (Revelation 1:7). The entire world will witness His return.

How is it possible that every eye will see Him? Since He is to descend in Israel, how will people in, say, Australia see Him? In this technological era, it isn't difficult to imagine that the second coming of Jesus Christ would be carried by every television network across the world and be shared on every social media outlet. Regardless of the role technology plays, God can bend light and curve space. It would be no challenge for Him to manipulate optics so the radiant glory of Jesus' return is visible over the entire planet.

Christ the victor looks like no other warrior in the history of the world. According to John, "His eyes were like a flame of fire, and on His head were many crowns. He had a name written that no one knew except Himself. He was clothed with a robe dipped in blood, and His name is called The Word of God" (Revelation 19:12-13).

Let's explore the meaning of these descriptors.

### HIS NAMES

In this passage, Christ is called "The Word of God." Here John employs a phrase he also used in the first sentence of his Gospel.

Just as words are tangible expressions of invisible thoughts, Jesus is a tangible expression of the invisible God, incarnated in human form. When Jesus descends to administer justice one day, we can be sure that this will be God's own justice.

Jesus is also called "Faithful and True" (Revelation 19:11) and "the Faithful and True Witness" (3:14; see also 1:5 and 3:7). It makes sense, then, that His sayings are "faithful and true" (22:6). These descriptions remind us that our Lord never fails. He promised that one day He would judge the earth for its wickedness, and His return demonstrates His faithfulness in fulfilling that promise.

As Christ leads His armies, John sees one more name written on His thigh: "KING OF KINGS AND LORD OF LORDS" (Revelation 19:16). Of all the kings on earth, Christ is the King. Of all earthly lords or rulers, He is the Lord. Every knee will bow before Him when He returns to earth (Isaiah 45:23; Romans 14:11; Philippians 2:10-11).

## HIS EYES

Christ's fiery eyes will burn up all that is false as He gazes upon people's hearts and minds. This description signifies the Lord's ability to see deep into hearts and deal with all injustice (Revelation 1:14; 2:18; 19:12). Just as fire blasts through ore to reveal whether there is pure metal inside, the eyes of Christ will do the same for people's hearts. He will pierce through the motives of nations and individuals and judge them for what they really are.

## HIS CROWNS

When Jesus came the first time, His enemies mocked Him by putting a crown of thorns on His head. When He comes again, His many crowns will point to the fact that no rule, might, or authority will be able to stand against Him. He will, in effect, wear the crown of every nation on earth.

## HIS ROBE

At first it may seem that the description of Christ's garment as being dipped in blood is antithetical to the majesty and glory of His appearance, but the opposite is true. It speaks of the very essence of His victory—the redemption Jesus secured for us on the cross as "the Lamb slain from the foundation of the world" (Revelation 13:8). For all eternity, God's people will celebrate the shed blood that redeemed them from the penalty of sin.

### The People with Him at His Return

> The armies in heaven, clothed in fine linen, white and clean, followed Him on white horses.
>
> REVELATION 19:14

When Christ returns, He will bring His armies with Him. Note that the word used in verse 14 is *armies* (plural); it isn't just one army of heaven. These armies are the believers from all ages—the Old Testament saints, the New Testament saints, and the Tribulation saints—along with the angels of God, standing shoulder to shoulder in one massive force.

Zechariah's prophecy says, "The LORD my God will come, and all the holy ones with him" (14:5, NIV). Jude echoes these words: "Behold, the Lord comes with ten thousands of His saints" (verse 14). Paul also speaks of those who will accompany the Lord when He returns. At the Second Coming, Jesus Christ will appear "with all His saints" (1 Thessalonians 3:13). And on Judgment Day, Christ will be "glorified in His saints" (2 Thessalonians 1:10).

Notice how these hosts will be dressed. The white linen, clean and fine, represents righteousness. Jesus will wear the bloodstained garment so that we might wear the white linen of His righteousness. "These legions are dressed not in military fatigues but in dazzling white. Yet they need not worry about their pristine uniforms getting soiled because their role is largely ceremonial and honorary; they will not fight. Jesus Himself will slay the rebels with the deadly sword darting out of His mouth."[3]

### The Purpose of His Return

In righteousness He judges and makes war.
REVELATION 19:11

This description in verse 11 gives the central purpose for Christ's return to the earth: to judge and make war. Verse 15 reveals some of the details of that war: "Out of His mouth goes a sharp sword, that with it He should strike the nations. And He Himself will rule them with a rod of iron. He Himself treads the winepress of the fierceness and wrath of Almighty God."

Jude describes the kind of world Christ will find when He returns to the earth: "Enoch, the seventh from Adam, prophesied about these men also, saying, 'Behold, the Lord comes with ten thousands of His saints, to execute judgment on all, to convict all who are ungodly among them of all their ungodly deeds which they have committed in an ungodly way, and of all the harsh things which ungodly sinners have spoken against Him'" (verses 14-15). In one short verse, the word *ungodly* is used four times. This repetition is not accidental. This passage emphasizes that when Christ returns, His long-suffering patience will have run its course. He will impose judgment on those who have defied Him, and with the sharp sword of His mouth, He will smite the ungodly from all nations.

This particular sword does not represent the Word of God, as does the one in Ephesians 6:17. Rather, a sword is used symbolically to refer to a sharp instrument of war with which Christ will bring down opposing nations and establish His absolute rule.

## The Punishment at His Return

> I saw an angel standing in the sun; and he cried with a
> loud voice, saying to all the birds that fly in the midst of
> heaven, "Come and gather together for the supper of the
> great God, that you may eat the flesh of kings, the flesh of
> captains, the flesh of mighty men, the flesh of horses and
> of those who sit on them, and the flesh of all people, free
> and slave, both small and great." . . . And all the birds were
> filled with their flesh.
>
> REVELATION 19:17-18, 21

The punishment of the wicked at this moment will be so horrific,
and death so extensive, that an angel from heaven will summon the
birds of the sky to gather for a grisly feast of human flesh.

The word used for "birds" here is *orneois*, which is literally
translated "vulture." All the vultures of heaven—not God's heaven,
but what Jews called the first heaven, or the atmosphere—will be
invited to feast on the carcasses of those who fall before the sword
of the Lord. Notice that those who fall in battle will be the "mighty
men" of earth—the captains and kings—as well as "free and slave,
both small and great" (Revelation 19:18). Death is the great leveler.
It recognizes no rank, treating all equally.

## The Penalty at His Return

> The beast was captured, and with him the false prophet. . . .
> These two were cast alive into the lake of fire burning with
> brimstone. And the rest were killed with the sword which
> proceeded from the mouth of Him who sat on the horse.
>
> REVELATION 19:20-21

When John uses the word *captured*, he chooses an interesting term. In the original Greek, it means "to grab or snatch." When the time comes—when the cup of iniquity has been filled—the Lord will snatch up the Beast and the false prophet from the earth, and these two evil creatures will have the unwanted honor of going to hell before Satan. Satan will not join them in hell until the end of the Millennium, one thousand years later. "The devil, who deceived them, was cast into the lake of fire and brimstone where the beast and the false prophet are. And they will be tormented day and night forever and ever" (Revelation 20:10).

The "rest [who] were killed with the sword," as Revelation 19:21 describes them, will be the other enemies of God who perished in the war. They will include all who wore the number of the Beast. Like their masters, they also will be cast "into the everlasting fire prepared for the devil and his angels" (Matthew 25:41).

In June of 1944, the people of France had suffered for four years under the tyranny of Adolf Hitler. His armies had invaded France in 1940 as part of his unholy ambition to turn all of Europe into a Nazi superstate. But then, on June 6, 1944, General Eisenhower commanded Allied troops to cross the channel from England and invade the fortified beaches of Normandy to liberate the French nation from oppression.

Editor James M. Kushiner describes what happened on that fateful day, now known as D-day:

> Before dawn, then throughout the rest of the day, sea,
> land, and air were rent by flashes, thunder, flying metal,
> parachutes, while fresh wounds in the earth and men
> erupted in sand and soil, blood and guts. Beaches turned
> red. Trees exploded, cattle perished, men breathed their last.
>   D-Day was just the first day. The battle for Normandy
> raged on well into August, and Paris was liberated

August 25, 1944. The scarring of Normandy and the shedding of blood was the result of many men and their designs—either for conquest and occupation or for liberation.[4]

In many ways, what happened on D-day offers a scaled-down preview of the world's final battle. Like World War II France, we suffer under the heel of a brutal tyrant who illegitimately occupies our world, imposing death, destruction, and misery. Like the oppressed citizens of France in the 1940s, we, too, cry out for liberation from a cruel oppressor.

But as we are assured in Revelation 19, liberation will come. We have a Supreme Commander who has never lost a battle, and He is simply waiting for the strategic moment when He will descend and crush forever the forces that have invaded His world. And because He is the "Faithful and True," we can rest assured that He will not fail. Victory over our archenemy is absolutely certain. "We await the final trumpet, the last command, when . . . every knee shall bow and every tongue confess: Greater love hath no Man than this Jesus, the Lion of Judah, who has conquered."[5]

*chapter nine*

# THE KING

IT WAS NEAR SUNSET, and Eva McLennon stood ankle deep in a river while bathing her two-year-old daughter. The water, lead gray and covered with scum, reeked with decay. She hated to dip little Sophie into it, but she had no better alternative. The river was in its death throes, as were all the rivers that hadn't dried up during the past seven years.

The river was fifty yards from the wooded camp where she and her husband, Ryan, and a dozen others were hiding. She never imagined when she was growing up that she'd be a fugitive from the law one day. She and the rest of the people at the camp were Christians, converted by a zealous Messianic Jew after the sudden disappearance of Christians all over the world. Since that time, the president of the European Union, Judas Christopher, had amassed enough power to annex the United States and the rest of the civilized world as part of his growing empire. His edicts had grown increasingly repressive against religious minorities.

Eva well remembered the day the decree had gone into effect requiring all citizens to carry a government-issued number that would allow them to exchange goods, land, food, and services. But there was a condition attached: everyone who received the number had to swear to worship no god but Judas Christopher.

Many members in Eva's house church had consented to the order. But for Eva and Ryan, yielding was unthinkable. They knew from reports coming out of other cities that if they did not accept the number, they would forfeit all their property and be barred from selling and buying. If they refused to worship Judas Christopher, they would be herded like cattle into boxcars and shipped off to some undisclosed location, where their fate would be sealed.

Ryan, Eva, and about forty other Christians had stuffed all the food and necessities they could fit into their vehicles and drove to a remote mountain, where they pushed their cars into a lake. Then they hiked deep into the woods and set up camp. They survived by foraging for roots, nuts, fruit, and berries and by hunting small game with bows and arrows.

Life was a continual struggle for survival. The forest, like the rest of the planet, was reeling from the catastrophic disasters that had ravaged the earth—volcanic eruptions, earthquakes, fires, and diseases. Pollution had contaminated the water and the air, and the sun burned as red as an infected sore against the smoggy sky. Though the fugitives boiled their water to purify it, they had already lost several members to sickness. Eva couldn't remember the last time it had rained.

President Christopher had made clear his intent to cleanse the earth of all Jews and Christians. The group always had to be on the lookout, and they'd been forced to relocate twice when troops had come too close to their camp.

On Sundays, the little company always gathered for worship. One Sunday, troops searching the forest had heard them singing and conducted a raid. Half the group managed to escape on foot, but the rest were captured. The survivors moved deeper into the woods, not daring to return for their tents and supplies.

\* \* \*

Eva gazed at little Sophie splashing happily in the putrid water. She wondered whether her daughter had any future at all. How much longer could they survive?

She lifted the child from the water and began to dry her with her skirt. Suddenly, terrified screams erupted from the camp. Eva scooped her daughter into her arms, clapped her hand over the toddler's mouth, and crouched behind a hedge of briars. She heard a scuffle, followed by the unmistakable crack of a rifle.

When the clamor ceased, a gravelly voice bellowed, "March, you rebels! That way."

The woods grew silent. Eva trembled violently but remained hidden. Just before dark, she crept back to the campsite and found it empty.

"Where Da Da?" Sophie asked.

Eva tried to respond, but no words would come out. She knew Ryan wasn't coming back.

She considered staying at the campsite and using its supplies, but the glow of distant flashlights made her change her mind. She frantically bagged the little food that remained and grabbed a gallon of boiled water. Then she fled into the woods.

Eva wandered through the forest carrying Sophie for most of a week. Every time the child asked for Da Da, hot tears welled up in Eva's eyes. She knew they would never see Ryan again. Had it not been for Sophie, she would have dropped to the earth and smothered her grief under the blanket of death.

But she plodded on. During the day she found shade to protect them from the fevered sun, and in the evenings she searched for berries and nuts. The water began to run low. She lost all sense of direction and had no idea whether she was moving toward danger or away from it. Every night she heard wolves howling in the distance. She shuddered at their unearthly wails and hugged little Sophie closer.

A few days after the raid, the moment Eva had been dreading finally arrived: their water ran out. Without a way to start a fire, she couldn't purify the sludgy water from the dead streams. Exhausted, hungry, and thirsty—like Hagar of Scripture—Eva placed her child in the shade of a bush, dropped down beside her, and wept.

"My poor little darling, you never had a chance at life. I'm so sorry. But soon we shall both see the face of God."

The heat closed in, and Eva's eyelids grew heavy. The last thing she heard before sleep overtook her was the eerie sound of the wolves in the distance.

When she awakened, the entire atmosphere had changed. A cool breeze caressed her skin. A cloud covered the sun—not the usual ashy haze from an erupting volcano or an incinerated city, but a deliciously fresh-looking rain cloud. The boom of distant thunder rolled across the heavens. The brilliance of the sun behind the cloud created an effect that looked almost like a warrior riding his horse down from the heavens.

Moments later it began to rain. Glorious rain! Eva exulted in its freshness on her parched skin. She opened the jug and let it fill with water. She and Sophie drank deeply. The wine of Cana could not have tasted better.

As the rain continued, Eva took Sophie in her arms, dancing in the downpour the way she'd seen Gene Kelly do in one of his classic movies.

Before nightfall she found a cave and made a bed of leaves for her and Sophie. Again she heard the eerie wail of wolves. *They sound so much closer now,* she thought as she drifted off to sleep.

Eva slept soundly through the night until Sophie's laugh awakened her. She struggled to open her eyes as sunlight streamed through the mouth of the cave.

"Doggie," she heard Sophie say.

Eva rolled over to join her daughter's little game. Suddenly her eyes widened in horror. Sophie was toddling toward a huge gray wolf that stood just six feet away. Several other wolves lay about the cave.

"Doggie," the child repeated.

"No, Sophie!" Eva screamed. "Come back!" She threw herself toward her daughter, determined to die with her. But to her shock, the wolf began wagging its tail. It lowered its head and came closer, licking Sophie's face as she giggled with delight.

"I must be dreaming," Eva muttered.

But it wasn't a dream. She picked up her child, and the other wolves gathered around her, wagging their tails and gazing at her expectantly. With a tentative hand, she reached down and stroked the head of the nearest animal. Its happy tail shifted into high gear, and other wolves pressed toward her, jostling for equal treatment.

Astounded, Eva stepped through the pack to leave the cave and find food. Several wolves followed her. She found a pecan tree and stuffed her pockets full of nuts, surprised that the birds nearby didn't scatter as she walked among them. A squirrel scampered down a tree as she approached. On impulse, she held out a pecan to it. The creature boldly took it from her hand. *Something really odd is going on here*, she thought.

Still carrying Sophie, Eva reached a clearing filled with deer grazing. She expected the animals to bolt for the woods, but they merely looked up briefly and continued their foraging as she and two of the wolves passed through.

"Sophie," she said to her daughter, "this is utterly surreal."

The sky was now as clear and as blue as a sapphire—the bluest Eva had seen it for almost seven years. She breathed deeply, the air cool and fresh, as she imagined it would have been in Eden. She spent the day finding food, and when evening approached, it rained again.

She and Sophie returned to the cave, and the wolves followed. The creatures plopped down at their feet and promptly went to sleep.

Somewhere in the corner of her mind, Eva remembered that the prophet Isaiah spoke of a time when animals and humans would no longer fear each other. She couldn't quite explain it, but she decided to accept the animals into their temporary home.

*   *   *

The next evening, Eva put Sophie down for the night when out of the darkness came the sound she'd been dreading: human voices. Peeking her head out of the cave, she blanched in terror. Bright beams of flashlights sliced through the night, and there was no doubt they were moving directly toward the cave.

In a panic, Eva grabbed Sophie and fled. In her haste, she tripped and fell into a bush. Sophie, unhurt but scared, began to cry.

"This way!" a male voice shouted from behind them.

Eva clapped her hand over the child's mouth and ran until she reached a ravine. She half jumped, half slid down the muddy slope to the bottom, where they crouched and waited. The flashlights passed by, not more than four feet overhead. A moment later Sophie squirmed free, and a small cry escaped her lips. Eva silenced her, but it was too late. The flashlights turned back and aimed their blinding beams into her face. She was cornered.

"Do what you will with me," she pleaded, "but please don't hurt my baby."

"Why would I hurt my own daughter?" a familiar voice replied.

Eva clambered out of the ravine and flung herself into her husband's arms. "I thought you were dead!" she sobbed as she covered his face with tears and kisses.

"Far from it," he replied. "Now that I've found you, I've never felt better. We've been searching for more than a week."

Ryan took Sophie from his wife and pressed the little girl to his chest, kissing the top of her head. "I'm so glad we found you, princess. I was afraid I'd never see you or your mother again."

Ryan's fellow searchers led the reunited family back through the woods to their car. Ryan said to the driver, "Eva and Sophie are starving. Let's stop at the nearest restaurant before we drive to the city."

"Ryan, what are you thinking? We can't go into the city," Eva protested. "Our photos are plastered on wanted posters everywhere. And with no authorized number, we can't buy food."

"Just relax and trust me." A smile spread across Ryan's face.

At the restaurant, Eva gorged herself, and Ryan fed Sophie as he told his story. "Our captors locked us in holding cells to wait for the next death train. But on the day it was supposed to arrive, news came that the armies of Judas Christopher and his allies had been annihilated in battle, and Christopher did not survive. His worldwide governmental system unraveled, and not knowing what else to do, his troops released their prisoners. We began searching for you and Sophie immediately."

"How could such a thing have happened?" Eva was stunned.

"Are you ready for this? Christopher's conqueror was none other than Christ Himself. He has come back! And it gets even better. He has resurrected all the martyrs from the Tribulation period, along with the Old Testament saints and those who were raptured. He has set up His throne in Jerusalem, and He is now the sole Ruler of the entire world."

Eva could hardly absorb such astounding news. "How is all this possible?"

"Christ has sent these resurrected men and women everywhere around the globe as His subregents, cabinet officers, governors, and mayors to rule the planet under His direction. They have already been set up in the national and state capitals all over the world."

"But how could all this have happened so quickly?"

"It seems that these resurrected humans are like the resurrected Christ of the Gospels," Ryan said. "They can travel instantly to any place on earth. We're told that they were all selected for their tasks based on their pre-resurrection lives. It's the parable of the talents unfolding before our eyes."

"So what will we do? How will we live?"

"Christ will assign a certain task to us. He has chosen redeemed men and women to serve in every capacity you can imagine—school administrators and teachers, building contractors, carpenters, engineers, heavy-equipment operators, long-haul truckers, artists, musicians, computer programmers—you name it."

Eva smiled, still trying to take it all in.

"Christ intends to rebuild everything that has been destroyed over the past seven years," Ryan continued. "He has organized the project with proven experts to assure that it will be done with highest quality and efficiency."

As Eva assimilated the news, Ryan asked how she and Sophie had survived in the forest. She related the hardships they'd experienced and how she'd been on the edge of despair until the rains came and the wild animals turned harmless.

"The same change has come over all the people of the earth," Ryan said.

"I don't understand. How could the entire world change so suddenly?"

"Well, from what I've gathered, Christ didn't just destroy Christopher and his demonic forces; He also chained Satan deep in a bottomless pit. It was Satan's influence that threw nature off kilter and infected animals with fear. His influence, along with that of his demons, also provoked and multiplied people's sins. With Satan and his hordes thrown overboard, the world can now steer a straight course."

As they drove toward the city, Ryan turned to look at his wife. "I hope you won't be too shocked when you meet resurrected people you knew before they died."

"Why would I be?"

"Just wait—you'll see."

Eva snuggled against her husband and dozed as Sophie slept soundly in her arms. Hours later, the car stopped in front of a small but neat frame house.

"This is ours for now," Ryan said. "An emergency committee has been working to find housing for all fugitive Christians. Another committee has rounded up clothing, bedding, and furniture for us."

* * *

Finally allowing herself to relax, Eva slept throughout the day and the following night. After breakfast the next morning, the doorbell rang.

"Good morning, Eva." A young woman was standing on the doorstep. "I'm Kathryn. I've volunteered to take you grocery shopping today."

Eva stared at the woman. She was the most flawlessly beautiful human Eva had ever seen, both in face and form. What surprised her nearly as much, however, was that in spite of the woman's physical perfection, Eva already felt comfortable with her. *Why does Kathryn look so familiar?* she wondered.

"Ryan," she called into the house. "Would you mind looking after Sophie? I'm going shopping with—"

"Oh, don't bother your husband," Kathryn interrupted. "Let's take your daughter along. I insist. I love little girls."

As Eva was lifting the child to put her into the baby seat of the shopping cart, Kathryn reached out her arms. "Let me carry her. It's been awhile since I've held a baby."

Throughout the trip Kathryn was helpful, friendly, kind—and amazingly good with Sophie. Eva couldn't shake the feeling that she should know this woman. That feeling intensified as she listened to her chatter and play with the child. She used expressions and vocal inflections that Eva was sure she recognized.

"Kathryn," she finally said, "I've felt all morning that I know you somehow. Have we met before?"

"We certainly have." Kathryn's silver laughter brightened the air. "I'm your mother."

"My mother?" Eva tried to register this new shock. "But my parents were martyred three years ago, when my mom was forty-four. You can't be a day over twenty. And while my mother was very beautiful, you make Miss Universe look like a troll."

"Yes, but I've been resurrected! I am perfect now—exactly as God meant me to be before human genetics were corrupted in the Fall."

Eva shook her head. "It's going to be strange having parents who look younger than I do. Why didn't you tell me right off who you are?"

"Well . . ." Kathryn smiled. "I guess I just wanted to see how long it would take you to figure it out."

Eva soon learned to identify the resurrected people. Not only were they young, beautiful, and perfectly healthy, they were also exceptionally intelligent and perceptive. They never made wrong decisions, they always treated others with respect, and they radiated a love that clearly flowed from Christ Himself.

As Ryan had told Eva, Christ's goal for the planet was restoration. The first task was to clean up the damage inflicted by the natural disasters, judgments, and wars of the Tribulation period. The mayor called on Ryan to head an excavation company assigned to clear away rubble in preparation for new construction. He found managing people much easier than it had been before the Millennium. His workers didn't complain, and they poured themselves wholeheartedly into their tasks.

The same attitude prevailed everywhere. People worked together to restore neighborhoods. They conducted house raisings, much like the Amish barn raisings of previous centuries. People now preferred the company of friends, family, and neighbors to television. Balls, square dances, community sings, and chats on front porches became common evening activities.

Natural disasters ceased altogether. Rain fell regularly over all the earth, and former deserts—even the Sahara—became arable. Crop failures were merely a distant memory. Hunger was now nonexistent, and tyranny and persecution no longer poisoned the earth. The influence of Christ the King was felt in every facet of life.

It didn't take long for a worldwide civilization to arise—one better than anything since Eden, yet not quite Eden. Though Satan had been banished, the unresurrected people of the earth still contended with their sinful nature. Infractions of the law still occurred. There were no courts, judges, or juries to try these cases, however. All offenders appeared before Christ Himself, who acted not only as King but also as Judge. His judgments were final, and since His justice was perfect, there was no need for plea bargaining and no point in appealing.

After Eva and Ryan raised ten children to maturity, they were delighted to discover that Eva was pregnant again. She stood before a bathroom mirror assessing herself. She was now over fifty, yet she had the looks and health of a woman in her twenties. Citizens of the Millennium aged slowly, and those who had been resurrected didn't age at all. *At this rate, she thought, I could live to be well over eight hundred.*

That evening Eva asked her father, "Won't it be hard on you and Mom to see me sink slowly into old age while you remain forever at the pinnacle of human perfection?"

"You don't need to worry about that, dear daughter," he replied. "The time is coming when you, too, will be resurrected to the same ageless perfection. You know that this world as it is will last several more centuries, and then it will be remade. The real heaven will come down to earth, and God will again live with human beings as He did in Eden. Then creation will experience true perfection throughout eternity."

"Yes." Eva sighed. "Then what all humanity has longed for since we lost Eden will become an eternal reality—and we owe it all to our glorious King."

* * *

# THE SCRIPTURE BEHIND THE STORY

A golden age, paradise on earth, utopia, a return to Eden—these phrases describe the dream that has filled the hearts of people since the fall of humankind. The good news is that according to the Bible, this isn't just a dream. An age is coming when all earthly problems and imbalances will be history.

When the apostle Paul wrote about this coming age, he saw it as a reversal of God's curse on the earth because of Adam's sin (Genesis 3). As this paraphrase of Scripture puts it: "All creation is waiting patiently and hopefully for that future day when God will resurrect his children. For on that day thorns and thistles, sin, death, and decay—the things that overcame the world against its will at God's command—will all disappear, and the world around us will share in the glorious freedom from sin which God's children enjoy" (Romans 8:19-22, TLB).

The whole world is groaning for Eden to be re-created—the time when life will return to the way it was before the Fall. That era, which is also referred to as the thousand-year reign of Christ, is mentioned in only one passage in the New Testament:

I saw an angel coming down from heaven, having the key
to the bottomless pit and a great chain in his hand. He laid

hold of the dragon, that serpent of old, who is the Devil and Satan, and bound him for a thousand years; and he cast him into the bottomless pit, and shut him up, and set a seal on him, so that he should deceive the nations no more till the thousand years were finished. But after these things he must be released for a little while. And I saw thrones, and they sat on them, and judgment was committed to them. Then I saw the souls of those who had been beheaded for their witness to Jesus and for the word of God, who had not worshiped the beast or his image, and had not received his mark on their foreheads or on their hands. And they lived and reigned with Christ for a thousand years. But the rest of the dead did not live again until the thousand years were finished. This is the first resurrection. Blessed and holy is he who has part in the first resurrection. Over such the second death has no power, but they shall be priests of God and of Christ, and shall reign with Him a thousand years. Now when the thousand years have expired, Satan will be released from his prison.

REVELATION 20:1-7

Notice that in these verses, the term "one thousand years" appears six times, and in each case it refers to a distinct feature of that era:

Verse 2: the length of time Satan will be bound
Verse 3: the length of time the nations will not be deceived
by him
Verse 4: the length of time the martyred saints will reign with
Christ
Verse 5: the length of time during which "the rest of the dead"
(the unsaved dead) will wait until their resurrection into
judgment

Verse 6: the length of time those who rise in the first
   resurrection will reign with Christ
Verse 7: the length of time that will elapse before Satan will
   again be loosed from the bottomless pit[1]

Some people have argued that since the Millennium is mentioned in only one passage in the New Testament, it should not be taken literally or treated as a serious Bible teaching. Prophetic scholar René Pache dismantles this argument: "The teaching of the Old Testament concerning the Millennium is so complete that the Jews in the Talmud succeeded in developing it entirely by themselves. . . . They affirmed before Revelation was ever written that the Messianic kingdom would last one thousand years. One should not therefore claim, as some have done, that without the famous passage in Revelation 20, the doctrine of the Millennium would not exist."[2]

The Bible uses various terms to identify this thousand-year period. It is referred to as "the kingdom of heaven" (Matthew 3:2; 8:11), "the kingdom of God" (Mark 1:15), "times of refreshing" (Acts 3:19), "times of restoration" (Acts 3:21), "the day of Jesus Christ" (Philippians 1:6), "the fullness of the times" (Ephesians 1:10), and "the world to come" (Hebrews 2:5). But this era is best known as the Millennium.

The English word *millennium* is made up of two Latin words: *mille*, which means "thousand," and *annum*, which means "year." So the term simply means a period of one thousand years. Yet its long duration belies the speed of its arrival: "The coming of the Millennium will not be a gradual and imperceptible process but rather, sudden, supernatural, and apparent to the whole world. It will be preceded by a series of world wide catastrophic events—wars, plagues, famines, and cosmic disturbances. It will be ushered in by a special manifestation of God and His glory; 'all flesh shall see it together' (Isaiah 40:5)."[3]

As we examine the key characteristics and features of this incredible age, it is important to understand that it will be lived out in the lives of ordinary people who are following the everyday routines of life on earth. "Basic structures and institutions of society will probably continue. Lifestyles and patterns, with individuals manifesting their distinct personalities, will remain. People will eat, sleep, earn a living, marry, have children, and finally die. There will be cities, farms, schools, industries, and stores. The difference will consist in the presence of proper, enjoyable relationships among people and especially toward God. Righteousness will prevail, and people will think and converse about God."[4]

As we examine the writings of the prophets concerning the millennial kingdom, twelve features command our attention.

### The Anticipation of the Kingdom

> I have set My king on My holy hill of Zion. I will declare
> the decree: The LORD has said to Me, "You are My Son,
> today I have begotten You. Ask of Me, and I will give You
> the nations for Your inheritance, and the ends of the earth
> for Your possession. You shall break them with a rod of iron;
> You shall dash them to pieces like a potter's vessel."
>
> PSALM 2:6-9

The Old Testament prophetic books tell us a great deal about the millennial kingdom. In the book of Isaiah, entire chapters are devoted to the subject. Before Isaiah, David wrote these prophetic lines in Psalm 2, which describe God the Father gifting the Kingdom to His Son, Jesus Christ.

Some of the most vivid prophecies of the Kingdom age are found in the writings of Daniel. Chapter 2 records that he saw the whole course of the world's future revealed in the dream of pagan king Nebuchadnezzar. This dream featured the gigantic statue of a man formed with layers of descending quality, from a golden head to feet of clay. Each layer represented a succeeding world empire. The vision culminated when "a stone [that] was cut out without hands" shattered the image (Daniel 2:34) and grew until it filled the earth.

Here is Daniel's explanation of this vision: "In the days of these kings the God of heaven will set up a kingdom which shall never be destroyed; and the kingdom shall not be left to other people; it shall break in pieces and consume all these kingdoms, and it shall stand forever" (Daniel 2:44).

In a later vision, Daniel saw the King coming to take His Kingdom: "I was watching in the night visions, and behold, One like the Son of Man, coming with the clouds of heaven! He came to the Ancient of Days, and they brought Him near before Him. Then to Him was given dominion and glory and a kingdom, that all peoples, nations, and languages should serve Him. His dominion is an everlasting dominion, which shall not pass away, and His kingdom the one which shall not be destroyed" (Daniel 7:13-14).

One of the most famous prophecies regarding the coming of the King is found in the book of Isaiah: "Unto us a Child is born, unto us a Son is given; and the government will be upon His shoulder. And His name will be called Wonderful, Counselor, Mighty God, Everlasting Father, Prince of Peace. Of the increase of His government and peace there will be no end, upon the throne of David and over His kingdom, to order it and establish it with judgment and justice from that time forward, even forever" (9:6-7).

In the book of Revelation, the seventh trumpet sounds, and the message that accompanies it makes a bold statement about Christ's Kingdom: "The kingdoms of this world have become the kingdoms of our Lord and of His Christ, and He shall reign forever and ever!" (11:15).

## The Coronation of the King

Out of His mouth goes a sharp sword, that with it He should strike the nations. And He Himself will rule them with a rod of iron. . . . And He has on His robe and on His thigh a name written: KING OF KINGS AND LORD OF LORDS.

REVELATION 19:15-16

In this passage, John tells us how the King will arrive and begin His reign. He will come as a conqueror, taking back His world. As the Old Testament prophecies indicate, there is a close connection between our Lord's victory at the Battle of Armageddon and His reign as King over all the earth: "The LORD will go forth and fight against those nations, as He fights in the day of battle. . . . And the LORD shall be King over all the earth. In that day it shall be—'The LORD is one,' and His name one" (Zechariah 14:3, 9). Christ must rid the earth of its evil usurper before He can establish His reign.

In the Millennium, Satan will no longer be the prince of the world. His era will end, and Christ will initiate His eternal reign of righteousness, joy, prosperity, and peace. His glory will shine forth and bathe the universe with righteousness.

This is the same message Gabriel announced to Mary. He told her that one day her son Jesus would serve as the supreme Ruler of the world: "He will be great, and will be called the Son of the Highest; and the Lord God will give Him the throne of His father David. And He will reign over the house of Jacob forever, and of His kingdom there will be no end" (Luke 1:32-33).

Alva McClain, the founder of Grace Theological Seminary, describes Christ's Kingship this way:

The age to come, as [Jesus] liked to call it, will be ushered in by the exercise of His immediate power and authority. He has all power now; He will take this power and use it to the full when He returns. The age long silence of God, the taunt of unbelief, will be broken by the transition and resurrection of the church, by the unloosing of judgment long withheld; by the visible and personal presence of the Mediatorial King, and by the complete establishment of His Kingdom on earth for a period specified by our Lord as "1000 years." . . . During this period, every aspect of the Kingdom as set forth in Old Testament prophecy will be realized upon earth, truly the golden age of the world. Children will be born, life will go on, and men will work and play, but under ideal conditions.[5]

## *The Incarceration of Satan*

I saw an angel coming down from heaven, having the key to the bottomless pit and a great chain in his hand. He laid hold of the dragon, that serpent of old, who is the Devil and Satan, and bound him for a thousand years; and he cast him into the bottomless pit, and shut him up, and set a seal on him, so that he should deceive the nations no more till the thousand years were finished. But after these things he must be released for a little while.

REVELATION 20:1-3

In his vision, John learned that events surrounding Satan will bookend the Millennium. The thousand-year age will start when Satan is imprisoned in the abyss, and it will end when he is released.

Dr. Henry Morris paints a haunting picture of the place that awaits our adversary:

Somewhere deep in the center of the earth a prison cell has been reserved in the remotest recesses of the bottomless pit. . . . Located at the very middle of the earth, one could not fall any deeper down. . . . Such a place will be Satan's confine during the millennium, as far removed from human beings as is possible to be on this planet. . . . Not only will he be hurled to the center of the earth, but he will be shut up in his cell, with its entrance invincibly sealed so that he cannot even direct his own demonic hosts while so restrained.[6]

For one thousand years, Satan will be rendered powerless. He will have no power over anything or anyone. It will be his absence, in part, that allows the earth to be filled with great prosperity, peace, and joy.

## The Administration of David

> They shall serve the LORD their God, and David their king, whom I will raise up for them.
>
> JEREMIAH 30:9

The Lord Jesus Christ will be King supreme, but He will choose to rule through a vice-regent—the resurrected King David. Jeremiah's words were written four hundred years after David's death, so Jeremiah could not have been referring to David's historical reign as Israel's king. The prophets Ezekiel and Hosea also affirm David's kingly position during the Millennium (Ezekiel 34:23-24; 37:24-25; Hosea 3:5).

Dr. John Walvoord explains the logic of David's administrative role in the Millennium: "In the light of many prophecies which promise saints the privilege of reigning with Christ, it would seem most logical that David, the king raised from the dead, should be given a place of prominence in the Davidic kingdom of the millennial reign of Christ. As indicated in Revelation 19:16, Christ is 'KING OF KINGS AND LORD OF LORDS.' This would certainly imply other rulers."[7]

## *The Participation of the Saints*

> I saw thrones, and they sat on them, and judgment was committed to them. Then I saw the souls of those who had been beheaded for their witness to Jesus and for the word of God, who had not worshiped the beast or his image, and had not received his mark on their foreheads or on their hands. And they lived and reigned with Christ for a thousand years. . . . Blessed and holy is he who has part in the first resurrection. Over such the second death has no power, but they shall be priests of God and of Christ, and shall reign with Him a thousand years.
>
> REVELATION 20:4, 6

Daniel anticipated this moment when the saints will reign with Christ. He wrote, "The saints of the Most High shall receive the kingdom, and possess the kingdom forever, even forever and ever. . . . Then the kingdom and dominion, and the greatness of the kingdoms under the whole heaven, shall be given to the people, the saints of the Most High" (Daniel 7:18, 27).

There will be a hierarchy of rulers and judges in the Millennium. We have noted David's high-ranking role and the lower role of the ruling saints. Between these tiers of authority will be the twelve apostles, who will already have been given their assigned thrones for the purpose of judging Israel (Matthew 19:28).

So who are these additional saints who will reign with Christ? Dr. Henry Morris contends that they will be "the same saints, dressed in fine white linen . . . who comprised the armies accompanying Christ as He returned to earth (Revelation 19:8, 14, 19). All those who had been redeemed by His blood, resurrected from the grave, raptured into His presence, and evaluated for their rewards at His judgment seat will apparently be assigned individual thrones of authority and judgment."[8]

The apostle Paul took it almost as common knowledge that saints would participate with Christ's ruling work one day: "Do you not know that the saints will judge the world?" (1 Corinthians 6:2).

## The Elimination of War

Everyone shall sit under his vine and under his fig tree, and no one shall make them afraid.

MICAH 4:4

Isaiah describes this unprecedented time in human history as one when people "shall beat their swords into plowshares, and their spears into pruning hooks; nation shall not lift up sword against nation, neither shall they learn war anymore" (Isaiah 2:4).

Isaiah then explains one of the most astounding things about this era of peace: "In that day there will be a highway from Egypt to Assyria, and the Assyrian will come into Egypt and the Egyptian into Assyria, and the Egyptians will serve with the Assyrians. In that day Israel will be one of three with Egypt and Assyria—a blessing in the midst of the land, whom the LORD of hosts shall bless, saying, 'Blessed is Egypt My people, and Assyria the work of My hands, and Israel My inheritance'" (Isaiah 19:23-25).

"Can you imagine a thing like that?" W. A. Criswell writes. "Think of the years of hatred ever since Ishmael and Isaac grew to despise one another. From that day until this has there ever not been war between Israel and the Arabs? But there is coming a time, says the Lord when the Lord of hosts will bless them all. . . . All of us, saved Jews, and saved Gentiles, are to be together in the glorious and ultimate kingdom of our Lord."[9]

The absence of hostility between humans will be mirrored in the animal kingdom: "The wolf also shall dwell with the lamb, the leopard shall lie down with the young goat, the calf and the young lion and the fatling together; and a little child shall lead them. The cow and the bear shall graze; their young ones shall lie down together; and the lion shall eat straw like the ox. The nursing child shall play by the cobra's hole, and the weaned child shall put his hand in the viper's den. They shall not hurt nor destroy in all My holy mountain, for the earth shall be full of the knowledge of the Lord as the waters cover the sea" (Isaiah 11:6-9; see also 65:25; Hosea 2:18).

Criswell goes on to explain that this era of peace will fulfill God's original intention for His creation:

> God never intended for animals to eat one another, to lie in wait, to destroy, to drink blood. This is a mark of sin in the world. God never intended for one man to kill another man, much less for one nation to go to war and slay millions of his fellow men. The Lord made His creation to be filled with light, goodness, glory, holiness, love and happiness. But all that we lost in Eden, God will give us back at the new creation. Think of a day when the wolf and the lamb, the leopard and the kid, the lion and the fatling will lie down together! When the vicious, ferocious, carnivorous lion is a vegetarian! He will eat straw like an ox. Oh, what God has prepared in that millennial day![10]

### The Realization of Prosperity

> In His days the righteous shall flourish, and abundance of peace, until the moon is no more.
> PSALM 72:7

The perfect labor situation and ecological changes in the Kingdom age will produce economic abundance. There will be no want. All people will have what they need. It will be a time of unparalleled prosperity. "The wilderness and the wasteland shall be glad for them, and the desert shall rejoice and blossom as the rose" (Isaiah 35:1).

The prophet Joel describes the ecological changes that will contribute to this prosperity:

> Do not be afraid, you beasts of the field; for the open pastures are springing up, and the tree bears its fruit; the fig tree and the vine yield their strength. Be glad then, you children of Zion, and rejoice in the LORD your God; for He has given you the former rain faithfully, and He will cause the rain to come down for you. . . . The threshing floors shall be full of wheat, and the vats shall overflow with new wine and oil. . . . You shall eat in plenty and be satisfied, and praise the name of the LORD your God, who has dealt wondrously with you.
>
> JOEL 2:22-24, 26

According to Mark Hitchcock, "The millennial kingdom will have no need for rescue missions, welfare programs, food stamps, or relief agencies. The world will flourish under the hand of the King of heaven."[11]

### The Integration of Holiness

> It shall come to pass that he who is left in Zion and remains in Jerusalem will be called holy—everyone who is recorded among the living in Jerusalem.
>
> ISAIAH 4:3

The millennial kingdom will be a holy Kingdom. Not only will the King be holy, but so will the land, the city, the Temple, and the King's subjects. Holiness will be integrated into every aspect of life during the reign of King Jesus. "Jerusalem shall be called the City of Truth, the Mountain of the LORD of hosts, the Holy Mountain" (Zechariah 8:3).

Holiness does not imply, as many people assume, a head-in-the-clouds religiosity that disdains earthly pursuits. It simply means being like God and being submitted to Him. True holiness means that our heads, our hands, and our hearts belong to Him and our whole desire is to do His work by the power of His Spirit. In the Kingdom to come, that ideal will be a universal reality.

### The Prolongation of Life

The eyes of the blind shall be opened, and the ears of the deaf shall be unstopped. Then the lame shall leap like a deer, and the tongue of the dumb sing. For waters shall burst forth in the wilderness, and streams in the desert.

ISAIAH 35:5-6

In the Millennium, sickness and death will not exist among the resurrected saints, and among the survivors of the Tribulation it will be a rare occurrence. Jeremiah writes, "'I will restore health to you and heal you of your wounds,' says the LORD" (Jeremiah 30:17).

As a result of the pristine conditions of the universe during the Millennium, people will live long lives. It appears that life spans will revert to those of the era before the Flood, when humans lived to be more than nine hundred years old. "No more shall an infant from there live but a few days, nor an old man who has not fulfilled his days" (Isaiah 65:20).

Not only will people live much longer, but there will also be a significant increase in the birthrate as children are born to those who survive the Tribulation. "I will multiply them, and they shall not diminish; I will also glorify them, and they shall not be small. Their children also shall be as before, and their congregation shall

be established before Me; and I will punish all who oppress them"
(Jeremiah 30:19-20).

Alva J. McClain writes: "Disease will be abolished. . . . The crisis
of death will be experienced only by those incorrigible individuals
who rebel against the laws of the kingdom. The ordinary hazards of
physical life will be under the direct control of One whose voice even
the 'winds and the waves obey.'"[12]

## The Celebration of Joy

> With everlasting joy on their heads, [the ransomed of the
> LORD] shall obtain joy and gladness, and sorrow and sighing
> shall flee away.
>
> ISAIAH 35:10

When Isaac Watts wrote "Joy to the World" some three centuries ago, he didn't intend for it to be a Christmas song. Instead,
the lyrics were meant to announce the second coming of Christ
and His rule over the Kingdom. The verses echo the joy of Christ's
eternal reign:

> *Joy to the world! The Lord is come;*
> *Let earth receive her king; . . .*
> *No more let sins and sorrows grow. . . .*
> *He rules the world with truth and grace.*

This is a song of the Millennium.[13]

Isaiah spoke often about the joy of the Millennium:

> "They rejoice before You according to the joy of the harvest."
> (Isaiah 9:3)

"With joy you will draw water from the wells of salvation."
(Isaiah 12:3)

"We have waited for Him; we will be glad and rejoice in His
salvation." (Isaiah 25:9)

"You shall have a song as in the night." (Isaiah 30:29)

"Sing to the LORD a new song, and His praise from the ends of
the earth." (Isaiah 42:10)

"Break forth into song, sing together." (Isaiah 52:9)

"I will greatly rejoice in the LORD, my soul shall be joyful in my
God." (Isaiah 61:10)

"Rejoice with Jerusalem, and be glad with her, all you who love
her." (Isaiah 66:10)

These passages are merely a sampling of the many expressions of
millennial joy found in the Old Testament. Other prophetic books,
such as Jeremiah, Zephaniah, and Zechariah, also include descriptions of the celebratory nature of this era. Clearly, the Millennium
will be a time of unparalleled joy.

### The Centralization of Worship

It shall come to pass in the latter days that the mountain
of the LORD's house shall be established on the top of the
mountains, and shall be exalted above the hills; and all
nations shall flow to it.

ISAIAH 2:2; SEE ALSO MICAH 4:1

In the Millennium, Jerusalem will become the world center of
worship. The worship of God during the Kingdom era will be more
prolific and more genuine than it has been at any time since the
Garden of Eden. This worship will also be universal. The Lord says,
"It shall come to pass that from one New Moon to another, and from

one Sabbath to another, all flesh shall come to worship before Me" (Isaiah 66:23).

Isaiah tells us that in that day the gates to the city of Jerusalem will be "open continually," never shutting day or night. All nations shall worship the Lord, and the ones who do not will perish (Isaiah 60:11-12). In that day everyone will know that there is but one God, and everyone will worship Him. "Many people shall come and say, 'Come, and let us go up to the mountain of the LORD, to the house of the God of Jacob; He will teach us His ways, and we shall walk in His paths.' For out of Zion shall go forth the law, and the word of the LORD from Jerusalem" (2:3).

The prophet Zechariah describes how different life will be for Jews in the Millennium. Instead of being persecuted, they will be exalted and sought after because of their relationship to King Jesus. "In those days ten men from every language of the nations shall grasp the sleeve of a Jewish man, saying, 'Let us go with you, for we have heard that God is with you'" (Zechariah 8:23).

### The Continuation of the Kingdom

Then comes the end, when [Jesus] delivers the kingdom to God the Father.

I CORINTHIANS 15:24

The millennial kingdom will not be temporary. The earthly Kingdom, when Christ rules out of Jerusalem, will last one thousand years, but at the end of that time it will merge into God's eternal rule.

Daniel describes the Kingdom rule of Christ as "an everlasting dominion, which shall not pass away" (Daniel 7:14). Considering all the characteristics of the Millennium, Dr. John Walvoord writes, "Taken as a whole, the social and economic conditions of the millennium indicate a golden age in which the dreams of social reformists through the centuries will be realized, not through human effort but by the immediate presence and power of God and the righteous government of Christ."[14]

After the completion of the Millennium, Christ's Kingdom will continue without end as heaven comes to earth.

The story of King Arthur is one of the best known in all literature. The young king begins his reign with bright hope over a kingdom founded on the ideals of equality, justice, purity, courage, and integrity. At first the kingdom prospers greatly, drawing the best knights from other lands who lend their strength to further the nation's ideals. But human weakness in the form of lust and treachery eventually bring the kingdom crashing down.

No one knows how much of the Arthurian story is fact and how much is legend. But we do know this: it embodies two hard-and-fast truths. One, the longing for ideal perfection is embedded in every human heart. Two, fallen humans are unable to maintain those ideals. Every kingdom ruled by a human being, no matter how glorious its beginning, eventually falls—either by conquest or by the internal flaws and weaknesses of the people.

As we have discussed in this chapter, Revelation 20, the Old Testament prophecies, the New Testament Epistles, and the Gospels attest to the fact that the ideal of a perfect and happy empire is not a vain one. God does not give us desires that cannot be realized. A day is coming when the desire for a perfect world will be accomplished in full.

That worldwide Kingdom will not fail, as all human kingdoms do, for it will be ruled by the perfect Son of God—the resurrected Jesus Christ. He will reign over a world and over people who will reflect His perfection. In such a Kingdom ruled by such a King, nothing can ever go wrong again. That is why the Bible promises, "Of His kingdom there will be no end" (Luke 1:33).

It is a truth we can depend on.

*chapter ten*

# THE JUDGE

MORGAN WILSON had his four-foot putt lined up perfectly. He was about to tap the ball when he suddenly clutched his chest and collapsed onto the green. The panicked voices of his buddies faded away as he felt himself traveling through a dark tunnel. Then all at once, he was in a mode of existence unlike anything he'd experienced on earth. Unknown to him, he was in Hades, the abode of the wicked as they await the Day of Judgment.

Many other souls surrounded him, and more continued to flock in. Their bodies were like his own—wispy and insubstantial, but with all senses intact. At one end of the room guarding a massive door stood a manlike figure who was so bright Morgan could hardly look at him.

"How many earth years have passed since I died?" he asked the man.

"Well over a thousand," the doorkeeper answered.

"Only a thousand? In this dreadful place, it seems like a million. Where am I? And why am I here?"

"Christ has defeated Satan and his agents once and for all and hurled them into the lake of fire. Now He has begun the final judgment of all souls. You are here to await your turn."

One by one, the waiting souls were called to the door. When Morgan's turn came, he passed through the door, and what he saw took his breath away. His eyes strained to take in the otherworldly beauty and majesty. Directly before him towered a great white throne. He looked into the face of the One sitting on it, and he was undone. The face radiated pure love and infinite sorrow. In that instant, Morgan realized that this face, this being, had somehow always been the reality behind every longing he'd ever had.

The Man's hands were scarred, as if they had been impaled by some sharp instrument. With a stab of fear, Morgan realized that he was in the presence of Jesus Christ. Panic welled up as he reflected on his earthly life, which had not always been what it ought to have been. But he also remembered being told that Christ was merciful. He clung to that thought as if it were a rope dangling over a bottomless pit.

In a rich, pure voice, Christ called Morgan by name. Morgan was drawn forward like a magnet. For the first time he noticed six books stacked on a table beside the throne. Christ picked up the first one, and Morgan got a glimpse of its title: the Book of the Law. Christ opened the book and placed it on His lap.

"Morgan Wilson," He said, "what do you have to say regarding your life on earth?"

In spite of his violent trembling, Morgan found his voice. "Well, uh, I tried my best to obey Your laws. And when I think of other people I know, I figure I did it a little better than most."

"So you think your salvation depends on your keeping of the law. Very well. Since you expect to be saved by your good works, let's consider what that requires." Looking at the book, Christ reviewed aloud each point of the law and then looked at Morgan. "Have you done all these things?"

"Well, not perfectly, of course. But I think the good outweighs the bad."

"I'm afraid that's not good enough," Christ said. "If you base your salvation on the law, you must keep all the law, obeying every point without fail."

"But, Lord, that's impossible. No one is perfect except You. But on the whole, I think I've earned enough points to call myself a pretty good man."

"My dear Morgan, these laws are not ways for you to earn merit. No one can earn salvation by keeping the law; it is My free gift to those who love Me. The law describes what God meant the human race to be—what Adam and Eve were like before they sinned. Only those who obey every law perfectly are fit to inhabit heaven."

"But if that's the case, no one can be saved," Morgan countered. "The Bible says, 'All have sinned and fallen short.'"

"You are exactly right. That's why I died for you. I never sinned, and I took the penalty for your sin in order to free you from it."

"If You knew we couldn't keep the law, why did You inflict it on us?"

"It was your diagnostic tool—a standard you could compare yourself to. That standard of perfection was there to show you how afflicted you were with the disease of sin. You needed to accept that diagnosis before you would accept My remedy. But instead of using the law to diagnose your condition, you tried to make it your cure. All that did was allow your disease to fester."

Christ closed the Book of the Law and picked up the next volume: Morgan Wilson's Book of Works. As He opened it, Morgan's fear began to ease. He had done many good works; he felt sure the Lord would be impressed.

"It says here that you gave one thousand dollars to your church's new building fund."

"That's right," Morgan replied. "I even set an example by being the first to contribute."

"So you were. It says here that you came forward when the fund-raising campaign was announced. You made a little speech telling how much you were giving, and you wrote your check right there in front of the entire church."

"Indeed I did." Morgan smiled broadly.

"The book also says that the primary motivation for your contribution was not to further the cause of My church; it was to draw admiration to yourself."

"But that's not—" Morgan stopped, realizing how futile it would be to argue with Christ. "But I—well, I did many other good things. I was a deacon in my church. I occasionally taught Sunday school. I never missed a church service—even on Wednesday nights. I seldom fell asleep during sermons. I even contributed half the funds for a new building wing."

"Yes, all those things are recorded here. But it's also recorded that you made sure all those deeds were visible to others."

"Didn't You tell us to let our light shine before men so they could see our good works and glorify You?"

"According to this book, you did none of these things with My glory in mind. You drew all the glory to yourself. You even withheld the money for that building wing until the deacons agreed to name it after you."

Suddenly Morgan felt exposed. He could muster no response.

Christ continued, "Your public deeds made you look dedicated and noble, and people praised you for them. That was the reward you sought, and that was the reward you got. Therefore you need no reward from Me. You did none of your deeds because you loved Me. You merely used Me as a means of gaining respect and admiration.

Even when you professed Christianity, your public acceptance of Me was an empty show. You never gave Me your heart."

Christ closed the book and reached for the next one: Morgan Wilson's Book of Secrets. As He opened the cover, Morgan's apprehension grew. So far, things had not gone well for him. He trembled to think what these pages might reveal.

"You have a lot of entries in this book," Christ said. "Let's look at some of the things you did in secret.

"It says here that many of your customers paid you in cash, and you reported none of those payments to the IRS. You also reported business losses you did not incur and inflated the amount of your charitable gifts. You cheated on your income tax, and according to these records, you did so every year."

"But taxes were exorbitantly high, Lord! And the government used billions of dollars of our tax money to support immoral causes."

"My faithful servant Paul told you to obey the laws of the land, and I told you to render to Caesar what belongs to Caesar. You said moments ago that the law was important to you. But as I look over your entries, I see consistent infractions. Whenever you thought the police weren't around, you habitually drove over the speed limit."

"Oh please, be reasonable," Morgan pleaded. "That was such a tiny, insignificant thing. Everybody did it."

"Insignificant maybe, but this was the law of your land, which you were charged to obey. All of these acts undermine your claim to respect the law. Such cavalier disobedience for even 'tiny' laws shows you had no real respect for the law at all. When no one was looking, you did whatever you wanted and believed you could get away with. This self-centered focus shows that within your heart resided the same impulse that motivates mass murderers—to do what you wanted to do instead of what was right. It's a difference not of kind, but of degree."

"I never thought such little things would get me in such big trouble."

"Well, then," Christ responded, "let's look a little deeper and see if all your secret acts were 'little things.' It says here that in the early years of your air-conditioning business, when you made repair calls yourself, you regularly loosened the Freon valves on your customers' AC units, letting the expensive gas escape slowly, which would lead to another service call soon after. It also says that you visited Internet porn sites late at night. And to top it off, these records indicate that you had a long-running affair with a woman at your church. None of these deeds were ever found out, and since they never damaged your reputation, you never repented of them."

"But nothing I did ever hurt anyone."

"No? How much did your porn and adultery destroy the intimacy of your marriage? What did your tampering with those AC systems cost families who couldn't afford it? How much did your lawless driving endanger others on the roads? What you never understood, Morgan, is that your deeds hurt you. They kept your focus on yourself and drew it away from Me. They seared your conscience until you lost your regard for right and wrong. But I'll say more about that in a moment."

"But surely, Lord, even the best people have a few misdeeds to hide."

"The bottom line is that you did your good works in public and your evil ones in secret. You should have done the opposite. You should have done your good works in secret so that your reward would have been My riches instead of the praise of people. And you should have aired your evil deeds in confession and repentance."

Morgan looked down in shame as Christ closed Morgan Wilson's Book of Secrets and reached for the next one: Morgan Wilson's Book of Words.

"I see two categories of words in this book," He said. "Those that reflected the attitude of your heart and those that hid it. The two categories are sometimes paired. For example, when you were an employee, you flattered your supervisor in your salary-review meeting and then, at lunch on the same day, you told your coworkers he was so dumb that if he was going to speak his mind, he'd be speechless."

"But that was just a joke."

"You hardly ever read your Bible, yet you often quoted from a list of Scriptures you'd memorized to impress other church members. You taught a Sunday school class on purity in marriage at the very time you were involved with the other woman. You spoke to your church's youth group about keeping their speech clean while your own jokes with your golfing buddies were not even fit for the gutter."

"Lord, you know how a group of guys are. We were just—"

"You cursed at your employees. You were rude to your wife, criticizing her incessantly. You lost your temper with your kids over their slightest lapses. You made comments to hurt those you didn't like, and you lied to cover your own indiscretions. When church members came to you—a deacon—with private problems or confessions, you couldn't wait to tell others. Your gossip ruined the reputations of several people."

Christ shook His head and closed the book. He picked up the next one: Morgan Wilson's Book of Conscience. As He opened it, hope drained from Morgan's heart. He dreaded what this volume might reveal.

As Christ opened the book, He said, "Every individual has within him a deep, ingrained standard of right and wrong that will sometimes rise to the surface, expose the truth about himself, and spur him to repent. That embedded standard reveals itself through one's conscience."

Morgan's hopes rose. He could not remember his conscience giving him any trouble since he was a teenager.

"When a man is young," Christ continued, "his conscience is often less contaminated, which makes it a clearer conduit for the basic principles of right and wrong. When the conscience speaks with such clarity, the young person usually recognizes when he has done wrong. Let's open this book and see what your conscience did for you."

"I'm ready."

Christ looked at the first page. "Here it says that you skipped school one day and went to the beach. That night you lied to your mother about where you'd been. You spent a sleepless night feeling guilty for both the deed and the lie, but when the same opportunity arose several weeks later, you skipped school and lied again. After doing this a few more times, you stifled the voice of conscience until it no longer bothered you. And from that moment on, your secret behavior and lies came easily."

Morgan felt that long-forgotten shame wash over him as the events of his life flashed before him.

"Your conscience managed to surface when you began your secret affair," Christ went on. "Had you heeded its warning, guilt over your sin might have led you to turn your entire life around. But your conscience was so atrophied by that point that it came naturally for you to shut it out. Eventually it didn't bother you anymore."

"I—I desperately wish I'd listened," Morgan said. "I don't know why I didn't."

"I'll tell you why. You replaced the voice of your conscience with another: the voice of self-justification. That voice convinced you that both your porn indulgence and your secret affair were justified because you felt your wife had lost her youthful beauty and you had a right to seek what you were missing elsewhere. Not only was your wife growing older, but she had also become sharp tongued and unresponsive. The younger woman was alluring—she excited your senses and stroked your ego. You believed you had a right to happiness, and you thought she would make you happy while your wife did not. Had your conscience remained engaged, you would have understood that your wife was bitter because you treated her with such disdain. And that awareness might have led to your repentance and true conversion."

Tears welled up in Morgan's eyes—not in remorse over what his deeds had done to his wife, but over what they were doing to him now.

"Shutting down your conscience allowed you to replace truth with the self-justifying lies you told yourself. Those lies became your truth. You convinced yourself that God would not condemn anyone who believed anything sincerely. He finally gave you over to your desires and allowed you to be deceived by your own lies."

Morgan, now in utter despair, grabbed at one last strand of hope. He remembered grace. He would make a plea for the grace of God, which he'd been told was vast enough to cover all sins. *Maybe that's why this last unopened book is so enormous*, he thought. *Maybe it's a book of grace.*

"I see that You have one more book to open," Morgan said. "Is there any chance it might somehow override all that has been written in the others?"

Jesus picked up the heavy volume. "This is the Book of Life. The name of every person ever born has been entered into it. Tragically, however, many of the names no longer appear. They have been blotted out."

"Please—" Morgan pleaded. "Please open that book and see whether by some chance my name is still there."

Jesus turned slowly through the pages, scanning each one. Finally He closed the volume and looked at Morgan sadly. "I am sorry; your name is not here. You do not belong to Me, and I must banish you forever from My presence."

"But Lord—Lord!" Morgan cried. "You're forgetting all I did for You. Remember? I never missed a church service! I taught Sunday school, I was a deacon, and I gave money to the church. Surely all that counts for something!"

"Morgan, as your books have already shown, you did the visible things that brought you praise. But you never fed a hungry person, you never visited anyone in jail, you never sat up with a sick friend, you never clothed a poor family, you never stopped to assist a stranded motorist. Everything you did was for you, not for the love of others. You cannot love Me if you do not love others. You never loved Me, Morgan. Though you wore My name, you were an impostor. You said the right words, but your heart belonged to you."

"But what about grace?" Morgan cried, "Can't You give me grace?"

"My grace was always available to you. All you had to do was place your trust in Me and make Me the Lord of your life. Had you done that, My grace would have freely covered your sins and failures. But you never surrendered yourself and allowed Me into your heart. Therefore, you never knew Me, and I never knew you."

"Oh, please, Lord, please!" Anguish welled up in Morgan's voice. "I know that You are Lord and that I have sinned. Just give me one more chance. Please!"

One of the bright beings approached to lead Morgan away. He wailed bitterly as he looked for the last time on the one face whose presence would have meant perpetual joy throughout eternity—a face he would never behold again except in his moments of bitter regret.

The angel led him toward another door, this one dark and ominous, on the far side of the great hall. There he was thrust into the darkness. The door slammed behind him, echoing in the empty blackness. Morgan couldn't see anything—no sun, no moon, no stars, not a single ray of light.

He groped about with his hands and tried to find footing for his feet. There was nothing. Though he had no weight, he had the sensation of falling through the darkness. Sensing no other presence but himself, he called out into the emptiness, but his voice seemed to get swallowed up. He heard nothing but the horrible sound of his own weeping. He was isolated from all humanity—and he would be for all eternity.

He had lived for himself. He had made himself the most important entity in his life. Now in death, he had been granted exactly what he'd always loved best: the company of himself and nothing else, forever.

Eons passed, and Morgan Wilson had decayed into something less than human, becoming nothing more than a perpetual hunger and an incessant wail. For all eternity, he would writhe in a lake of fire, his torment never ceasing. He would never be reclaimed; he would never again have hope.

* * *

# THE SCRIPTURE BEHIND THE STORY

The account of the Great White Throne Judgment in Revelation 20:11-15 is one of the most sobering passages in the Bible. It tells of the final judgment of the inhabitants of planet Earth. The last sentence of the passage is chilling: "Anyone not found written in the Book of Life was cast into the lake of fire." No one can read that sentence without realizing that how we live our lives matters.

Almost all Christians have some idea about a future judgment when everyone will stand before God. One of the most common beliefs is that He will evaluate our lives—our good works and our bad—and then, like a high school teacher grading on a curve, He will decide who gets into heaven and who does not. Nothing could be further from the truth. God's program of judgment is far more sophisticated than that.

A final judgment is coming—of that we can be certain. "It is appointed for men to die once, but after this the judgment" (Hebrews 9:27). But few Christians realize that there will be not one but two days of judgment—first the judgment seat of Christ and second the Great White Throne Judgment. Our relationship with Christ will determine which court will try our case.

The judgment for Christians will occur at the first court, the judgment seat of Christ, immediately after the Rapture. "We must all appear before the judgment seat of Christ, that each one may receive the things done in the body, according to what he has done, whether good or bad" (2 Corinthians 5:10). The purpose of this judgment is not to pronounce condemnation. No one judged in this court will be condemned, for all will be followers of Christ who submitted their lives to Him. All their bad deeds will be covered by grace. The purpose of this judgment is for Christ to assess every believer's earthly works to determine rewards for faithfulness.

At the Great White Throne Judgment, however, unbelievers and those who pretend to be Christians, like Morgan Wilson in our story, will stand before God. Here they will face the consequences of rejecting Jesus Christ as Savior and Lord. This judgment is the final bar of justice in God's plan for the inhabitants of planet Earth, and there will be no grading on a curve. The accused will be judged by the black-and-white standard of absolute truth: "The White Throne Judgment will be nothing like our modern court cases. At the White Throne, there will be a Judge but no jury, a prosecution but no defense, a sentence but no appeal. No one will be able to defend himself or accuse God of unrighteousness."[1] It will be a judgment of grim finality.

These two judgments bring into focus the two different resurrections mentioned in the Bible. The prophet Daniel writes, "Many of those who sleep in the dust of the earth shall awake, some to everlasting life, some to shame and everlasting contempt" (Daniel 12:2). Jesus said, "Do not marvel at this; for the hour is coming in which all who are in the graves will hear His voice and come forth—those who have done good, to the resurrection of life, and those who have done evil, to the resurrection of condemnation" (John 5:28-29).

A growing number of people today have fallen for the doctrine of conditional immortality—the belief that only the righteous will be resurrected and the wicked will be annihilated. Seventh-day Adventists and Jehovah's Witnesses, as well as some evangelicals, teach this doctrine. But the Bible clearly teaches that everyone—every man, woman, boy, and girl—will be alive somewhere forever. Every individual who has ever lived, whether saved or unsaved, will be resurrected.

More than two thousand years ago, Christ was raised from the dead. At the Rapture, the saved of this present age will also be raised from the dead. Seven years later, at the close of the Tribulation, the saints who were martyred during the Tribulation will be raised from the dead along with the Old Testament saints (Daniel 12:1-2; Isaiah 26:19). This will mark the first resurrection, also referred to as the "resurrection of life"—eternal life (John 5:29). When Christ returns to reign during the

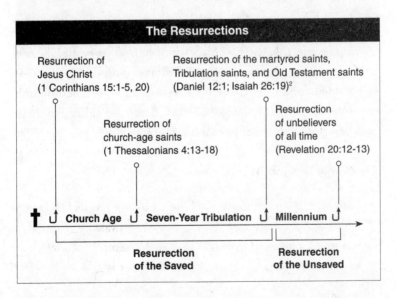

The Resurrections

Resurrection of Jesus Christ (1 Corinthians 15:1-5, 20)

Resurrection of the martyred saints, Tribulation saints, and Old Testament saints (Daniel 12:1; Isaiah 26:19)[2]

Resurrection of church-age saints (1 Thessalonians 4:13-18)

Resurrection of unbelievers of all time (Revelation 20:12-13)

Church Age　Seven-Year Tribulation　Millennium

Resurrection of the Saved

Resurrection of the Unsaved

Millennium, not one believer's body from Adam onward will be left in the grave. The first resurrection will have been completed.

In Revelation 20, we learn about the second resurrection, also called the "resurrection of condemnation," or judgment (John 5:29). It is the resurrection of the unbelieving or uncommitted dead—and they will live in eternal death:

> The rest of the dead did not live again until the thousand years were finished. . . . And I saw the dead, small and great, standing before God, and books were opened. And another book was opened, which is the Book of Life. And the dead were judged according to their works, by the things which were written in the books. The sea gave up the dead who were in it, and Death and Hades delivered up the dead who were in them. And they were judged, each one according to his works. Then Death and Hades were cast into the lake of fire. This is the second death. And anyone not found written in the Book of Life was cast into the lake of fire.
>
> REVELATION 20:5, 12-15

This resurrection will take place one thousand years after the end of the Tribulation. It will include all the unsaved dead from Creation to the Millennium. After this resurrection, there will be no grave occupied by the dust of its inhabitant. Every individual will have been resurrected to either eternal life or eternal death.

### The Place of the Great White Throne

> I saw a great white throne and Him who sat on it, from whose face the earth and the heaven fled away. And there was found no place for them.
>
> REVELATION 20:11

While God's Word does not specify where the Great White Throne Judgment will be, we do know where it will not be: not in heaven, and not on earth. It cannot take place on earth because, at the appearance of the Lord, "the earth and the heaven fled away" (Revelation 20:11). And it cannot take place in heaven, because no sinner can enter the presence of God there. The Great White Throne Judgment takes place somewhere between heaven and earth.

One writer has imagined it this way: "It will not happen in our present universe, either on earth or in the atmospheric, stellar, or divine heavens. No planet in our solar system will qualify. It could take place somewhere beyond our universe that has not been affected by angelic sin. Whether the assigned place actually exists today, it is hard to say."[3]

Perhaps the name of the throne itself is more important than its location. *Great* speaks of the infinite One who is the Judge. *White* speaks of divine holiness, purity, and justice. And *throne* speaks of the majesty of the One who has the right to determine the destiny of His creation.

### The Person on the Great White Throne

I saw a great white throne and Him who sat on it. . . . And I saw the dead . . . standing before God.

REVELATION 20:11-12

The Judge upon the great white throne is none other than the Lord Jesus Christ. We discover this through Jesus' own words: "The Father judges no one, but has committed all judgment to the Son . . . and has given Him authority to execute judgment also, because He is the Son of Man" (John 5:22, 27).

In his letter to the Romans, Paul wrote, "God will judge the secrets of men *by Jesus Christ*" (2:16, emphasis added). In Acts, Peter declares that Christ was "ordained by God to be Judge of the living and the dead" (10:42). Christ will judge the spiritually living at the judgment seat of Christ and the spiritually dead at the Great White Throne Judgment. "Jesus Christ Himself will conduct the trial, and no one is better qualified. He did all He could to save man. Since man has rejected Him, he must be judged by Him."[4]

### The People before the Great White Throne

I saw the dead, small and great, standing before God. . . .
The sea gave up the dead who were in it, and Death and
Hades delivered up the dead who were in them.

REVELATION 20:12-13

As John viewed the great white throne, he saw the dead—all who died without a relationship with Jesus Christ. Their bodies were summoned from their graves and from the sea, and their souls were called from Death and Hades to stand before the Judge of all the earth.

John says that this group will be made up of both "small and great"—an expression found often in the Old Testament and occurring five times in the book of Revelation (11:18; 13:16; 19:5, 18; 20:12). The term indicates that all classes of people will be present, from all ranks in the church and in the world.

There will be many religious people at the great white throne—philanthropists and preachers, miracle workers, and laypeople like the antihero in our story. As Erwin Lutzer writes, "This multitude is diverse in its religions. We see Buddhists, Muslims, Hindus, Protestants, and Catholics. We see those who believed in one God and those who believed in many gods. We see those who refused to believe in any God at all. We see those who believed in meditation as a means of salvation and those who believed that doing good deeds was the path to eternal life. We see the moral and the immoral, the priest as well as the minister, the nun as well as the missionary."[5]

What will happen to these religious people when they stand before the great white throne? Jesus tells us, "Many will say to Me in that day, 'Lord, Lord, have we not prophesied in Your name, cast out demons in Your name, and done many wonders in Your name?' And then I will declare to them, 'I never knew you; depart from Me, you who practice lawlessness!'" (Matthew 7:22-23). Contrary to popular opinion, believing in your chosen "truth" does not make it true for you. There is only one Truth, and that is Jesus Christ. Believe in Him or perish.

Cultural standing will mean nothing before the great white throne. "Both the small and the great of this life (as men view other men) will be there: the banker and the beggar, the prince and the pauper, the statesman, the scientist, the lawyer, the doctor, the professor, the author, the mechanic, the housewife, the bricklayer, the farmer, and the criminal. In this life men have station, but before Christ, there will be no respect of persons. Although they will stand there in mass, they will be judged individually."[6]

Everyone who stands before the great white throne, rich or poor, famous or obscure, beautiful or plain, powerful or weak, intelligent or slow, religious or not, will have this one thing in common: they died without Christ, and they have no hope. As Donald Grey Barnhouse puts it, "Only one group will be seen at this judgment, the dead . . . the spiritually dead."[7]

### The Purpose of the Great White Throne

I saw the dead, small and great, standing before God,
and books were opened. And another book was opened,
which is the Book of Life. And the dead were judged
according to their works, by the things which were written
in the books.

REVELATION 20:12

This verse tells us that when all were gathered before the throne of God, "books were opened." In other words, the evil works of the unsaved will be exposed. Every individual will be judged according to the Book of Life and other books. Though we are not told specifically what the other books are, we have some indications from Scripture about their contents and about how they will be used to judge sinful men and women at the great white throne.

### THE BOOK OF LAW

The Jewish leaders of Jesus' day thought they could merit salvation through obedience to the law, and many Christians today make the same mistake. But as Paul points out, people cannot earn salvation through the law unless they keep it perfectly, which we fallen humans cannot do. "By the deeds of the law no flesh will be justified in His sight . . . for all have sinned and fall short of the glory of God" (Romans 3:20, 23). Paul goes on to tell us that salvation comes only through submitting to Christ and claiming His grace. As a result, there is "no condemnation to those who are in Christ Jesus" (Romans 8:1). Anyone who stands before Christ the Judge and claims to be justified by the law will be condemned by the law. Only those who are in Christ will be found not guilty in the eyes of the law.

### THE BOOK OF WORKS

Revelation 20:13 tells us that the rebellious "were judged, each one according to his works." Paul speaks also of those "whose end will be according to their works" (2 Corinthians 11:15). Jesus said, "The Son of Man will come in the glory of His Father with His angels, and then He will reward each according to his works" (Matthew 16:27).

God will have a complete record of every moment of every person's life—everything done in secret and everything done in public. Who you are will be borne out by what you have done and how you have lived. For those who believe they will go to heaven by their good works, this will be their ultimate moment of truth. By their works they will be judged, and by their works they will be condemned.

Here we encounter a major difference between the judgment seat of Christ, where the saved will stand, and the Great White Throne Judgment, where the unsaved will fall. The saved will also have their share of sins and failures. But because they have placed their faith in Jesus Christ as Savior, the record of their sins will be erased, and their debt of sin will be paid in full.

This truth is confirmed throughout Scripture:

- "He who overcomes shall be clothed in white garments, and I will not blot out his name from the Book of Life; but I will confess his name before My Father and before His angels" (Revelation 3:5).
- "Most assuredly, I say to you, he who hears My word and believes in Him who sent Me has everlasting life, and shall not come into judgment, but has passed from death into life" (John 5:24).
- "There is therefore now no condemnation to those who are in Christ Jesus" (Romans 8:1).

## THE BOOK OF SECRETS

Scripture makes it clear that although we may be able to hide things from other people, there is nothing we can hide from God. Jesus said, "Nothing is secret that will not be revealed, nor anything hidden that will not be known and come to light" (Luke 8:17). The apostle Paul writes, "God will judge the secrets of men by Jesus Christ" (Romans 2:16). And Solomon says that "God will bring every work into judgment, including every secret thing, whether good or evil" (Ecclesiastes 12:14).

D. L. Moody, the famous evangelist, used to say that if a camera were ever invented that could take a picture of the heart of man, the inventor would starve to death because no one would buy such a thing—no one wants his or her secrets exposed. But at the Great White Throne Judgment, there will be no more secrets. Every secret the unsaved think they've safely hidden will stand as testimonies against them at the great white throne.

### THE BOOK OF WORDS

Scientists tell us that no word we speak is ever lost; the sound waves continue on indefinitely, available to be recaptured at any time in the future. Scripture affirms that spoken words may act as accusers of the unsaved at the Great White Throne Judgment: "I say to you that for every idle word men may speak, they will give account of it in the day of judgment. For by your words you will be justified, and by your words you will be condemned" (Matthew 12:36-37).

When people's excuses begin to pour out, the book of words may be opened. By a person's own utterances, he or she will stand condemned before the Lord.

### THE BOOK OF CONSCIENCE

In his letter to the Romans, Paul wrote of people's consciences "bearing witness." Their thoughts are responsible for "accusing or else excusing them" (2:15). This suggests that the human conscience may play a role in the judgment of unbelievers. No person, saved or unsaved, follows the dictates of conscience all the time. Neither is the conscience an infallible guide to right and wrong. But when that inner voice is brazenly violated, it shows a careless attitude toward sin that may be used as condemning evidence.

### THE BOOK OF LIFE

The Bible speaks of the Book of Life several times (Exodus 32:32-33; Psalm 69:28; Daniel 12:1; Philippians 4:3; Revelation 3:5; 13:8; 17:8; 21:27; 22:19). Some first-century cultural background will help us understand the nature of this book.

The cities of John's day had a register that listed the names of every citizen. If people committed crimes or otherwise dishonored their standing in the city, they could be called before a tribunal to have their names removed—literally blotted out—from the city's register. Such individuals would no longer be considered citizens and would be forced to live elsewhere.

I believe this is the concept behind the Book of Life. The names of all people born into this world were originally contained within its pages, but those names are subject to removal.

One can speculate that beside each person's name as entered in the book at time of conception will be recorded the time of his "age of accountability," the date of his conversion to Christ as His Savior, and evidence demonstrating the genuineness of that conversion. However, if there are no entries for the last two items by the time that person dies, the entire entry will be blotted out (Revelation 3:5), and an awful blank will be left in the book at the place where his name would have been. Exhibiting this blank spot in the book will be the final and conclusive evidence that the person being judged must be consigned to the lake of fire.[8]

### The Punishment at the Great White Throne

Then Death and Hades were cast into the lake of fire. This is the second death. And anyone not found written in the Book of Life was cast into the lake of fire.

REVELATION 20:14-15

When Death and Hades are cast into the lake of fire, the totality of sinful humanity's judgment is set. When a person stops living in this world, we say that he or she dies. The meaning of death is separation. This is the first death—the separation of the soul from the body. One's body goes into the grave in death, and one's soul goes to Hades—the place of intermediate suffering—awaiting the final judgment. When Death and Hades are cast into hell, both the body, which has been resurrected from the grave, and the soul, which has been in Hades, will be cast into the lake of fire to be separated from God forever. This, according to John, is "the second death."

Dr. Isaac Massey Haldeman writes: "From this second death there is no resurrection. . . . [The condemned] will be sent out into the wide universe, into the 'outer darkness.' They will be as 'wandering stars, to whom is reserved the blackness of darkness forever.' They shall wander through this unlit darkness of eternity as derelicts of humanity, tossed upon an endless and shoreless sea; souls that have missed the purpose for which created—union and fellowship with God."[9]

Both Revelation and Matthew clearly teach about eternal punishment in hell. It is not a popular doctrine, but there is no way around it in Scripture. Jesus spoke three words about hell for every one word He spoke about heaven, including these: "[The King] will also say to those on the left hand, 'Depart from Me, you cursed, into the everlasting fire prepared for the devil and his angels.' . . . And these will go away into everlasting punishment" (Matthew 25:41, 46). Paul writes that those who do not know God "shall be punished with everlasting destruction from the presence of the Lord" (2 Thessalonians 1:9).

The most graphic portrayal of hell in the Bible is the description of the fate of those who receive the mark of the Beast (the Antichrist) during the Tribulation. Those who agree to worship and serve the Antichrist will be "tormented with fire and brimstone in the presence of the holy angels and in the presence of the Lamb. And the smoke of their torment ascends forever and ever; and they have no rest day or night, who worship the beast and his image" (Revelation 14:10-11).

Scripture offers a grim picture of hell. It is a place of torment and flames (Luke 16:20-28), a place of "wailing and gnashing of teeth" (Matthew 13:42), a place where the "worm does not die and the fire is not quenched" (Mark 9:48), and a place of "fire and brimstone" (Revelation 14:10-11; 21:8).

Revelation 19 tells us that after the Beast and the false prophet are captured, they will be "cast alive into the lake of fire burning with brimstone" (verse 20). One thousand years later, at the end of the Millennium, Satan will join the Beast and the false prophet in hell: "The devil, who deceived them, was cast into the lake of fire and brimstone where the beast and the false prophet are. And they will be tormented day and night forever and ever" (Revelation 20:10). And finally, "Anyone not found written in the Book of Life was cast into the lake of fire" (Revelation 20:15).

Just as the believer at the judgment seat of Christ will receive rewards based on his or her good works, so the unbeliever at the great white throne will receive degrees of punishment in the lake of fire based on his or her sinful works. While everyone's punishment will be severe, not everyone's punishment will be the same. A number of New Testament passages communicate this truth, but it is most clearly taught in our Lord's parable of the steward and his two servants: "That servant who knew his master's will, and did not prepare himself or do according to his will, shall be beaten with many stripes. But he who did not know, yet committed things deserving of stripes, shall be beaten with few. For everyone to whom much is given, from him much will be required; and to whom much has been committed, of him they will ask the more" (Luke 12:47-48).

In Matthew 11:20-24, Christ tells us that He did mighty works in Chorazin, Bethsaida, and Capernaum that were intended to induce repentance. But these three cities did not repent. Because they neglected such an opportunity, Jesus said that their punishment on the Day of Judgment would be more severe than that of Tyre, Sidon, and Sodom—all of which perished by destruction, conquest, or fire. Because they were given so much light but chose to stay in the darkness, their darkness will now be eternal.

Scientist and scholar Dr. Henry Morris suggests one way that this gradation of punishment might be carried out:

> It may also be that the resurrection bodies designed for [the unsaved] by God at "the second resurrection" will be designed with individual nerve systems whose sensory responses are graduated in proportion to the degree of punishment appropriate to the individual, so that the actual pains of hell will be felt differently by each one. . . . God is surely able to inflict His punishments in perfect justice, individually tailored.[10]

For those of us who have been given the privilege of growing up in Western nations where the gospel has been abundantly available, our punishment will be greater if we do not repent and receive God's forgiveness and grace.

I think of the city where I live and the church that I have the joy of leading. We preach the Word of God in all our services. We have Sunday school for the children and youth, and Bible fellowships for adults. We are blessed with women's ministries and men's ministries. We have recreational ministries and international ministries. Our ministry is available on the radio and on television and through the Internet and in printed form. We have a study Bible and small-group Bible studies. We have been given much. And because of that, we are more responsible before God than those who have not been given as many opportunities.

In Revelation 21:8, John tells us what kind of people end up in the lake of fire. Read the list carefully: "The cowardly, unbelieving, abominable, murders, sexually immoral, sorcerers, idolaters, and all liars shall have their part in the lake which burns with fire and brimstone." Did you notice that the "unbelieving" are included with all the morally perverted people on this list? You don't have to be a great sinner to get into the lake of fire; you can be merely an unbelieving sinner.

Since you are reading this chapter, there is still time for you to make sure you avoid the lake of fire. There is still time for you to put your trust in Jesus Christ as your personal Savior. I urge you to read these words from John's Gospel and make your decision for Jesus Christ today: "He who believes in Him is not condemned; but he who does not believe is condemned already, because he has not believed in the name of the only begotten Son of God. . . . Most assuredly, I say to you, he who hears My word and believes in Him who sent Me has everlasting life, and shall not come into judgment, but has passed from death into life" (John 3:18; 5:24).

Believe today!

# *epilogue*
# THE OVERCOMERS

He who overcomes shall inherit all things,
and I will be his God and he shall be My son.

REVELATION 21:7

I AM THANKFUL that the book of Revelation does not end with the Great White Throne Judgment described in chapter 20. The last sentence of that chapter is a grim one indeed: "Anyone not found written in the Book of Life was cast into the lake of fire" (verse 15). It's a message of divine justice and ultimate condemnation—a fitting climax to the terrifying scenes of plagues, death, and destruction that fill the previous chapters.

But then we come to chapter 21, and the heavy cloud of judgment lifts to reveal the most glorious vision in the Bible—a peek at the perfect home God has prepared for His people as their inheritance forever. And the best thing about John's vision here is that it is more than merely a vision; it is a picture of reality that sets our hearts longing for the home God intended for His people. This chapter reveals the journey of faith for believers, showing it to be, first, one of perseverance and endurance and, ultimately, one of triumph, glory, and happiness.

In the final chapters, John opens the doors to the heavenly city and gives believers their first mouthwatering look at their eternal home with God. John reveals a heaven that is beyond all expectation—a place where there is no more pain, no more weeping, and no more death. This is what God had in mind from the beginning. When Adam and Eve fell, bringing sin and all of its resulting miseries into God's perfect world, it appeared that Satan was winning. But God was not about to allow Satan to ruin a creation that He had pronounced good. Revelation reveals that although God's plan has been thousands of years in the making, all creation will soon cease its groaning and be restored to its original perfection.

One day this scarred and battered world will pass away, and all things will be made new. There will be a new heaven, a new earth, and a new Jerusalem. As we uncover these wonders in Revelation 21, we are invited to whet our appetites for the magnificent future that awaits the saints of the Lord.

## A New Heaven and Earth

> I saw a new heaven and a new earth, for the first heaven and the first earth had passed away. . . . Then He who sat on the throne said, "Behold, I make all things new."
>
> REVELATION 21:1, 5

Revelation 21 tells us that after the Great White Throne Judgment at the end of the Millennium, God will make everything new. As wonderful as that announcement is, John tells us very little about the new heaven and the new earth. He does reveal that the new earth will have no sea, but he doesn't offer any clues about what that means. We can, however, imagine an earth with no vast expanses of unusable, salty water that separate people from each other the way our seas do today. Perhaps all water will be fresh, with clear rivers emptying into multitudes of lakes distributed across the globe.

We read about the new heaven and the new earth in two other places in the Bible. The apostle Peter says that righteousness will dwell there (2 Peter 3:13). In other words, there will be no more sin, no more evil. Isaiah 66:22 says that the new heaven and the new earth will "remain before [God]." They will be not only perfect but also eternal—there will be no more upheavals and no more judgment.

How is God going to bring the new heaven and the new earth into existence? Some people refer to 2 Peter 3:10-12 and suggest that heaven and earth will be renovated by intense heat and fire. In our nuclear age, it's easy to imagine the world being burned to a crisp by an unbridled nuclear war. But I really don't think God is planning to blow up the planet and remake it from scratch. Rather, I think He will do essentially what landscapers do to lawns that have become matted with years of layered undergrowth: He'll burn away the contamination to restore the original purity. It will be the first step toward remaking, renewing, refreshing, and refurbishing His existing creation so it can become our home throughout all eternity.

## A New City

I, John, saw the holy city, New Jerusalem, coming down out of heaven from God, prepared as a bride adorned for her husband. And I heard a loud voice from heaven saying, "Behold, the tabernacle of God is with men, and He will dwell with them, and they shall be His people. God Himself will be with them and be their God. And God will wipe away every tear from their eyes; there shall be no more death, nor sorrow, nor crying. There shall be no more pain, for the former things have passed away."

REVELATION 21:2-4

People have longed for a city of God as far back as the book of Genesis. We learn in the book of Hebrews that Abraham, living in tents in the land God had promised him, "waited for the city which has foundations, whose builder and maker is God" (Hebrews 11:10). Every saint of God feels a deep longing for something beyond this life, but it is not until Revelation 21–22 that we see the city that fulfills this longing.

How do we interpret the astounding things John wrote about this city? Of the many approaches we could take, I think the best is merely to read the Bible as it was written. This introduces us to wonders that will stretch any human mind and honor the power of God.

### The Dimensions of the City of God

We will start with the dimensions of the new city. It is staggering to imagine how many saved individuals have walked the earth since the beginning of time. To accommodate them all, this city will have to be enormous. And so it is. Scripture gives its basic dimensions as a cube measuring about 1,500 miles per side, depending on how one translates the exact measurement of a furlong (Revelation 21:15-16). Think of a box that is 1,500 miles high, 1,500 miles wide, and 1,500 miles long (approximately the driving distance between Dallas and New York). In other words, this city would occupy a land area of 2.25 million square miles. One writer calculated that the base of the city is roughly ten times the size of France or Germany, and forty times the size of England.

We are not given clues as to the layout of this city, although our minds immediately conceive of different levels, like a tall office building. We just have to take it on faith that the mansion Jesus has been preparing for us will fill us with delight (John 14:2-3).

### The Description of the City of God

Though John divulges few insights about the workings and organization of the Holy City, here are the few descriptive details he does offer:

### 1. A HOLY CITY

In Revelation 21:2, John calls the new city "holy"—pure as a virginal bride. No metropolitan area currently on planet Earth even comes close to that description, contaminated as they are by sin, filth, pollution, crime, poverty, disease, anger, and turmoil. This new city, however, will be free of these contaminations. No words of boasting or anger will ever be heard; no unkind deeds will ever be committed.

Why? Because every resident will have been made holy by the redeeming grace of God and will remain in that state for eternity. Since God and everyone in the city are holy, the city itself will be holy.

### 2. THE PEARLY GATES

The term *pearly gates* has become such a part of colloquial language that few people realize it comes right out of the book of Revelation: "The twelve gates were twelve pearls: each individual gate was of one pearl" (21:21). With descriptions such as this one, it's easy to understand why some commentators think these descriptions aren't meant to be taken literally. After all, what kind of monster oyster could produce such a pearl? The answer, of course, is that it comes from God, not from an oyster. There are no limitations on God's creativity. If He can create a galaxy, He can certainly make a pearl of any size.

Inscribed on each pearl gate will be the name of one of the twelve tribes of Israel. The gates will be set into the four walls around the city, which will be made of jasper. The purpose of the walls won't be to keep people in or out; they will simply define the dimensions of the city. Remember that all enemies will have been destroyed, so there will be no more need for protection. The gates will be open at all times.

### 3. THE FOUNDATIONS OF PRECIOUS STONES

The foundations of the city wall will consist of twelve precious stones layered one on top of the other like sheets of plywood (Revelation

21:19-20). We are not familiar with many of these stones today, but we can imagine this scene by picturing translucent layers of the gems we do know, such as amethysts, emeralds, diamonds, or opals. The dazzling beauty of such a wall would refract dancing beams of iridescent color from all directions.

### 4. THE STREETS OF GOLD

Scholars have also engaged in debate about whether the city's streets will literally be made of gold. John says they are made of pure gold, "like transparent glass" (21:21; see also verse 18). The pure gold in our world is not like transparent glass; it is opaque. But the gold of the Holy City will be so pure that it won't repel light the way opaque objects do; instead, it will absorb light and bathe in it. I imagine it will look something like a gold-hued pane in a stained-glass window. Regardless of what we imagine, we can be sure that, like everything God creates, this gold is simply another reflection of His own beauty.

### 5. THE LIGHT OF THE CITY

In the Bible, light is often associated with the appearance of God. The light that will reflect off the gold and gems in this city will not be that of the sun or the moon. Scripture says the city will be illuminated solely by the glory of God (Revelation 21:23). We can be sure that this light is unlike anything in the natural universe, produced by some combustible fuel and always in need of replenishment. It will be more like the light that emanated from the burning bush Moses encountered. The light of God is the light of glory, not of heat or fire.

### 6. A TREE OF LIFE

We find the last description of the Holy City in Revelation 22:1-2, where John talks about the tree of life. Crystal-clear water will flow from the throne of God, and on each side will grow the tree of life. This tree was first planted in the Garden of Eden, but when Adam and Eve fell, they were barred from it lest they eat its life-giving fruit and live eternally in their fallen state. But in the Holy City, that tree will be restored. The redeemed will be invited to eat freely of it and live eternally in their newfound perfection.

This fruit-bearing tree raises a question: Will we eat food in heaven? The answer is clearly yes. Heaven is essentially a restored Eden, where its inhabitants will live the kinds of lives in the kinds of bodies God originally intended.

The Bible records various examples of heavenly beings eating. When the angels visited Abraham, they ate a meal (Genesis 18:2-8). When Jesus appeared to His disciples after His resurrection, He ate fish (Luke 24:42-43). It appears that even in our heavenly bodies, we will enjoy the taste of food and drink (Matthew 26:29). The fact that the fruit on the tree of life will renew itself monthly indicates that it is to be consumed (Revelation 22:2). Gluttony will never be a problem, since we will be eating to the glory of God.

### The Last Invitation in the Bible

> Let him who thirsts come. Whoever desires, let him take the water of life freely.
>
> REVELATION 22:17

Why do people come to Christ? They are thirsty! All human beings are born with an empty place in their lives that can only be filled with what John calls "the water of life" (Revelation 22:17). Most people try to quench that thirst with pleasure, accomplishment, possessions, human relationships, or power, but in time, they see that these things are not satisfying. As Solomon said after trying wealth, sex, power, and glory, it is all meaningless vanity.

When people realize that nothing on earth will satisfy their longing, they begin to identify their thirst. That is when they are poised to come to Christ. They realize that they are thirsty and He is not. He has—no, He *is*—the living water every human craves. It is He who fills the empty place that all of us since Adam have been born with. As Blaise Pascal put it, "There is a God-shaped vacuum in the heart of every man which cannot be filled by any created thing, but only by God, the Creator, made known through Jesus."

The restrictions on who might come to Christ are nonexistent! The invitation is open to all. John says, "Whoever desires." Who can come to Christ? Anyone who wants his or her thirst quenched forever.

If medical or psychological technicians were to invent an electronic scanning machine to uncover just where in the human organism salvation occurs, what would they find? Does salvation occur in one's intellect? Does a person gather and retain a quota of information that triggers salvation? If that quota is found to be deficient, would a larger dose of education do it? Apparently not, since we all know highly educated, intelligent people who are not saved. We cannot educate people into the Kingdom of God.

What about the emotions? Do people become saved when they feel saved? If so, what happens when they have a bad day and don't feel saved? Does that mean they have lost their salvation? Is the Christian life such a roller-coaster experience that salvation comes and goes depending on one's mood? That is utterly foreign to the assurance of the gospel. Salvation does not come through our emotions.

The truth is, we are saved in our will—"whoever will," or "whoever wants to." We are saved when we submit ourselves to Christ and say, "Lord, I will place my faith in You to forgive my sins and grant me Your free gift of eternal life."

Eternal life. That means life forever. How long is forever? Charles Swindoll provides a stunning illustration.

If you have a steel ball, solid steel, the size of this earth, 25,000 miles in circumference, and every one million years a little sparrow would be released to land on that ball to sharpen his beak and fly away only to come back another million years later and begin again, by the time he would have worn that ball down to the size of a BB, eternity would have just begun.[1]

As we conclude this study of the key players in the book of Revelation, only one question remains: Where do *you* fit into the story? Have you accepted the living water that God offers in the person of Christ? If so, you can be assured that no matter what you may encounter in the days ahead, your earthly life and your eternity are in His hands. As a result, you are an overcomer. Let the book of Revelation be a glorious confirmation of the fact that you will never thirst again.

If you have not taken a drink of that water, I encourage you to do so today. The Bible says, "*Whoever* calls on the name of the LORD shall be saved" (Romans 10:13, emphasis added). Call upon Him and quench your thirst, both now and forever.

# ACKNOWLEDGMENTS

IN MANY WAYS, the writing of this book began nearly thirty years ago when I first preached through the book of Revelation for the congregation I serve at Shadow Mountain Community Church. It took me forty-three sermons and twenty months to make it through the entire book, and I couldn't have done it without the encouragement of my wife, Donna. Thank you, Donna, for your faithful love and strengthening presence from those early days until now.

For almost twenty years my older son, David Michael, has worked alongside me at Turning Point. As the chief operating officer, David has been a faithful and visionary leader, helping us deliver the unchanging Word to an ever-changing world in many new and exciting ways. Thank you, David!

Many times in life and ministry we are faced with choices between what is good and what is best. Those decisions would be nearly impossible for me to make if it were not for Diane Sutherland and Barbara Boucher. Thank you for protecting my schedule and helping me accomplish the assignments God has given me.

Once again, Paul Joiner and the Turning Point Creative Department have done a superb job planning and preparing for the release of this book. Paul, I am amazed by the vision you have for getting our books into as many hands as possible. I would also like to thank Martin Zambrano, who created the charts throughout the book.

When we finished this project, we realized that we had way too much material. Editing down a manuscript might sound like an easy task, but I assure you it is not. Kris Bearss took on that assignment, and she was magnificent. Thank you, Kris, for your excellent work. Thanks, also, to my theological friends Dr. Chuck Emert and Dr. Gary Coombs for their many valuable suggestions.

Beau Sager and I have been working together now for several years. When it is time to begin a book project, I look across the hall to see if he is there. I would not want to begin such an undertaking without his diligent, patient, and determined assistance. Beau is a former star basketball player and, in his day, he was a deadly shooter. When it is time for us to begin a book project, I look at Beau to see if he has his game-face on, and then I start to write. For several months each year, the two of us live in "the zone" and block out everything we can until the game is over!

I am blessed to have had the same literary agent for more than twenty-five years. Thank you, Sealy Yates, for all you do!

I also want to express my gratitude to Ron Beers and the people at Tyndale for their commitment to this project. It has been a great joy to work alongside such a great publishing team.

Most of all, I am thankful to my Lord and Savior, Jesus Christ. This book—and my life—are about Him. Blessing and glory and wisdom and thanksgiving and honor and power and might be to our God forever and ever!

*Dr. David Jeremiah*
SAN DIEGO
JULY 2014

# NOTES

## INTRODUCTION

1. C. S. Lewis, *Surprised by Joy* (New York: Harcourt, Brace and Company, 1955), 181.
2. C. S. Lewis, *The Collected Letters of C. S. Lewis*, vol. 2 (New York: HarperOne, 2004), 1.
3. C. S. Lewis, "Bluspels and Flalansferes: A Semantic Nightmare" in *Selected Literary Essays* (London: Cambridge University Press, 1969), 265.

## CHAPTER 1. THE EXILE

1. John R. W. Stott, *What Christ Thinks of the Church* (Grand Rapids: Eerdmans, 1958), 12.
2. Eugene H. Peterson, *Reversed Thunder: The Revelation of John and the Praying Imagination* (New York: HarperCollins, 1988), xi–xii.
3. Ethelbert Stauffer, *Christ and the Caesars* (Philadelphia: Westminster Press, 1955), 150.
4. Martyn Lloyd-Jones, *True Happiness* (Wheaton, IL: Crossway, 2001), 88.
5. Louis T. Talbot, *The Revelation of Jesus Christ* (Grand Rapids: Eerdmans, 1937), 15.
6. Justin Martyr, *The First Apology of Justin, the Martyr*, Christian Classics Ethereal Library, www.ccel.org/ccel/richardson/fathers.x.ii.iii.html.
7. William E. Blackstone, *Jesus Is Coming* (Grand Rapids: Kregel, 1989; originally published in 1908), 14, 18.
8. Denis Lyle, *Countdown to Apocalypse* (Belfast: Ambassador Books, 1999), 21.
9. Vernard Eller, *The Most Revealing Book of the Bible: Making Sense out of Revelation* (Grand Rapids: Eerdmans, 1974), 48.
10. Roni Caryn Rabin, "A Glut of Antidepressants," *New York Times*, August 12, 2013, http://well.blogs.nytimes.com/2013/08/12/a-glut-of-antidepressants/?_php=true&_type=blogs&_r=0.

11. Walter B. Knight, *Three Thousand Illustrations for Christian Service* (Grand Rapids: Eerdmans, 1947), 602, 605.

12. Phil Moore, *Straight to the Heart of Revelation* (Oxford, UK: Monarch Books, 2010), 17.

## CHAPTER 2. THE MARTYRS

1. "Jewish Population of Europe in 1945," *Holocaust Encyclopedia*, www.ushmm.org/wlc/en/article.php?ModuleId=10005687.

2. Jacob Presser, *Ashes in the Wind: The Destruction of Dutch Jewry* (New York: Dutton, 1969), 336.

3. Henry M. Morris, *The Revelation Record: A Scientific and Devotional Commentary on the Prophetic Book of the End Times* (Carol Stream, IL: Tyndale, 1983), 119.

4. Richard Bauckham, *Climax of Prophecy: Studies in the Book of Revelation* (Edinburgh: T. & T. Clark, 1993), 424–25.

5. W. A. Criswell, *Expository Sermons on Revelation*, vol. 3 (Grand Rapids: Zondervan, 1962), 106–7.

6. Ibid., 105.

7. Louis T. Talbot, *The Revelation of Jesus Christ* (Grand Rapids: Eerdmans, 1937), 99.

8. Donald Grey Barnhouse, *Revelation: An Expositional Commentary* (Grand Rapids: Zondervan, 1971), 133–34.

9. John F. Walvoord, *The Revelation of Jesus Christ* (Chicago: Moody Press, 1966), 134–35.

10. Adapted from "Death of a Martyr: 203 AD" on the website Eyewitness to History.com (2004), www.eyewitnesstohistory.com/martyr.htm, accessed May 15, 2014.

11. Adapted from Angie Bring, "Modern Martyrs," Worldwide Challenge, November 1, 2005, http://worldwidechallenge.org/content/modern-martyrs.

12. "World Watch List," Open Doors, www.worldwatchlist.us/world-watch-list-countries.

## CHAPTER 3. THE 144,000

1. J. A. Seiss, *The Apocalypse: An Exposition of the Book of Revelation* (Grand Rapids: Zondervan, 1865), 161.

2. Mark Hitchcock, *The End: A Complete Overview of Bible Prophecy and the End of Days* (Carol Stream, IL: Tyndale, 2012), 291.

3. Jonathan Edwards, *The Great Awakening*, The Works of Jonathan Edwards series, vol. 4 (New Haven, CT: Yale University Press, 1972), 118.

4. Jeremy Begbie, "The Sense of an Ending," October 27, 2001, http://veritas.org/talks/sense-ending/?view=presenters&speaker_id=1955.

## CHAPTER 4. THE TWO WITNESSES

1. See John C. Whitcomb, "The Two Witnesses of Revelation 11," www.pre-trib.org/data/pdf/Whitcomb-TheTwoWitnessesFirst.pdf.
2. For more on this topic, see David Jeremiah, *Escape the Coming Night* (Nashville: Thomas Nelson, 2001), 122.
3. Timothy J. Demy and John C. Whitcomb, "Witnesses, Two," in *The Popular Encyclopedia of Bible Prophecy*, ed. Tim LaHaye and Ed Hindson (Eugene, OR: Harvest, 2004), 402–3.
4. William R. Newell, *Revelation: Chapter-by-Chapter* (Chicago: Moody Press, 1935), 152–53.
5. Henry M. Morris, *The Revelation Record: A Scientific and Devotional Commentary on the Prophetic Book of the End Times* (Carol Stream, IL: Tyndale, 1983), 201.
6. Tim LaHaye, *Revelation Unveiled* (Grand Rapids: Zondervan, 1999), 188.
7. Newell, *Revelation*, 155.
8. Morris, *Revelation Record*, 204.
9. J. A. Seiss, *The Apocalypse: An Exposition of the Book of Revelation* (Grand Rapids: Kregel, 1969), 266.
10. John Phillips, *Exploring Revelation* (Grand Rapids: Kregel, 2001), 150.

## CHAPTER 5. THE DRAGON

1. Adapted from W. A. Criswell, *Expository Sermons on Revelation*, vol. 4 (Grand Rapids: Zondervan, 1966), 85–87.
2. Donald Grey Barnhouse, *Revelation: An Expository Commentary* (Grand Rapids: Zondervan, 1971), 229.
3. Carolyn Arends, "Satan's a Goner," *Christianity Today*, March 25, 2011, www.christianitytoday.com/ct/2011/february/satansagoner.html.

## CHAPTER 6. THE BEAST FROM THE SEA

1. Quoted in Robert Glenn Gromacki, *Are These the Last Days?* (Old Tappan, NJ: Revell, 1970), 110.
2. Arthur W. Pink, *The Antichrist* (1923; repr., Grand Rapids: Kregel, 1988), 8.
3. Henry M. Morris, *The Revelation Record: A Scientific and Devotional Commentary on the Prophetic Book of the End Times* (Carol Stream, IL: Tyndale, 1983), 241.
4. Mark Hitchcock, *The End: A Complete Overview of Bible Prophecy and the End of Days* (Carol Stream, IL: Tyndale, 2012), 262.
5. Solomon Zeitlin, *The Rise and Fall of the Judean State*, vol. 1 (Philadelphia: Jewish Publication Society, 1962), 92.
6. Quoted in Gromacki, *Are These the Last Days?*, 117.
7. Pink, *The Antichrist*, 119–20.

## CHAPTER 7. THE BEAST FROM THE EARTH

1. John Phillips, *Exploring Revelation* (Grand Rapids: Kregel, 2001), 171.
2. Donald Grey Barnhouse, *Revelation: An Expository Commentary* (Grand Rapids: Zondervan, 1971), 240.
3. Robert H. Mounce, *The Book of Revelation: The New International Commentary on the New Testament*, rev. ed. (Grand Rapids: Eerdmans, 1998), 255.
4. W. A. Criswell, *Expository Sermons on Revelation*, vol. 4 (Grand Rapids: Zondervan, 1962), 115.
5. Craig S. Keener, *The NIV Application Commentary: Revelation* (Grand Rapids: Zondervan, 2009), 357.
6. J. A. Seiss, *The Apocalypse: A Series of Special Lectures on the Revelation of Jesus Christ*, rev. ed. (New York: Charles C. Cook, 1901), 345.
7. Henry M. Morris, *The Revelation Record: A Scientific and Devotional Commentary on the Prophetic Book of the End Times* (Carol Stream, IL: Tyndale, 1983), 251.
8. Ibid.
9. David Jeremiah, *The Coming Economic Armageddon* (New York: FaithWords, 2010), 145.
10. Mark Hitchcock, *The End: A Complete Overview of Bible Prophecy and the End of Days* (Carol Stream, IL: Tyndale, 2012), 275.
11. Fredk A. Tatford, *Prophecy's Last Word: An Exposition of the Revelation* (London: Pickering & Ingles, 1947), 154.
12. Barnhouse, *Revelation*, 250.

## CHAPTER 8. THE VICTOR

1. Adapted from Matt Woodley, "The Grieving Heart of God," PreachingToday.com, accessed June 12, 2014, http://www.preachingtoday.com/sermons/sermons/2007/july/gospelingenesis4.html.
2. N. T. Wright, *Surprised by Hope* (New York: HarperCollins, 2008), 137.
3. David Jeremiah, *What in the World Is Going On?* (Nashville: Thomas Nelson, 2008), 224.
4. James M. Kushiner, "Onward Christian Soldiers," *The Fellowship of St. James,* accessed June 6, 2014, http://campaign.r20.constantcontact.com/render?ca=fa215191-1d64-43db-8712-3e2c19d97687&c=a9340410-417e-11e3-b22b-d4ae527557ea&ch=aa4489b0-417e-11e3-b32d-d4ae527557ea.
5. Ibid.

## CHAPTER 9. THE KING

1. Adapted from Leon Wood, *The Bible and Future Events* (Grand Rapids: Zondervan, 1973), 166.
2. René Pache, *The Return of Jesus Christ* (Chicago: Moody Press, 1955), 380.

3. Adapted from unpublished notes by Alva J. McClain, Grace Theological Seminary, Winona Lake, Indiana.

4. Wood, *The Bible and Future Events*, 161.

5. From unpublished notes by Alva J. McClain, Grace Theological Seminary, Winona Lake, Indiana.

6. Henry M. Morris, *The Revelation Record: A Scientific and Devotional Commentary on the Prophetic Book of the End Times* (Carol Stream, IL: Tyndale, 1983), 408.

7. John F. Walvoord, *The Millennial Kingdom* (Findlay, OH: Dunham, 1963), 300–301.

8. Morris, *The Revelation Record*, 412.

9. W. A. Criswell, *Expository Sermons on Revelation*, vol. 5 (Dallas, TX: Criswell Publishing, 1995), 79.

10. Ibid., 80.

11. Mark Hitchcock, *The End: A Complete Overview of Bible Prophecy and the End of Days* (Carol Stream, IL: Tyndale, 2012), 428.

12. From unpublished notes by Alva J. McClain, Grace Theological Seminary, Winona Lake, Indiana.

13. David Jeremiah, *Escape the Coming Night* (Dallas, TX: Word Publishing, 1990), 229–30.

14. Walvoord, *The Millennial Kingdom*, 319.

## CHAPTER 10. THE JUDGE

1. Warren Wiersbe, *Be Victorious: In Christ You Are an Overcomer* (Colorado Springs: David C. Cook, 2010), 176.

2. "The Scriptures are silent on how God will deal with saints living on earth at the end of the Millennium or saints who have died in the Millennium. . . . It is probable that the righteous who die in the Millennium will be resurrected, much as the church will be at the Rapture, and that living saints will be given bodies suited for eternity like those living church saints receive." John Walvoord, *End Times* (Nashville: Word Publishing, 1998), 178.

3. Quoted in Robert Glenn Gromacki, *Are These the Last Days?* (Old Tappan, NJ: Revell, 1970), 175.

4. David Jeremiah, *Escape the Coming Night* (Dallas: Word, 1997), 236.

5. Erwin Lutzer, *Your Eternal Reward* (Chicago: Moody Press, 1998), 166.

6. Gromacki, *Are These the Last Days?*, 178.

7. Donald Grey Barnhouse, *Revelation: An Expository Commentary* (Grand Rapids: Zondervan, 1971), 390.

8. Henry M. Morris, *The Revelation Record: A Scientific and Devotional Commentary on the Prohetic Book of the End Times* (Carol Stream, IL: Tyndale, 1983), 433.

9. Isaac Massey Haldeman, *Ten Sermons on the Second Coming of Our Lord Jesus Christ* (New York: Revell, 1917), 739.

10. Morris, *The Revelation Record*, 433.

## EPILOGUE. THE OVERCOMERS

1. Charles R. Swindoll, *The Tale of the Tardy Oxcart and 1501 Other Stories* (Dallas, TX: Word, 1998), 183.

# ABOUT THE AUTHOR

DR. DAVID JEREMIAH serves as senior pastor of Shadow Mountain Community Church in El Cajon, California. He is the founder and host of Turning Point, a ministry committed to providing Christians with sound Bible teaching relevant to today's changing times through radio and television, the Internet, live events, and resource materials and books. A bestselling author, Dr. Jeremiah has written more than forty books, including *Captured by Grace, Living with Confidence in a Chaotic World, What in the World Is Going On?, The Coming Economic Armageddon, God Loves You: He Always Has—He Always Will,* and *What Are You Afraid Of?*

Dr. Jeremiah's commitment to teaching the complete Word of God continues to make him a sought-after speaker and writer. His passion for reaching the lost and encouraging believers in their faith is demonstrated through his faithful communication of biblical truths.

A dedicated family man, Dr. Jeremiah and his wife, Donna, have four grown children and twelve grandchildren.

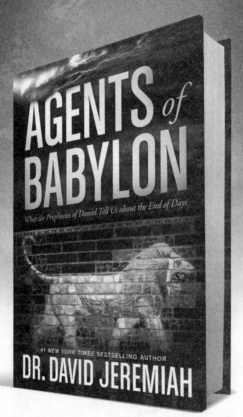

AVAILABLE
FALL 2015

AGENTS *of*
BABYLON

*What the Prophecies of Daniel Tell Us about the End of Days*

#1 NEW YORK TIMES BESTSELLING AUTHOR
DR. DAVID JEREMIAH

*stay connected to the teaching series of*

# DR. DAVID JEREMIAH

· · · · · · · ·

Publishing | Radio | Television | Online

##### · · · · ·

# COMPLETE YOUR STUDY
# THROUGH THE BOOK OF
# REVELATION

*With These Additional Titles from*
## DR. DAVID JEREMIAH

CP0821

• • • • •

### What in the World Is Going On?
Many theories try to depict the end times, and the Bible itself is filled with prophecies explaining this subject. In this book, Dr. Jeremiah identifies ten essential prophecies in the Bible to help us gain an understanding of the mysteries of the future.

### The Coming Economic Armageddon
The chaotic global financial market and widespread debt surround us daily. In this book, Dr. Jeremiah explores these economic disasters and answers questions like, "How did we get to this place?" and "Are the last days of Earth's history fast approaching?" to help us better prepare for the future.

### Living with Confidence in a Chaotic World
It is an undeniable truth that there is turmoil and trouble in our world today; however, it is possible to live confidently in the midst of the chaos by practicing ten biblical principles that God has provided for us. *Living with Confidence in a Chaotic World* is your personal guide to discovering and enjoying a confident life in the midst of chaos.

# FURTHER YOUR STUDY OF THIS BOOK

· · · · · · · ·

### *Agents of the Apocalypse* Resource Materials

To enhance your study on this important topic, we recommend the correlating audio message album, study guide, and DVD messages from the *Agents of the Apocalypse* series.

### Audio Message Album

The material found in this book originated from messages presented by Dr. David Jeremiah at the Shadow Mountain Community Church, where he serves as senior pastor. These ten messages are conveniently packaged in an accessible audio album.

### Study Guide

This 128-page study guide correlates with the *Agents of the Apocalypse* messages by Dr. Jeremiah. Each lesson provides an outline, overview, and application questions for each topic.

### DVD Message Presentations

Watch Dr. Jeremiah deliver the *Agents of the Apocalypse* original messages in this special DVD collection.

---

To order these products, call us at 1-800-947-1993
or visit us online at www.DavidJeremiah.org.

CP0820

# STAY CONNECTED

· · · · · · · ·

Take advantage of two great ways to let
Dr. David Jeremiah give you spiritual direction every day!
**Both are absolutely free!**

**①** *Turning Points* Magazine and Devotional

### *each magazine features:*

- A monthly study focus
- 48 pages of life-changing reading
- Relevant articles
- Special features
- Devotional readings for each day of the month
- Bible study resource offers
- Live event schedule
- Radio & television information

---

## Request your free subscription today!

**CALL:**     (800) 947-1993
**CLICK:**    DavidJeremiah.org/Magazine

Start your day off right! Find words of inspiration and spiritual motivation waiting for you on your computer every morning! You can receive a daily e-devotional from Dr. Jeremiah that will strengthen your walk with God and encourage you to live the authentic Christian life.

**Request your free e-devotional today!**

**CLICK:**     DavidJeremiah.org/Devo

CP0823

# BOOKS WRITTEN BY DAVID JEREMIAH

· · · · · · · ·

Escape the Coming Night

Turning Toward Joy

The Handwriting on the Wall

Invasion of Other Gods

Angels—Who They Are and How They Help...What the Bible Reveals

The Joy of Encouragement

Prayer—The Great Adventure

God in You

Until Christ Returns

Stories of Hope

Slaying the Giants in Your Life

My Heart's Desire

Sanctuary

The Things That Matter

The Prayer Matrix

31 Days to Happiness—Searching for Heaven on Earth

When Your World Falls Apart

Turning Points

Discover Paradise

Captured by Grace

Grace Givers

Why the Nativity?

Signs of Life

Life-Changing Moments with God

Hopeful Parenting

1 Minute a Day—Instant Inspiration for the Busy Life

Grand Parenting—Faith That Survives Generations

In the Words of David Jeremiah

What in the World Is Going On?

The Sovereign and the Suffering

The 12 Ways of Christmas

CP0825

What to Do When You Don't Know What to Do
Living with Confidence in a Chaotic World
The Prophecy Answer Book
The Coming Economic Armageddon
Pathways, Your Daily Walk with God
What the Bible Says About Love, Marriage, and Sex
I Never Thought I'd See the Day
Journey, Your Daily Adventure with God
The Unchanging Word of God
God Loves You: He Always Has—He Always Will
Discovery, Experiencing God's Word Day by Day
What Are You Afraid Of?
Destination, Your Journey with God
Answers to Questions About Heaven
Answers to Questions About Spiritual Warfare
Agents of the Apocalypse

---

To order these books, call us at 1-800-947-1993 or
visit us online at www.DavidJeremiah.org.

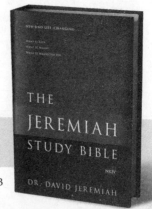